Praise for *Flight of Passage*

"It was the giddy, crazy adventure of a lifetime . . . The boys . . . squeaked through a Pennsylvania storm, had a run-in with redneck crop dusters, inadvertently spent a night in a roadside brothel and barely made it over the Rockies. [*Flight of Passage*] is part memoir, part tribute to the cocksure restlessness of a couple of teenagers."
—Hubert B. Herring, *The New York Times*

"[*Flight of Passage*] is an adventure full of fraternal jealousy, . . . boneheaded hubris, and unbridled fun and freedom."
—Douglas Bailey, *The Boston Globe*

"This is more than a flying adventure—it is also a warm, affectionate account of an unusual family, with characters presented as if they were created by a master novelist."
—Jack Elliot, *The Newark Star-Ledger*

"Lovers of adventure stories . . . will be exhilarated by this loosely told, very American memoir."
—Sophia Sackville-West, *The London Sunday Times*

"Rinker Buck is a virtuoso storyteller in a very American vein."
—Phillip Lopate, author of *The Art of the Personal Essay*

". . . colorful, exhilarating, heart-stirring . . . The journeys of miles and spirits that led to these resolutions Rinker recounts with such verve and love that *Flight of Passage* bids fair to become a coming-of-age classic."
—*A.L.A. Booklist*

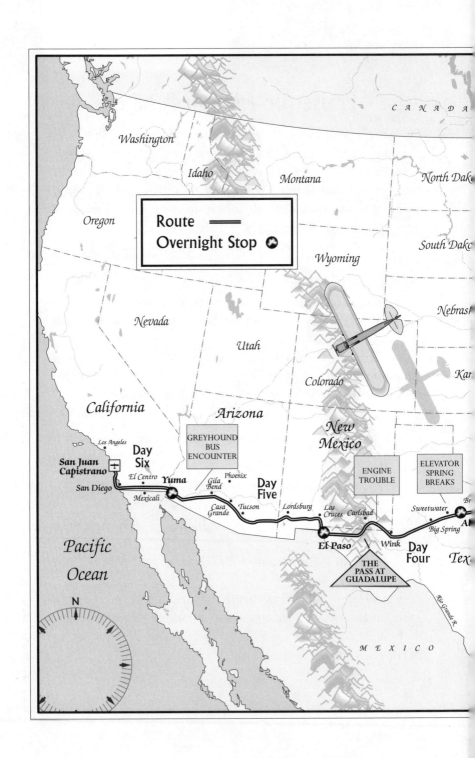

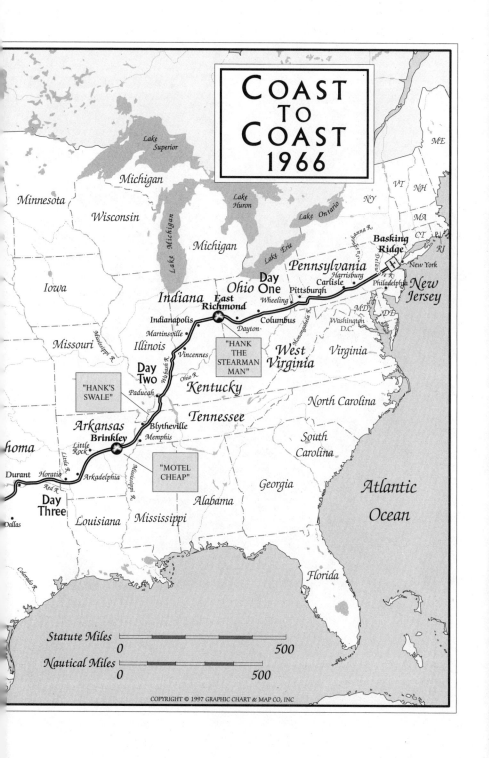

COAST
TO
COAST
1966

FLIGHT OF PASSAGE

RINKER BUCK

HYPERION

NEW YORK

Photo credits: p. ii—A Carmine Photo; pp. 4, 6—Nicholas Buck; p. 12—
Newark Star Ledger; p. 47—Kernahan Buck; pp. 65, 84—Rinker Buck;
p. 108—Jack Sharon; p. 136—Rinker Buck; p. 247—Robert and Ellen
Pate; p. 276—*Newark Evening News*; pp. 294–295—*Los Angeles Time, Morris County Record, New York Daily News, Newark Star Ledger, El Paso Times*;
pp. 316, 338—Rinker Buck

Piper Cub art by Michael Gellatly

Opening map by Graphic Chart and Map, Inc.

Library of Congress Cataloging-in-Publication Data
Buck, Rinker.
Flight of passage / by Rinker Buck. — 1st ed.
p.   cm.
ISBN 0-7868-6100-2
1. Transcontinental flights (United States)   2. Buck, Rinker—
Journeys—United States.   3. Buck, Kernahan—Journeys—
United States.   4. United States—Description and travel.
I. Title.
TL721.B83A3   1997
629.13'097—dc20   96-27745
CIP

Paperback ISBN 0-7868-8315-4

Book design by Holly McNeely

FIRST PAPERBACK EDITION

4   6   8   10   9   7   5   3

This book is for my brother, Kernahan Buck,
who got us there,
and for my father, Thomas Francis Buck,
who taught us to dream
and then had the sense to let us go.

ACKNOWLEDGMENTS

MANY MINDS GO TO WORK ON A BOOK LIKE THIS, AND I WOULD like to thank the wide circle of family and friends who helped while I was writing it. Most of them know me too well to doubt that I would apply my sense of humor and perspective to events, and they were unstinting in their assistance all the same.

My brother Kern, who is a lawyer now, insisted that I divulge "nothing but the truth" about our relationship as boys, which gave me the courage to include events I might otherwise have fudged and to reveal other critical material that formed the backdrop of our coast to coast flight in 1966. In some cases my brother's memories and interpretations differed from my own. But he understands that a first-person narrative like this inevitably reflects the author's personal voice and view of events. No one will get very far in this book without realizing how fortunate I am to have him as an older brother.

My mother, Pat Buck, cringes at the language I use and sometimes is appalled by my cast of mind, but remains marvelously supportive of all that I do. My sisters Dempsey and

McNamara were particularly helpful in recalling events while my brother and I were crossing the country in 1966. Bryan and Nicholas contributed their memories of our flying days together in the 1960s. My uncle and aunt, Jim and Joan Buck, also helped a great deal, and they continue to be the model family leaders described in this book.

Jack Elliott, the aviation columnist for *The Newark Star-Ledger*, covered my family and its various aerial exploits back in the 1960s, and thirty years later he and his wife, Esta-Ann, proved invaluable in digging up clips and reuniting me with many old friends in aviation. Jack is an extremely lucid and perceptive writer, and his insights into my father's personality and flying style were immensely helpful while I was sorting out the events leading up to our 1966 flight.

A number of old flying companions from New Jersey—Valerie Mahler, Lee Weber, Bill Machauer, Jack Sylvester, Tom Morley, Helen Yankaskas, Tom Kanach, Art Storm and Jan Mock—dug into their logbooks and pulled clips from their attics, patiently enduring all of my questions. Joseph Heller, Iggy Wolfington, Sterling Dimmitt, John King, Barclay Morrison, Father John Corr, Sarah and Paul Feakins, Louis DeChiaro, Terry and Natalie Gallagher and Nicholas Platt contributed their recollections about my father and family. The monks of St. Mary's Abbey/Delbarton School were also generous with their time, and I particularly want to thank my former English teacher, Gerard Lair, O.S.B., now the abbot at St. Mary's. His capacious intelligence and wit helped greatly while I was writing this book and, indeed, have been a lifelong source of support.

The inimitable Robert Warren Pate continues to delight me as a friend and correspondent, some thirty years after we first met in El Paso in 1966. I wrote from memory the long soliloquy by him in Chapter 17 before I tracked him down again in northern California. Pate was kind enough to carefully read it and confirm its accuracy.

My agent, David Black, prodded me for years to write this book, and his assistants, Lev Fruchter and Susan Raihofer, cheerfully attended to the all the details of representing a writer. My editor, Brian DeFiore, displayed admirable patience between revisions, and his insistence that I probe more deeply into the psychological motives behind our flight greatly improved my own understanding of the material. My attorney, Kenneth P. Norwick, puts up with me and provides thoughtful counsel well beyond the confines of law.

Anyone who marries a writer comes to doubt the wisdom of their choice during a book project. But my wife, Amelia, never lost patience or faith, even on the many nights when I didn't return home and remained at my office computer until dawn.

A number of people who knew and respected my father might be surprised by some of the things I have written. But much understanding comes from writing a book, and there is one thing I know for certain now that I only suspected before. If he were any different a man, any different a father, my brother and I would never have taken on the things we did.

FLIGHT OF PASSAGE

INTRODUCTION

WE WERE JUST TWO BOYS, SEVENTEEN AND FIFTEEN, FLYING TO California in an airplane built before either of us was born. Later that summer a reporter for the Associated Press would make us briefly famous by writing that we were the youngest aviators ever to fly America coast to coast, but it wasn't records or fame we were after. What we were really doing was proving ourselves to my father.

It seems inconceivable today that we could have been Tom Buck's sons and not flown to California as soon as we were able. My father was a dreamer, a magnificent dreamer, and what he dreamed about most was flying. Aviation was the most important thing in his life not simply because of its adventuresome aspects, though he was too starry-eyed to discount that. He was moved instead by the symbolism of flight.

In 1933, at the age of seventeen, my father had put the disappointments of a Depression upbringing in Pennsylvania behind him by running away from home to join a flying circus. He spent his teenage years barnstorming around the country as an air-show performer and ferry pilot—a romantic, carefree escape that sent him on his way. By the age of twenty-one he had already quit the barnstorming life and established himself in New York, beginning a highly successful career in magazine publishing that helped tide his family through the hard times and then supported the enormous brood of children he fathered after World War II. For the rest of his life, however, he was self-conscious about being a high school dropout without a college degree. His vagabond years, when he was a dashing young pilot with little more to his name than a grease-stained change of khakis, some maps, and a parachute, were in fact his education and loomed large in memory, defining his triumph over economic hardship and girding his self-image.

His nostalgia for those years grew with age, and raising sons brought it out. On the long winter nights while we were growing up in the 1950s, my older brother Kern and I used to sit up with my father before the glowing Franklin stove in our farmhouse in New Jersey, helping him ward off his chronic insomnia, hangar-flying until almost midnight. We listened raptly to his endless tales of pushing out past the Ozarks and the Mississippi and into Oklahoma and east Texas, crisscrossing the great western plains in a succession of open-cockpit Fairchilds and Pitcairn Mailwings.

That barnstorming blarney was a wonderful thing for a father to share with his sons, fraught as it was with the oily grit and hell-for-leather gumption of early aviation. There were perilous Appalachian ice storms and desperate landings by moonlight at remote Alabama strips. My father's storytelling technique was deeply emotive and physical. He was a big, theatrical man, standing six feet and four inches, with immense table-top shoulders and a broad chest that heaved in and out like an organ bellows as he spoke. While he talked in front of the fire he would sway back and forth in his rocker, kicking out his legs at imaginary rudder pedals or jabbing his arm over with the "stick" for a crosswind landing, rotating a four-point arc between his legs for a snap roll or Immelman turn. Sometimes his voice broke into a falsetto pitch. "The field was *short* boys, way too short." In the hiss of the fire we could hear the flying wires wail.

Behind my father as he spoke, on the paneled wall of his library, hung framed photographs of his flying career—faded, silver-tinted images of the young British airmen he had trained in Canada for the Battle of Britain, the row upon row of sprightly yellow Stearman trainers at Love Field in Texas, where he was an aerobatics instructor with the Army Air Corps after Pearl Harbor. One of our favorite pictures was a black-and-white news photo taken on Easter Sunday morning, 1942. In it, my father was taxiing a rickety KR-31 biplane past a waving, smiling crowd in front of Philadelphia City Hall, escorted by motorcycle cops on each wingtip. He had landed the open-cockpit ship in downtown Philadelphia as a publicity stunt for the wartime scrap drive, and the admonition *SCRAP IT!* was painted in large white script on the side of the plane.

I would later learn that not all of my father's stories were true. But it is a mistake to rate yarners like my father according to orthodox standards of truth. Boys are not particularly in need of that, and we could see for ourselves that my father existed in a realm beyond all need for proof. On sunny weekend days in the spring and summer, my father rose early, called for my brother and me to wheel his big, black BMW motorcycle up to the side door, and then he roared out of our driveway for the airport. There, he strapped on a parachute, pulled on his flight helmet and growled off the strip in the loudest airplane in general aviation, a military-surplus fighter plane named the AT-6 Texan. Sometimes he flew off for the air-shows and warmed up the gathering crowds by buzzing in at tree-top level and barrel-rolling over their heads, other days he dive-bombed our soccer games and swim meets. As boys, my brother and I loved nothing more than to lay prone on the soft grass along the airport flight-line, squinting up into the sun as my father stunted over the field. The big, sexy Texan made a hellacious racket in the sky, wailing and howling like a cigarette boat every time my father looped or rolled, all six hundred horses blurt-blurting and coughing and farting out through the stack. My father liked to practice aerobatics open-cockpit style, with the glass canopy over his head thrown wide open. When he rolled upside-down, the stray maps and runaway corn cob pipes collected among the floorboards dropped down and sprayed out past the tail in a black nimbus of dust.

My father's vagabond years in the 1930s, when he was a dashing young pilot barnstorming around the country, loomed large in memory and girded his self-image.

My father was in his late-forties by then and he had eleven children. But age and family responsibilities did not deter him from flying the way he liked, just as he had not been deterred as a younger man by a spectacular air wreck. In 1946, he had spun in from 2,000 feet and crashed into remote woods outside Wilmington, Delaware. His passenger was killed and my father's left leg, crushed on impact by the hissing engine, had to be amputated three years later. The artificial leg he wore gave him a noticeable limp, and he was frequently disabled by excruciating phantom pains. But he refused to regard this as a handicap or to heed the doctors who advised him to lead a quieter life. His missing limb gave him a kind of Ahab mystique, and he considered it expressive of his unconventional style. Indeed, he was the kind of man who prospered by turning glaring liabilities into stunning assets. In 1949, the year before I was born, he joined the nascent Alcoholics Anonymous organization to stop drinking, and soon after the witty, discursive "testimonials" he delivered made him a star performer on the AA lecture circuit. A virtual unknown in the late-1950s when he became interested in politics, by 1960 he was serving as state cochairman for John F. Kennedy's presidential campaign. He enjoyed the attention and acclaim these accomplishments brought him, even craved it, and his life was structured to receive as much of it as possible. Joseph Heller, the writer, worked with my father at *McCall's* in the late 1950s, and later based a character in one of his novels on Tom Buck. "He was a self-made man," Heller wrote, "and unable to hide it."

My father always made it clear that he expected Kern and me, his two oldest boys, to be just as successful and known. Unfortunately, children rarely respond according to plan. As a boy, my older brother was private and shy, self-conscious about being small for his age. Kern was the classic oldest son of a strong, iron-willed father, secretly afraid that he couldn't live up to the model, and thus quite skittish and sensitive to criticism. Even his appearance suggested vulnerability. He had feathery auburn hair with red highlights, broad cheeks and trusting brown eyes that opened wide with disappointment when he was hurt. He mostly excelled at things that required a lot of solitude and a minimum of social contact, math and science, and his best friend was a science nerd and ham-radio freak who lived in the village nearby, Louie DeChiaro.

Kern and Louie spent long afternoons up in Kern's room in the attic working on old radios, howling with excitement and jumping up and down on the floor whenever they rigged up a receiver powerful enough to "drag down Chicago." Their science projects—balsawood oil derricks that pumped "real crude," mock-up Mercury space capsules, boxes of electrified rocks that somehow lit up forty-watt lightbulbs—won top prizes every year at the grammar school science fair. Kern never developed a competitive instinct for sports and he was painfully bashful around girls. When he reached high school and decided that it was finally time for him to try a date, my

*On Easter Sunday morning, 1942, my father landed his open-cockpit
ship in front of Philadelphia City Hall as a publicity stunt
for the wartime scrap drive.*

sister Macky picked out the shyest girl in her class, scripted
an entire phone conversation with her on a yellow legal pad,
then held it up for Kern while he nervously dialed the number.

Nobody ever accused me of winning the school science
fair. I had watched my older brother play the role of diffident
recluse and was determined to be exactly the opposite. I was
the extrovert who was popular and did well in school, starred
in the class play, and became captain of our undefeated soccer
team. These achievements of mine were not based on merit,
but instead on criminal behavior. I was popular because I was
the class cutup, expert in such delicate and locally prized
work as the cherry-bomb demolition of the school principal's
mailbox, or the upgrading of the baseball coach's jockstrap
with an invisible but medically effective layer of Atomic
Balm. With me, trouble arrived in waves. During the spring

that I was in the seventh grade, a neighbor caught me making out in the woods with a beautiful sixth-grader and reported this fact to my mother. A few nights later my friends and I found an old jalopy in the woods up on Tea Mountain, rolled it onto a bridle path and careened down the hill, coming to a halt after a head-on collision with a tree on the lawn of best-selling writer Sterling North. The famous author himself, clutching a martini and nude except for a pair of silk boxer shorts, came outside and cursed us hysterically before he called the cops. The week after that my homeroom teacher, Blair Holley, threatened to have me expelled for stuffing a dead rat into Betsey DeChiaro's book bag. My spring campaign of mischief brilliantly coalesced during the last week of school in June, when I ran for president of the student council and got elected by a landslide margin.

My brother was miserable about this. He was shattered by the injustice of the world. He had behaved himself and followed all the rules and nobody seemed to notice whether or not he was even alive. I broke every rule and got all of the attention. He was terrified that I was either going to end up in prison, or become the President of the United States, outrageous behavior in a kid brother. More than anything in the world he longed for a quieter, understated younger brother who melted into the background and didn't upstage him all the time. I longed for a more outgoing, assertive older brother who could socially pave my way in school and act as a foil against my father. Meanwhile, I was mortified by the brother I had. Even the way Kern and Louie dressed—plaid shirts, clashing plaid dork shorts, black socks, and black hightops—drove me insane with embarrassment.

Everyone did their best to encourage Kern. One day, coming in from school and infuriated by some stunt I had pulled off, he complained to my mother about me. My mother was petite and very pretty, quintessentially Irish, and so youthful no one could believe that she had delivered eleven children. Like a lot of mothers at the time, even the Protestant ones, she was a devotee of the Rose Kennedy school of child-rearing. The small things, such as how you dressed and

7

whether or not you were polite to priests, mattered, and children could be pushed toward greatness by modeling themselves on someone who was unquestionably successful.

"Well, Kern," my mother said. "Maybe you should try being *more* like your brother. Rinker likes people, he works hard in school, and he never gets cavities."

My mother did a splendid job raising eleven children, but it was the wrong thing to say. Kern never got over it. A few years ago, when I was undergoing painful root-canal work, Kern called nearly every night to ask after me and flooded me with get-well cards. I've never seen him so solicitous about my welfare. And he was cheerful about it too, almost jubilant.

"Listen Rink, don't let this thing get you down," he said to me, as I lay moaning in bed, gingerly holding the phone up to my ear. "Eventually, everybody gets tooth decay."

A lot of my problems with my brother began to change for the better in the early 1960s, when we entered our teens and my father started teaching us to fly. Flying seemed to be a divine remedy for us. From the moment my father strapped him into the pilot's seat of a rented Piper Tri-Pacer for his first flying lesson, it was obvious that Kern was a born pilot. The self-confidence and poise that he lacked on the ground miraculously blossomed in the air, as if it had been held in reserve for this. Kern was naturally graceful and coordinated at the controls, and what he couldn't learn by just handling a plane he picked up by memorizing all twenty-eight chapters of *The Student Pilot's Handbook*. My father, though a very patient, gentle instructor, enforced exacting standards, insisting that we learn to fly by the old-fashioned, seat-of-the-pants method, with lots of emergency landing practice, spin-training, and aerobatics. My brother effortlessly mastered it all.

Most remarkable, at least to me, Kern was absolutely fearless in the air. Nothing rattled him. One cold, rainy November afternoon in 1962, when Kern was fourteen, he and my father were swinging in for a landing in the Texan when the engine sputtered and quit on the downwind leg. The Texan weighed almost two tons, and when you lost an engine in that plane all you had left was a flying manhole cover. Raking over the wings, they dove for the runway and landed "short" in an orchard. Rumbling and creaking like a D day tank, the big stubby fighter tossed aside several large apple trees, two fence lines, some farm implements and a chicken coop and then sleighed down through a cornfield before nosing over on the edge of the runway. Sliding down a crumpled wing together, my father and Kern landed in the mud and stood there cheerfully analyzing the wreckage. A throng of pilots and mechanics raced down to the crash site, and everybody was amazed by my brother's aplomb. "Hey guys, check this out!" Kern beamed. "How about the fact that we made it to the runway?"

My own progress in the air was less satisfying. Except for navigation, which I enjoyed and worked hard at, I was less graceful than my brother as a pilot and, worse, afraid most of the time. The unfamiliar physical sensations and bizarre optical effects of holding the nose of a plane level on the horizon, while simultaneously banking the wing below the horizon for a turn, were too much for me. In turbulence I shivered all over with spasms and broke out into a cold sweat, and I was terrified of stalls and spins. My father found it hard to hide his disgust.

"Ah shit, Rinker," he would moan from his instructor's seat in the rear of the plane. "Do you call that a 360-degree turn? Your brother can do this. Try it again."

When I still couldn't get it right my father would call forward his favorite instructional ode. "Son, an airplane is just like a woman. Treat her gently, but firmly." This was mystifying to me. By then I did have some experience with women, teenage women, and while my father's advice worked wonders with them out in the woods, it wasn't worth a damn inside an airplane. As soon as I rolled into the next 360-degree turn, the nose plunged right back through the horizon, so I yanked back harder on the stick. "Son, *please*, gently but firmly!" When my father screamed that at me for the tenth time in a single flight lesson, I wished we were back on the ground and had decided as a family to take up golf.

Eventually my father decided that I was still too young, slacked off on my lessons, and concentrated instead on my brother. I was relieved to be off the hook and, in one important respect, mediocrity never felt so good. Finally, indisputably, my older brother was better than me at something. I was actually proud of him now, even envious of his prowess in the air. Sitting in the back of the four-seat Beechcrafts and Cessnas we rented on weekends to fly off somewhere together, I loved the way Kern adroitly ran through his checklist, started the engine, and then managed a whole flight alone while my father sat with his arms crossed in the instructor's seat. At the end of our long flying days together, I would suddenly realize that I was happy to be around Kern now, merely because *he* was happy, a refreshingly new sensation for me. Kern was euphoric about his success as a pilot and his entire psychology became wrapped up in aviation. At last he could concentrate on what he liked in himself and forget about what he detested in me.

Best of all, my father was a lot more relaxed about both of us. Nothing bothered him now that he had a son who was a crack pilot. We were blissfully happy for the next four years, and all summer we spent weekend after weekend flying off the ramshackle grass strip a few miles from our home. In the fall, we picked up a burnt-out Taylorcraft or Aeronca trainer, disassembled it and towed it home behind our Jeep, and then spent the cold months inside our barn contentedly rebuilding our "winter plane."

Kern progressed as a pilot in the style that my father adored. In August 1964, he turned sixteen, the legal age for first solo. It would not be enough for the firstborn son of Tom Buck to merely circuit the field once in a nondescript Cessna trainer, the usual first-solo drill. Instead, he and my father concocted a multiple event. On his sixteenth birthday, they decided, Kern would solo four separate airplanes four times, for a total of sixteen hops around the strip. It was the kind of preposterous stunt that my father was known for, and Kern went right up and did it. Round and round the grass field, in plane after plane, my brother monotonously droned. My father had done his usual competent job of turning out a large crowd of family and friends to witness the event. But it was a sweltering hot day and everybody watching at the airport soon felt lazy and bored—sixteen consecutive arrivals and departures by a teenager in a light plane being about as entertaining as sixteen arrivals and departures by a crow. When Kern got to the last plane, which was a turd-brown Ercoupe, even my father had had enough. Stepping over to the shady side of the hangar, he lay down on the grass, removed his wooden leg, and took a nap.

To my father, an event wasn't an event until it was also a headline, and that too was arranged. That night my father called an old friend of his, Jack Elliott, the aviation writer for the *The Newark Star Ledger*, and we all sat around my father's library listening to Kern describe his sixteen solos to Jack. The story ran the following week in Jack's regular Sunday column, "Wings Over Jersey." The piece appeared under the headline SOLOS 16 TIMES AT AGE 16, and it was illustrated with a three-column picture of my brother sitting at the controls of the family's battered Piper Cub. Kern was still quite adolescent and small for his age and didn't look much past fourteen. But his innocent *Leave It to Beaver* good looks only made the accomplishment seem brighter. Jack was an experienced newspaperman who knew how to take material gathered over the phone and gussy it up so that readers felt they were receiving an eyewitness account. "Kern took her up and brought her down again like it was something he'd been doing all his life and could do with one hand tied behind his back," Jack wrote of my brother's first hop. "Then he did it again."

Kern had trouble adjusting to his new status as the young star of the strip. One fall day shortly after he soloed, we were all out at the airport together, but it was a very windy afternoon and none of the instructors were allowing their students to fly. But my father considered the conditions a good challenge for Kern and told him to go up and practice his takeoffs and landings. Kern circuited the field for an hour or so, expertly crabbing into the wind and planting the wheels down without a bump as he did his "touch and gos."

16-year-old Kern Buck . . . old enough to fly

Solos 16 times at age 16

He didn't look a day past fourteen, but Kern's innocent Leave It to Beaver *good looks only made the accomplishment seem brighter.*

As my brother circuited the field, another student pilot who we liked a lot, Nick Stone, stood by the gas pumps and watched. Every time Kern touched down Nick would say, "Jesus, what a landing. Perfect."

Then my brother would come around again and Nick would say, "Jesus, what a landing."

I got so sick of hearing Nick say "Jesus, what a landing" that I started to pray that my brother would botch a couple, just for the record. He didn't have to dig in a wingtip and seriously damage the plane, just touch down at an angle in the brisk crosswind and skid sideways hard enough to blow a tire, or let the drift push him over into the patch of gopher holes that lined the runway over by the windsock. Maybe he

12

could even manage to hit the windsock. It would be good for Nick's ego—hell, it would be *great* for mine—to see Kern screw the pooch, just once.

But no, this was my brother. Every landing was perfect.

After he made his last landing, Kern coasted the plane to a stop on the gas ramp, shut down and hopped out.

More out of admiration than envy, Nick said to him, "Jesus, what a landing. Kern you're good. You're just so damned good."

. When we got home that night, Kern was upset about it.

"Rink, this just isn't fair," he said. "Did you hear what Nick said to me?"

"Yeah. I heard what he said."

"Well, it isn't fair. To be good at something, you're supposed to *work* at it. But flying's easy for me. I don't even have to think about it."

I couldn't understand my brother. He never overlooked an opportunity to question himself. Suddenly I felt terribly guilty about him, and guilty about all of the things that I thought I could do better than he could, and I decided right then and there that I would turn over a new leaf and become a better brother for him. It was my job to build him up, compliment him, make him feel better about himself.

"Kern," I said, "You're being an asshole. What's *work* got to do with it? You're a good pilot, a great pilot! If you've got it, flaunt it."

"Okay Rink," he said. "Look, I'm going to make an agreement with myself that it's okay for me to be good at flying. I'm not going to feel guilty about this, no matter how good I get. And then you know what?"

"No, what?"

"I'm going to *stick to it.*"

You can begin to appreciate my problems. I spent a great deal of time then cursing my fate and wondering how I ended up with a brother like this.

In August 1965, on his seventeenth birthday, Kern effortlessly passed the flying test for his private pilot's license, and by that fall he had almost one hundred hours of logged time. Kern was also quite methodical and organized, the sort of boy who had his "career" all planned out at an age when most boys were merely planning their first date. He was determined to have his commercial pilot's license before he left for college in 1966. This was vital, he thought. We were all aware that my parents, though reasonably well off, turned out children at fantastic production rates, and they could never afford to put us all through college. Kern planned to "fly his way through school" as a charter pilot and flight instructor. To qualify for the commercial flight test, Kern needed an additional one hundred hours in his logbook, mostly of cross-country flying time.

That was the practical side of my brother. But Kern also had a brooding, dreamy side, the Irish in him, I guess. And he had inherited from my father a desperation to prove himself, but he was still too young to know what to do with his ambition. But it was there. Now that he was good at something, aviation, there had to be something more he could do, a way to apply it and stand out. Nobody should be able to forget that he was a great flyer.

He was obsessed about it. One night, shortly after he passed his private pilot's test, I found him upstairs in his room glumly pacing back and forth across the floor.

"Rink, you want to hear something pathetic? I mean, really pathetic?"

"Sure."

"Rink, I'm seventeen years old, and I haven't done a thing with my life yet. Not a thing!"

Damn. Here we go again. There had to be something I could say to cheer him up.

"Kern," I said, "Don't be such a weirdo. You've got a pilot's license already! Most of your friends don't even have their driver's licenses yet."

"Nah, nah Rink—that's nothing. I want to accomplish something, something everybody will be excited about and can respect. With aviation, maybe. But I don't know what it is yet. I'm going to shoot myself if I can't figure it out."

"Kern," I said. "Relax. If you shoot yourself, you won't figure it out."

For him, the situation called for something big, a lot bigger and better than SOLOS 16 TIMES AT AGE 16. Having grown up listening to rapturous tales of Pitcairn Mailwings and Waco 10s pushing out past the Ozarks and the Mississippi and into Oklahoma and east Texas, my brother had the advantage of great raw material to build on. The only plane available to him was the weatherbeaten, 85-horsepower Piper Cub my father had bought for $300 two years earlier, so that Kern could continue his flying lessons. So he began to dream big, harnessing his fantasies to the equipment at hand. That fall, as we returned to the Benedictine boys academy that we attended near our house, he seemed dreamier and more pensive than usual. His imagination was roaming west.

He announced his plan one weekend in late October. Working alone and without my father's help, Kern said, he and I would spend the winter rebuilding the Cub in our barn. Then, over the summer of 1966, we'd make a coast to coast flight to California. My brother insisted that he needed my help because he didn't think that he could finish the plane over the winter by himself. And he didn't believe that he could both navigate and handle the plane alone all the way to California either.

"Rink, I *need* you for this," my brother said. "I can't do it alone."

It was the most ludicrous idea I had ever heard. My brother barely had one hundred hours in his logbook. He had never piloted a plane beyond the Delaware River in Pennsylvania. Nobody flew a Piper Cub all the way to California. Nobody had even thought of it until my earnest, dreamy brother came along.

That fall, after Kern received his private pilot's license, we had flown a few times together, and I was surprised by how much we enjoyed ourselves in the air. Kern wasn't at all demanding like my father and, when he gave me the controls, he didn't mind the way I wallowed the plane around the sky. In fact, he was idiotically easy to please. All I had to do was sit in the backseat of the Cub and not complain while he "pulled a buzz job" over Louie DeChiaro's house, or pretend that I wasn't airsick when he threw a roll of toilet paper out the window and then screamed down through the clouds to slice up the unfurled rolls of paper with the prop. I wasn't doing anything back there, except turning green. But Kern was extravagantly grateful for my company and complimented me profusely on being a "great copilot."

Those flights revealed an important side of my brother to me. He was not only lonely, he was desperate for my approval. He didn't have a lot of close friends anyway, and those that he had didn't know a thing about aviation. I was the only one who knew what he was really like as a person, which to Kern at that age meant what he was like as a pilot. He enjoyed my company and wanted more of it, and I could tell that he was immensely frustrated by my failure to respond to him the way he felt a younger brother should. But it wasn't in Kern's nature to blame me for that, he blamed himself. Winning me over and earning my love was an enormous piece of unfinished business for him, another one of those things that he wanted out of the way and resolved before he left for college.

I was just fourteen that fall and in the throes of an awkward adolescence, and I was never going to admit that I experienced such nauseating emotions about my brother. I didn't want to talk about such things. So I assented to his plan, almost immediately, because if I didn't he would pester me endlessly about my obligations to him "as a brother." Besides, by then my teenage rebellion against my father was in full swing. I was still getting into trouble at school and my father and I fought a lot about that. Without really meaning to, Kern was finally doing what I had expected of him all along. His coast to coast plan, which would require a long winter rebuilding the plane in the barn, offered me a perfectly defensible excuse for dodging my father for almost a full year.

My father, too, was initially hesitant about my brother's plan, but one aspect was irresistible to him. Ever since the Depression, when he and his four brothers had worked all-night shifts at diners together and delivered papers at dawn, rescuing their family from financial ruin, the concept of brotherly collaboration was almost sacred to him. It pained him greatly that Kern and I had never been able to live up to that ideal. He viewed the coast to coast scheme as an opportunity for us to work together on something, transcending the jealous rages and petty squabbles that had marred our happiness as brothers and his happiness as a parent. And he was too much of a newshound to ignore another aspect. Two teenage boys flying coast to coast in a Piper Cub was a seductive adventure tale, a headline just waiting to happen. For him, the flight would be the ultimate opportunity to live vicariously through his sons and bask in the glow of their success.

The simple audacity of our trip, our complete naïveté and nonchalance, astounds me still. Our tiny, two-seat Cub, manufactured in 1946, had no battery, no radio, no lights, not even a starter. The four cylinder Continental engine was ignited by my brother yelling "Contact!" from the cockpit while I stood outside, swinging the propeller by hand. Our only navigational aids were an ancient magnetic compass bolted to the instrument panel and a shopping bag filled with airmen's charts. We nearly killed ourselves getting over the Rocky Mountains and, as we followed paved highways through the remote deserts of New Mexico and Arizona, the cars and pickup trucks traveling the blacktop the same way routinely overhauled us from behind and passed us, mocking us with their dust-devil wakes as they sped on west.

Most of all, we were naïve about ourselves. Setting out on our journey, my brother and I considered ourselves young adventurers in the style of the aviation greats—Wiley Post, Charles Lindbergh, Antoine de Saint-Exupéry. We would coax our frail plane across the continent, conquering every inch of terrain between New York and L.A., simply because "it was there." But this was bunk. In fact, we needed to discover each other as brothers. The love that had been bottled up inside us since we were boys had to be acknowledged and expressed somehow, and this was all we knew, flying. And there was redemption for us in the perils of a coast-to-coast flight. That is what we found out among unfamiliar deserts and high mountain passes, and that is what odyssey is all about I guess. The odyssey was us.

For years I wanted to write about that trip. Since college I have carried around from house to house an old Quaker State Oil box stuffed with mementos from our flight—our old flight logs and fuel records and maps, a yellowing pile of newspaper clips, a carousel of color slides that we took along the way. My wife and friends urged me to spill out the story just as I told it in person, mixing in the eccentric details of my family and the times. It was a classic tale of the 1960s, they said, and I needed to write it. This, in fits and starts, I gradually did.

Still, the full book eluded me. Any account of those years would have to confront the painful, unresolved feelings for my brother and my father that were boiling over in 1966. My father died in 1975, nine years after we made our flight, and I deluded myself for a long time with the excuse that the sorrow of losing him to an early death, the sorrow of just knowing a man as complicated as he was, was still too intense. In fact, I had neither the courage nor the detachment to confront my father and how I really felt about him. I was running away from my best material.

Then, one beautiful, cloudless August afternoon in 1994, I took my daughters for an airplane ride around Cape Cod. Sara was eight that year and Charlotte was four. We took off from Chatham in a four-seat Cessna and banked east for Pleasant Bay, flying low and slow with some flaps down and the engine power reduced, following the familiar white beaches up through Wellfleet and Truro and then swinging around Race Point at Provincetown. I was delighted with the way that Sara already could handle the controls from the copilot's seat. Little Charlotte, in the rear seat, took off her shirt—"To get a tan," she said—and fell asleep.

The night before had been Kern's birthday, and he had driven down from Boston with his family for a party. We sat out on the porch in Yarmouth Port and talked about our old flying days together, kicking out at imaginary rudder pedals and jabbing with our sticks as we sat in wicker rockers, our daughters falling asleep in our laps. Sara is a tomboy, a very determined and competent child who worships sports heros and Huck Finn. And she's a dreamer already, which all of the older children in our family always seem to be. I guess she was taking in a lot more than I realized.

After our sightseeing ride the next day, when we landed at Chatham Airport, Sara pretzeled up her body the way children do when they have something important to say and suddenly blurted it out.

"Dad, when I'm seventeen, can I fly to California with Charlotte?"

"Ah Jeez, Sara. C'mon. Kern and I were teenagers before we cooked up something like that."

"Big deal Daddy. You're just saying that because I'm a girl."

"Absolutely not Sara. If I've said it once I've said it a hundred times. Girls can do anything boys can do."

"Duh, Dad. So we can do it!"

"Sara I'm not saying that. I'm saying I'll think about it. Someday, if you're ready, I might let you go. Maybe we'll even go sooner, together."

"I don't want to go with you. I want to go with Charlotte. No parents. That's what *you* did."

"Sara. Uncle Kern and I took years of flying lessons from my father before we made that flight. We were ready."

"Big deal Daddy. You can teach me to fly, and then I'll be ready. Your father let you go, so you have to let me go. For now, all you have to do is say 'maybe.' "

"Sara I'm not saying maybe."

"Dad. Maybe."

"Oh all right. *Maybe*. But that's a big, fat maybe, I'm telling you. I'm only saying maybe, you understand?"

"Great! You said it. But you can't forget."

"I won't forget."

"Promise?"

"I promise. To think about it."

"Pinky-swear?"

"Pinky-swear."

So we pinky-sweared on it, and then Charlotte woke up from her nap in the backseat, saw Sara and I pinky-swearing about something, and she made me pinky-swear it with her too.

I knew then that I had to get the story down right away. I wanted my daughters to know more about the grandfather they had never met, what our lives with him were like, the forces that had swept through our family and propelled my brother and me on a daring flight to California. The truth couldn't hurt, and my daughters had never really heard the truth about me and the reasons that we made that trip.

Most of all, I was entranced by memories of innocence and exhilaration.

I wanted to convey the sweep of the land, the surprise of the terrain we crossed, the America of smalltown cafes and cheap motels and dusty landing strips wedged in among the ranches and the farms. I couldn't forget the faces of people and the generosity we found way out there. There were grizzled pilots and old kick-butt cropdusters, adventurers, and newsmen, all of them urging us on west. And my brother. Kern. He could fly like the blazes. I felt I should share what it was like to be fifteen and completely free, the side windows thrown open to the breeze, winging it out across the deserts and the mountains sustained by nothing more than four throbbing cylinders and a dream.

CHAPTER 1

MY BROTHER DUMBFOUNDED US WITH HIS PLAN ON A SATURDAY afternoon in October. My father, Kern, and I were an insep-arable threesome on weekends, and we were out in the back field chopping wood for my father's fire. I always enjoyed that time in the fall, splitting trunk logs with my father, because you couldn't be around the man and not feel virile. At forty-nine, he was still as strong and as handsome as a Percheron horse, and all two hundred pounds of him were muscle. Mow-ing through the logs with ferocious energy, he liked to swing his ax one-handed, just to show Kern and me that he could still do it, splitting big two-footers with a single blow. While he worked he filled the air with his lively banter and gently goaded us along, chiding Kern and me that we couldn't keep up "with the old man."

I liked the chill in the air and the feeling of winter coming on for another reason. The children of amputees are aware from the earliest age of the physical limitations placed upon a parent and develop their own accommodations for that. On winter evenings, when my father returned from work and his AA meetings, he generally worked for several more hours in his library downstairs, batting out a letter-to-the-editor or a political speech on his typewriter. He couldn't compose without a lit pipe in his mouth and a roaring fire in the hearth. But he was exhausted and sore from hauling his heavy wooden leg around all day and habitually took it off and tossed it in the corner as soon as he entered his library. Someone was needed to carry in his wood and stoke the fire all night. That became my job, for some reason having to do with the mysteries of personal desire and need, and I protected it like a sinecure. I did my homework every night on the antique cobbler's bench in front of his couch, getting up every fifteen or twenty minutes to throw another log on the fire, and then I read on the couch to keep him company until he was done. Many nights I fell asleep before my father was finished, and then he would hop one-legged across the floor to toss an afghan over me and another log or two into the fire. Even when we weren't getting along very well this was something my father and I could always do together. My memories of him and of winter are intimately bound up with the percussive tapping of his typewriter and the fragrance of cherry-scented tobacco and maple smoldering on the fire as I nodded off to sleep every night.

So, I always looked forward to that time with him. That day, while my father and I split the wood, Kern worked ahead of us, sectioning the logs with a chain saw. Midway through the afternoon, Kern switched off the saw and dropped it to the ground.

When he looked at my father, Kern's face was cocked sideways and his chin was angled high.

This generally meant trouble. Kern disliked confrontation, especially with my father. He tended to hold important things in until the last moment. By then the idea burned so intensely inside him that he tended to argue his case more insistently than he had to.

"Dad," Kern said. "Rinky and I are going to fly the Cub out to California next summer."

My father put down his ax.

"Whoa. Say again?"

"Dad. Rinky and I are going to fly the Cub to California next summer."

"Ah Jeez Kern. Where'd ya get an idea like that?"

"From you Daddy. You."

"Me? I never said anything like that. I mean, a thing like this takes time. Lots of time."

"No Dad. I've thought it all out. We'll rebuild the Cub in the barn over the winter and fly it west next summer. Think about that Dad, just think about it! Rinky and I flying coast to coast."

"Now listen here, son. When I was your age I *worked* my way across, piecemeal, over four years. I didn't even get to Texas until I was almost twenty. Hell, I bet you don't even know what comes after Ohio."

"Illinois."

"Wrong. Indiana."

"Big deal Daddy. Big deal. Who cares about Indiana? You're just saying no to say no."

"Big deal! Is that what you say to your father? Big deal? Well listen here Kern, this is a big idea. It scares the bejesus out of me. Have you thought about money? Have you thought about the deserts? And what about the mountains? How the hell are you going to get a Piper Cub over the Rockies? What pass are you going to fly?"

Kern wasn't sure about that yet.

"See Dad? See? You always turn a conversation into a quiz. How do I know what pass to fly? I'll figure that out later."

Even though the pipe in his mouth was already lit, my father reached into the pocket of his work jacket for his spare and nervously tapped in some tobacco.

"Oh Christ Kern. Why do you do these things to me?"

"Dad, you can't say no. I *have* to do this thing. I mean . . . Dad, I've been dreaming about this for a long time."

"Kern, I'm not saying 'no.' I'm saying 'maybe.' And that's a big, fat 'maybe' too. I've got to check my thinking on this."

"Fine Dad. Do all the thinking you want. But I've already made up my mind. We're going."

Kern pulled the chain saw back to life and roared through another log.

I was annoyed that my brother had included me in his scheme without consulting me first, but it never occurred to me to consider his plan unrealistic. We were very impulsive and barmy as a family and I was used to it by now. In 1958, when I was seven, my father decided that the ideal family vacation for us would be a horse-drawn tour of the Civil War and Revolutionary battlefields in Pennsylvania, so he went out and bought a team of horses and a large covered wagon and we spent a delightful summer doing just that, camping out by the roadsides or in farmers' fields every night. The year after that he bought an immense yellow school bus and we spent the next couple of summers bombing around in that. In the summer, when the weather was good, my father rode into his job in New York City on his motorcycle; in the winter, when there was snow, we rode to church on Sunday in a horse and sleigh. Now my brother was proposing that we fly coast to coast in the family Piper Cub. In the abstract, these ideas of ours always sounded insane. But then again they really weren't, considering us.

But the afternoon was ruined. My father was distracted by my brother's idea and was terrified that he was going to say yes too quickly, and he didn't have much heart for swinging the ax. Kern was distracted by the fear that my father would say no, which made him dangerous with a chain saw. Eventually they both lost interest in the wood pile and wandered off, and I finished splitting the wood myself.

My brother's timing could not have been worse for me. I was backsliding again, in trouble at school, and my father was furious about it. We had barely spoken in weeks. Any objections I might have had to my brother's coast to coast plan weren't going to count for much now.

That fall, I had enrolled as a freshman at Delbarton School, a Benedictine preparatory academy a few miles from our house. Kern had spent three years there and was now a senior. My father was very concerned about this step in my educational career. From kindergarten on I had been that most awful and perplexing kind of student—the academic star who was also a disciplinary terror—and my father was convinced that by sheer force of will and concern for my own future I could be cured of this schizophrenia. Because of AA, he was an advocate of the power of positive thinking. Several times over the summer he called me down to the library to deliver his favorite disciplinary chat, the "good kid" lecture. Essentially, my father said, I was a "good kid"—good at my studies, good at sports, good at making friends—but I was forever endangering my academic reputation with these "jackass stunts" of mine. He thought that I had done an excellent job of pulling the wool over the eyes of my grammar school teachers, but the Benedictines up at Delbarton were highly educated, sensitive monks, and they would see right through my antics. Over the summer, I was supposed to be "mentally preparing" myself for starting over at a new school, the enormous strides I was going to make in my behavior. For the duration of the lecture I nodded attentively and fixed my face with a purposeful, optimistic expression, and sometimes I even meant it. The conversation always ended the same way.

"All right son. That's the program. Cut out the bullshit, and behave. Kern's been up there for three years now and I haven't heard a single complaint. It's a new school for you, a clean slate. Deal?"

"Deal. Dad, I'm going to work on this."

Hazing was a big part of Catholic school life then. Every year, during the last week of September, the monks at Delbarton allowed the seniors to run this dumbass little institution called Freshman Initiation Week. Freshmen were required to run around the campus all day in these hideous green-and-white beanies, and to carry shoeshine kits, just in case a senior who had already had his shoes shined by twelve toadying freshmen decided that he needed still one more. At lunch, freshmen enjoyed the privilege of finishing off the seniors' half-eaten chocolate puddings. Afterward, the seniors stood around in a large group, calling out useful suggestions, while the freshmen made passionate love to the Greco-Roman statues in the formal gardens.

One morning that week, up at the bus stop in Morristown, a senior picked me out from the crowd of freshmen and instructed me to "moon my ass to traffic." It was a straightforward assignment. All a freshman had to do when a senior told him to moon his ass to traffic was hang his butt out on Route

24, shake it vigorously at a few passing cars, and then quietly drop back into the crowd and become an anonymous freshman again.

Of course, I could never comply with a request like that without adding some highly individualistic statement of my own. Besides, it was a beautiful, sunny morning, with the smell of crisp, dried leaves in the air and yellow and pink chrysanthemums shining in the courthouse beds across the road. Autumn weather inspired me. Why be an anonymous freshman, I thought, when I could go for broke and hang out a "total" bare-ass moon?

So, that's how I handled it. Unbuckling my belt, unzipping my fly and pulling my Fruit of the Loom briefs all the way down to my knees, I stepped out onto Route 24 and bent over with my butt facing the road, exposing a full bare-ass moon to traffic. The seniors howled with delight.

Nobody riding by in traffic seemed to care very much until this incredibly haggard old woman with saggy jowls and breasts screeched to a halt in her VW Bug. Jowls and breasts swaying, she leaned over, rolled down the window on the passenger side and screamed out.

"Young man, you're exposing yourself. Stop that!"

The Del boys loved that, and they all began to shout and cheer. For good measure, I gave the old lady another vigorous shake of my ass.

"Stop that! You're *exposing* yourself!"

When I wouldn't stop, the old lady squealed off in the VW, pulled to a stop at a pay phone, and called the cops. We heard the siren of a police cruiser just as our bus pulled up to the stop. By this time I had my pants buttoned back up and the old lady had run up from the corner. Jabbing a liver-spotted finger in my face, she pointed me out to the cops and demanded that I be "strung up" for exposure. To assure her that I'd be dealt with firmly, the cops placed me in handcuffs, stuffed me into the cruiser and we drove off for the station with the harridan in the VW following behind.

Down at the police station, it was the usual bogus routine. Most of the cops in that town were Catholic school dropouts, and most of the prosecutors were Catholic school graduates, and nobody got very excited about a Delbarton kid mooning traffic during Freshman Initiation Week. The police sergeant politely took down the lady's story on a yellow complaint sheet, thanked her for her trouble, and assured her that the department would "be in touch." As soon as the old bag left the police station the sergeant tossed the complaint form in a wastebasket and told one of the cops to drive me up to school.

It was a first for Delbarton. No student had ever been delivered to the monks in a police cruiser, and this caused quite a stir when we pulled up in front of Trinity Hall. As I stepped out of the cruiser and thanked the officer for the ride in fine Eddy Haskell style, students started leaning out of the classroom windows and cheering. Even a couple of priests were leaning out over the sills, smiling as they smoked their pipes. A bunch of students tore up their notebooks for confetti and threw it down for the ticker-tape parade effect.

"Nice ass Buck!"

"Way to go!"

"Fucking-A! Great moon!"

What the hell, I thought. It was the same old story for me. Fuck up, be a hero. I dropped my book bag and threw my arms over my head like a boxer to acknowledge the applause of my fellow students, and there were more cheers.

My brother usually drove up to school with a friend, and he wasn't at the bus stop that morning. But news of the mooning incident had traveled rapidly around school. When classes changed that morning, Kern came running down the hall toward me, all doe-eyed and worried.

"Rink! Jeez, what happened? Are you all right?"

"Kern. It's not a big deal, okay? Everybody's cheering for me."

"No way Rink. You're screwed. The priests are going to nail you for this. You'll get tons of detention."

But Kern had it all wrong. He'd been in so little trouble himself he didn't know the first thing about the disciplinary system. In the first place, the mooning incident had occurred while I was obeying the orders of a senior, during Freshman Initiation Week no less, which, technically, made it protected behavior. Second, I was an athlete—another thing Kern didn't know squat about—and athletes were never disciplined at Catholic schools. Father Peter "Skeet" Meaney, the school chaplain and freshman track coach, had recruited me for the cross-country team even before school began, and I had already won my first two races. Just before lunch, one of the seniors who had been at the bus stop that morning pulled me aside and told me how to handle the situation. Father Arthur, the school's red-haired, sclerotic dean of discipline, would scream at me and call me all kinds of nasty names, but all I had to do was yes-Father and no-Father him to death and I'd get off scot-free.

Artie cornered me up in the lunchroom. Clenching his fists inside his cassock and riding up on the balls of his feet, he screamed at me for ten minutes, calling me a "nudist creep" and telling me that I wasn't fit to shine my brother's shoes. But I could tell that the fix was in—Skeet, the track coach, had already interceded for me. Spewing invective, so angry I thought he was going to slug me, Artie assigned me two weeks of afternoon detention, but then he explained that this sentence would be "suspended" as long as I continued to win my cross-country races. The punishment was laughable, and Artie was obviously frustrated by his powerlessness. But he did think that he had a way of getting back at me.

"You know what else I'm going to do to you Buck?"

"No Father."

"I'm going to tell your father about this. In fact, I already have."

"Yes Father."

"I can't wait to see the look on your face after Tom Buck kicks your ass for this."

"Yes Father."

When I got home that night, my father's Oldsmobile was already parked in the porte cochere. He was home early, a bad sign. Only the most dire family emergency caused him to skip his AA meeting.

As I stepped onto the porch I saw him through the library window, sitting in his rocker while he stared into the fire and smoked his pipe. I couldn't possibly avoid him. The library was right there, at the front door.

"Godammit Rinker. You promised me. You're starting at a new school. You were supposed to stay out of trouble this time."

"Dad. A senior made me do it."

"Ah horseshit. If a senior told you to jump off the Brooklyn Bridge, would you do it?"

"Of course not. But this was different."

"Horseshit."

Lately, my father had been improvising techniques from the Alcoholics Anonymous program to deal with me. My behavioral problems, he thought, were like an alcoholic's, addictive and chronic, and they needed to be addressed systematically with an eye toward a long-term cure. He made me write out on one side of a sheet of paper all of the things that were wrong with me, and then on the other side I had to list all of the measures I could adopt to correct each defect. He made me read the biographies of AA founder Bill W. and the late Matthew Talbot of Dublin, a famous reformed drunk, who my father and his friends in AA were petitioning Rome to have declared the "patron saint of all alcoholics."

This time, my father decided to try a new approach—I think this one was the sixth or seventh step in the AA program. That's the one where recovering alcoholics contact all the loved ones and friends they had wronged while they were drinking and apologize for some grave offense that they still feel guilty about. Then they had to sit there and listen to all the negative things that their relative had to say about them. This was supposed to provide humbling but useful new material for the recovering alcoholic to work on.

"Rinker," my father said, "I want you to write a letter of apology to this woman. And no bullshit either. Just give me a no-nonsense, down-to-earth, bless-me-father-for-I-have-sinned letter for this old gal and maybe that'll help you understand why you did this."

"Dad, I'll do it."

I worked my ass off on that letter. Upstairs in my attic

room, banging away on my Smith-Corona typewriter, I wrote and rewrote, consulting my Webster's Dictionary and Roget's Thesaurus for just the right words. It had to be perfect. When I was done, I was so proud of the results that I made a carbon and saved it before I took the original down for my father's approval. Here's the last paragraph, which appeared just prior to "Sincerely Yours."

However, I am truly sorry and I *do* feel guilty. I had no way of knowing that my thoughtless actions would pro-voke such tortured consternation in a woman in your frail condition and of such advanced age. Please don't hesi-tate to contact me if I can be of any further assistance during your recovery from this most troubling and mem-orable event.

As he read the letter, my father's hands trembled and he fumbled for his pipe.

"Ah shit Rinker. Look at this thing. You booby-trapped it."

"Hey, c'mon Dad. It's a good letter. I worked hard on that."

"Ah, bull."

"Dad, let's just get this over with. I'll mail it in the morn-ing."

"Rinker, we can't send this thing. The goddam lady will die of a heart attack."

Terrified that I might actually mail it, my father crumpled up the letter and threw it into the fire. He stared into the flames for a while and then sighed.

"Ah hell Rinker. I don't know whether you're going to end up in the White House, or down on the Bowery. But right now, you're my biggest pain in the ass."

"Ah Dad."

"Look. Go upstairs and study or something, will you? Get out of my sight."

When I got to the door my father called out again. He was sitting in his rocker with his back toward me, facing the fire.

"You know what really bothers me about this?"

"No, what?"

"Kern. Your brother. This stuff really hurts him, Rinker. He's very upset and confused about you. Do you realize that? I've asked you not to antagonize him, but you always find a way."

I wasn't really that worried about my brother. I'd been antagonizing Kern for so long he practically expected it by now. But I felt awful about what my father said, because he wasn't really talking about Kern, he was talking about Kern and him together. My father had worked hard over the past four years bringing Kern along, teaching him to fly. His life then was enormously frustrating and complex—too many kids, too many bills, a job in New York that he no longer enjoyed—and watching Kern grow as a pilot had erased a lot of his pain and brought him joy. The day my brother soloed, I think, was the happiest day in my father's life. They were perfect together, and Kern was practically my father's alter ego now. Kern's happiness meant everything to my father, everyone in the family could see that. Bringing Kern out of his shell and boosting his self-confidence had been a major accomplishment for my father. By hurting one of them, he seemed to be saying, I was hurting both of them, threatening the one great contentment of his life over the past few years.

I hated myself for that, but I also hated my situation. Everything I did had to be considered in the light of my father and my brother's expectations. Their relationship was primary and intense, a given. I was secondary, the also-ran in our threesome. Perhaps I should have been able to figure all of this out. A lot of my behavior had to do with rebelling against what I considered my father's inordinate sympathy and love for my brother, and certainly I was envious of their relationship. But nobody figures very much out at the age of fourteen.

I never felt guilty for very long. This is just family, I thought, something to get away from. Why should I worry about my father and my brother when things were going so well up at school? Everybody loved the way I mooned that old lady, and I wasn't going to walk away from popularity that came as easy as that.

My father was impatient by nature and hated dwelling on a problem, and he knew that Kern had him trapped. My father had rushed us through childhood, always throwing us up onto a hotter horse, or into a faster plane, insisting that we accept manly responsibilities early. He was a grand eccentric himself, always spouting off some crazyass barnstorming scheme of his own, and now Kern had simply outdone him. A coast to coast flight was exactly the kind of dreamy, preposterously impractical act that he expected of his oldest son. If he withheld his permission now, he would be turning his back on the boy he had raised.

One night late that week my father called us down to his library. He was sitting on his rocker in front of the fire staring pensively into the flames, drawing on a long, curved briar.

"Ah screw it Kern," my father said. "I'm sick of thinking about this. You and Rinky can fly to California. Hell, it's even a good idea."

Kern launched off the couch.

"Yoweeee! Thanks Dad. Thanks! I promise we won't disappoint you. Jeez. This is great!"

Dashing out of the library for the staircase, he floated up the carpeted steps as if he were riding a cushion of air.

"Whoa! Hey Kern, whoa," my father called after him. "Where you going? I wanna talk about this thing. Plan the trip."

"Later Dad," Kern called down from the landing. "I want to order my maps."

My father sighed, shrugged his shoulders, and laughed.

"Jeez," he said. "Kern."

"Yeah," I said. "Kern."

My father had this enormously persuasive manner of leaning over almost perpendicular in his chair, joining the tips of his fingers from both hands into a steeple, and staring someone right in the face. I'd seen him do this at AA meetings, at political gatherings, and with the worshipful young salesmen flocking in and out of his office in New York. He tapped me on the knee.

"Now listen here young man," he said. "One thing."

"Dad, you don't have to say it. I know. Don't screw this one up. For Kern's sake."

"Well good, Rinker. Exactly. But think of yourself too. Your brother *likes* you, he wants you along on this trip. Think of the things you'll learn, working on the plane. And the country you'll see! Why, Jesus, Texas. Texas! Texas is magnificent from the air. This is a wonderful opportunity for you."

"Sure Dad. Texas."

"Deal?"

"Deal."

This was the kind of thinking I had to engage in. Because my brother liked me, because it was a wonderful opportunity for me, we would be flying out past Texas together, and then somehow we would hoist ourselves over the Rocky Mountains in an 85-horsepower Piper Cub.

CHAPTER 2

WE BROUGHT THE CUB HOME THE DAY AFTER THANKSGIVING. IN earlier years we disassembled our "winter planes" out at the airport, lashing the wings to wooden cradles mounted on the sides of our Jeep pickup and hitching the tail to the rear bumper, so that the plane towed backward on its landing gear. We inched the plane home that way, over twelve miles of back roads, and it usually took us all day. But Kern decided this year that this method wasn't efficient. He made arrangements with a neighbor, Barclay Morrison, to fly the Cub into the small private landing strip that Barclay maintained on his place. This would save us a lot of time and wear and tear on the plane.

Kern was excited about it. He planned to fly the Cub in himself, and he was determined to have the plane in the barn by the long Thanksgiving weekend, so we could get a head start on stripping off the old fabric and sanding down the airframe for repainting. He couldn't wait to get to work, and all through Thanksgiving dinner he bubbled over about his plans for the plane and his various dreams about our trip.

The next morning was blustery and cold. A ceiling of high cirrus blocked the sun and waves of low cumulus raked the hills. The wind was blowing straight out of the north, gusting to twenty-five knots or more, and we knew without even driving over there that we'd face a fierce crosswind at Barclay's east-to-west strip.

Barclay's field was narrow and short, just 800 feet. It sat atop a high, grassy hill with steeply sloping ravines on three sides. In winds like these, Kern knew that he couldn't possibly put the Cub down and get it stopped before he ran off the edge.

At breakfast, Kern was very glum about it, and his immense brown eyes were opened wide with dejection, as big as hubcaps.

"Dad. Rink," he sighed. "The mission is scrubbed."

My father sat with his elbows on the table, holding a cup of coffee in both hands. He hated to see Kern disappointed like that. He stared dreamily out the windows to the trees at the far edge of our field, which were bent over in the wind. Normally these were no conditions to fly in, but normally had never appealed to my father very much.

"Wipe that scowl off your face son," my father said. "I'll fly the Cub into Barclay's for you."

"Dad, no," Kern said. "It's too dangerous. There must be a 90-degree crosswind over there today. We can wait until tomorrow."

"Bull," my father said. "Tomorrow there might be snow. I can put the Cub down at Barclay's. It'll be fun for you, watching the old fart do it."

Little shivers of fear and pride trembled through me whenever my father gave himself a challenge like that. My father was good, very good at flying. There wasn't a pilot around who had quite his touch. He probably could put the Cub down at Barclay's. But it would be hazardous, and there wasn't much point to it. We could always break the plane down at the airport and haul it home from there.

But Kern and I knew that it was useless to challenge my father when he was in a mood to prove himself. In his repertoire of barnstorming blarney tales, precarious landings were his favorite. It was a matter of self-esteem for him. He could shoehorn a plane into places that other pilots wouldn't even look at.

After breakfast, Kern gypsied around the barn for his tools, and then we all piled into the chalky warmth of our battered Willys pickup and drove out to the airport in Basking Ridge.

At the airport, nobody was flying. There were reports of severe turbulence and a cold front with snow moving down the east coast. My father wiggled into his old sheepskin flying suit and sat by the gas stove in the pilots' shack to stay warm. Kern and I walked down the flight line, preflighted and started the Cub, and taxied it up to the shack. We tied it down near the shack with the engine still idling. My father told us to leave right away for Barclay's. The wind was blowing so hard he thought he might need us to hold down the wings once he landed.

When we got over to the Morrison place, Barclay walked down to his grass strip with his Irish wolfhounds. He was an elegant, quiet man, immaculately dressed in wool trousers, polished shoes, and a tweed cap. He sat with us on the warm hood of the Jeep waiting for my father and the Cub to show up. His own ship, a Helio Courier bush plane, sat nearby, its tiedown chains snapping and banging in the fierce wind.

Barclay glanced at his windsock up on the hill. It was rifled straight out, indicating a strong crosswind directly across the grass runway.

"That's quite a wind," Barclay said.

Kern felt defensive about it.

"Barclay," he said. "If he doesn't like the look of it he won't land. He'll wiggle the wings for us to pick him back up at the airport."

"That's all right son," Barclay said. "I know your father. He'll at least try to put the plane down."

Under normal wind conditions, landing a plane is a relatively straightforward business, no more difficult than docking a boat. Pilots land by pointing the plane directly into the wind, to retain lift and slow down the groundspeed before the wings are stalled just above the ground. Landing into the wind also helps avoid the dangerous crosswinds that can sweep the plane off the runway as it becomes vulnerable at slow speeds.

In a light crosswind, there's an accepted procedure for

landing. Lining the plane up with the runway, the pilot banks one wing into the wind to correct for drift. The tail rudder is pushed the opposite way to correct for the wing being down and to keep the plane straight. Thus cross-controlled, the plane crabs into the wind toward the runway. The crab is corrected and the wings leveled just before touchdown. There are all kinds of variations—side slips; approaching the runway at a slight angle; touching down on one wheel—for every pilot has his own "crosswind technique."

One thing a pilot is never supposed to do, according to the Federal Aviation Administration (FAA) rule book, is exceed a plane's published "crosswind component." Generally, that means winds deflecting more than 45 degrees to the runway, blowing above ten or twelve knots. According to the laws of aerodynamics, a plane simply can't be put down in such conditions. Most pilots learn the lesson for good by trial and error. Some of the finest flyers I've known have taken out trees and gas trucks before establishing their personal "crosswind limit."

Barclay's strip that day was so far beyond any known crosswind component that it was an FAA violation just looking at it.

My father had a distinct personality in the air. Whereas on the ground he was all bravado and blarney, inside a cockpit he had a jaunty, old-fashioned grace. He was strictly seat of the pants, a throwback to the barnstormers of the 1930s. When landing he approached high and fast, insurance against an engine failure, and then he spilled off the extra height and speed on final approach with a dramatic sideslip. Flying somewhere, he dreamily meandered off course to follow rivers and other landmarks.

There was no mistaking the Cub we saw darting around the low clouds that morning at Barclay's. We could see the wings rocking as my father fought the turbulence and the nose dipped down in level flight from running the prop too fast, which was the way that he flew. As he turned in toward the field he banked the wings over sharply, kicking out some top rudder to slip off the extra altitude.

My father was too gifted a hand to even consider fighting

a crosswind as strong as the one he faced that morning. He didn't linger either like most pilots would, circling carefully to check the wind and the field.

Instead, a quarter mile out, he simply turned perpendicular to the runway and pointed the nose of the Cub at the tip of the windsock, flying directly upwind. He ran the engine at half-power to penetrate the strong wind and held the nose high so the Cub dropped like a elevator. He threw open the side windows and stuck his head out into the air for better visibility. The long white scarf he liked to wear when he was flying fluttered out into the slipstream like the tail of a kite.

That's how he flew it, all the way down. Perpendicular to the runway, directly into the wind. It was the ultimate cross-wind technique. At 30 feet, dropping down below the trees, the nose was still pegged on the windsock.

It was all one graceful and unified motion, what he did next.

At the edge of the runway, right over our heads, my father gunned the engine. Then he made a sharp 90-degree turn to line up with the runway, banking so low and so hard that the wingtip looked as if it was pivoting against the ground.

When he was lined up with the runway he snapped the wings in the other direction back past the level point and planted the windward tire on the grass. He was still carrying a lot of power and he was fast, very fast, nowhere near a stall, but it was a brilliant stroke because he needed all that power and speed to keep air moving over the controls so he could fight the wind drift. Very few pilots would think of handling it this way, but then there very few pilots like him. He knew—actually, he was betting—that the motion of rocking the wheels back and forth on the grass to fight the plane onto the ground, and fish-tailing the fuselage to fight the wind, would load up enough drag to slow the plane in time.

The end of the runway and the ravine below were racing up quickly to swallow the plane. But there was nothing my father could do about that now because he was committed, and his only choice was to fight the wind all the way down the strip and keep the plane running straight and in one piece.

It was a hauntingly beautiful moment, those three or four seconds while my father and the Cub darted past. Plane and pilot and the elements they faced were locked in perfect combat, so evenly matched, so near disaster, that it was impossible to determine where skill left off and luck, or fate, or the divine protection extended to the truly foolhardy took over. The risk my father was taking, and the grace he handled it with, seemed transmitted from him and the plane into me. And he was really exerting himself now, working that plane for every last ounce of effectiveness. Through the windows of the Cub I could see him leaning into the controls and pumping his arms back and forth on the stick, beating the four-point arc all the way to the stops, and he was furiously walking the rudders to keep the plane tracking straight and to get the other wheel down, and all of these bodily movements were visible in the rapid deflections of the controls on the wings and the tail. The power and swiftness and peril of it all was entrancing, and there was something in the vision of that plane straining to get on the ground that transcended each of these things individually and became, whole, an act of supreme competence. As he skittered past us on one wheel my father had this grim half-smile of determination on his face.

Weather-cocking in the gusts, bouncing from wheel to wheel, the Cub jackassed all the way down Barclay's strip.

When he got to the end of the field, my father stood on the right brake. The Cub careened around on one wheel for a ground-loop. Ordinarily this was a maneuver to be avoided but my father didn't have a choice in this case, and he knew how to ground-loop a plane. He allowed the tail to sway up high before he corrected with down stick, so there would be enough air blowing over the tail controls for them to respond. He did one other thing at that moment that I've never heard of or seen since. Halfway through the ground loop, he fire-walled the throttle and the prop roared, yanking him the rest of the way around the ground loop. It was an extremely dangerous thing to do, but stylish too, and he was so skilled and dumbass-lucky that it worked for him.

Coming around, the right wingtip almost touched the ground and the locked tire threw up a spray of grass divots.

All of this occupied just a few seconds and it wasn't very elegant. But the plane was down and stopped and nobody cares about elegance when the crosswind component has just been exceeded by 100 percent. The little Cub stood alone on the grass, framed by the sky and the low clouds behind it so that it looked like it was still flying, because the ground all around it fell off steeply and buffets of wind were still catching the wings and lifting them slightly. My father gave the propeller one last blast and taxied up to gain the protection of the tree line. The Cub was splattered all over with mud, but it didn't have a scratch.

Kern and I ran down and hung off the wing struts to steady the plane. In the cockpit, my father was shivering and his face was bright red from taking all that slipstream with his head out the side. He looked over to Kern and shrugged with that gleeful, boyish smirk he always had when he'd done something insane in a plane and gotten away with it again. The prop shaft went click-click-click as he shut the engine down.

As I hung from the wing strut, my heart pounded like a ball-peen and tears stung the corner of my eyes. I never knew whether to love or detest my father at such moments. I was annoyed by not being able to control my emotions and even more by their frustrating lack of certainty. In just a few seconds, I had passed from certainty that my father was going to crash to the elation of watching him getting the plane stopped. Yet right now, I knew, I could just as easily be down at the bottom of the hill, pulling him out of an overturned plane.

These anguished feelings always passed quickly, though. Then suddenly the arresting beauty of the landing—the steep sideslip down over the trees, the turn low to the ground, then the wheels meeting the grass and the ground-loop—would go by as a blur and merge with another, dominant feeling. I forgot everything else I felt about my father and knew only pride. Maybe he lived too dangerously and was always frightening us by testing himself, but that was the father I had. He was a great old flyer and nobody could out-barnstorm the man.

Barclay walked down with his wolfhounds. He stepped underneath the wing and helped my father out, disentangling his legs from the rudder cables than ran along the floor of the cockpit.

Barclay was relieved and amazed, but he was too polite and understated a man to say the wrong thing.

"Well, that's a crosswind landing, Tom."

"Yeah. Thanks for letting us use your strip."

Then Barclay walked back up the hill with his dogs.

We could usually take apart a plane in less than an hour. It was more or less just a matter of removing the wings from the fuselage. The bolts holding the main beams of the wing, the spars, come out just above the cockpit. The strut supports that hold the wings up by triangulating down to the landing gear are also disconnected by removing bolts. Secondary parts such as the control cables and fuel lines are detached. Once lifted off the fuselage, the wings of a Piper Cub aren't that much heavier than a metal canoe, and Kern and I mounted them on the wooden cradles bolted to the fenders of our pickup.

We secured the wings on the cradles with hay-rope. Removing the propeller from the engine shaft, we wrapped it in a blanket and laid it on the bed of the pickup. Then we chained the Cub's tailwheel to the Jeep's rear-hitch and bounced off across Barclay's field toward home.

I always felt embarrassed in that leafy, plush community of winding country lanes and quaint horsefarms, riding home in our shitrigged pickup and plane. Our truck was an old beam-chassis Willys, blue and rusting out on the sides, with exhaust and smoke from the burning clutch wafting up through the floorboards. The muffler had blown a hole years ago and we'd never bothered to replace it. As we belched along Blue Mill Road, traffic backed up behind us and people stared. Barclay's place sat right in between the big Kirby and McGraw estates. Beyond that we had to pass the Colgate and

Francis homes, and then Congressman Freylinghuysen's vast spread. Most of our neighbors were quiet Protestant bluebloods, or rich Catholics aping Protestant bluebloods, projecting a veneer of effortless social perfection. They glided by in polished Jaguars or new Chevy Suburbans towing matching horse vans, and spent the Thanksgiving weekend riding with Jackie Kennedy in the local fox hunts. We were the neighborhood Joads, dragging home a 1946 Piper Cub behind our dilapidated Jeep.

But I could get over my social embarrassment, because my father was always revived by our annual rite of bringing home a plane. It reminded him of his salad days in the 1930s and 1940s, when he began every winter by stashing a plane in a barn somewhere. He was giddy and red-faced, laughing all the way home as the traffic clogged up behind us.

My father was particularly pleased with himself that day. He hadn't flown in quite a while and he was glad to have acquitted himself so well in front of us at Barclay's. But he was still shivering and cold when we pulled into our place. We left him at the porte cochere, so he could go inside and warm up in the bath. Kern and I could stow the plane in the barn ourselves.

My father stepped out of the Jeep, lit his pipe, and leaned into the cab beside Kern with his leg resting on the running board.

"Well good, boys, good. Now you've got your airplane."

"Dad," Kern said. "I'm very grateful for this. Thanks. Not many pilots could do what you did today."

"Nah, nah, nah, Kern," my father said. "I mean, shit. In my day, every pilot flew like this."

In his white scarf and sheepskin flying suit, he skipped brightly up the steps and across the porch of the house, whistling and pleased with himself, an old flyer who hadn't lost his touch.

Kern let out the clutch of the Jeep and steered for the barn.

"Rink, you wanna know something?"

"No, what?"

"Daddy's a hot shit."

This was the problem I had with my brother, the effect he had on me. He always insisted on looking at the bright side of life, half of the truth, bubbling all over with enthusiasm about something that had just happened, especially if it involved my father. They crashed airplanes together, and he was happy about it. They got into screaming matches, but, Kern thought, this was "good for their relationship." For Kern, at the end of every rainbow, there was a big, freaking pot of gold. His ebullience was so maddening to me that I would instinctively disagree with him about everything, even when he was right, and I would feel this desperate urge to look at the bleaker and more realistic side of life, simply because he refused to do it.

My silence riled him and I knew it, so I didn't say anything at first. When we got to the barn he tried again. He wasn't going to shut off the Jeep and stow the plane until I agreed with him.

"Rink, are you listening to me?"

"Yeah . . . I'm listening."

"I just said: Daddy's a hot shit."

"Ah Kern. He's a maniac. He practically killed himself in the Cub today."

"See? See? That's you, isn't it? You've always got to be shitting all over Daddy!"

"Kern, that's not shitting all over Daddy. It's the truth. I'm only saying, he's a maniac."

"But Rink. It's the same thing! You say maniac. I say hot shit. It just depends on how you look at it, that's all."

"Fine Kern, fine," I said. "If it's the same thing, let's call him a maniac."

"Okay Rink. Fine," Kern said. "Look, I'll make you a deal. I'll call him a maniac if you call him a hot shit."

Ah Jesus. This was another thing Kern did to me, the old Tom Sawyer–Huck Finn routine. You get my bag of marbles, I get your dead cat.

"Fine, Kern. Deal," I said. "Now let's just get this over with, okay? Daddy's a hot shit."

"Great! You said it. Now it's my turn. Daddy's a maniac. A maniac! Now, that wasn't so hard Rink, was it?"

"Oh no Kern, no," I said. "It was easy. Listen, one other thing."

"Yeah Rink?"

"Kern, you're a jackass."

We stripped the old fabric off the Cub that afternoon. As the shop lights cast spooky shadows of us on the walls, we ran our pen-knives down across the fuselage fabric, pulling the stiff linen off the plane in long rectangular sheets. When we got to the wings, the stench of stale butyrate dope greeted us from inside the rib compartments. It had seeped in there and been trapped for years as the Cub baked outside in the hot sun. The smell assaulted our nostrils and filled the barn, and I always liked that first whiff of airplane dope in the fall. It reminded me of the long winter of inebriation that we faced re-doping the plane.

The metal airframe was in better shape than we expected. Here and there the tubular steel framing was pitted with rust, but that could be easily fixed by sanding and then applying a new coat of rustproof paint. The wing structure consisted of aluminum ribs arrayed in a parallel row, held in place by the two metal spars. Except for a dent or two in the sheet metal that formed the leading edge of the wing, the wings were in excellent shape.

Kern and I baled the old fabric with twine and carried it outside to burn in a one hundred-gallon drum. We started a fire with newspaper and kindling, piled on the bales of fabric, and stood back as the highly flammable linen ignited. Then we warmed up some apple cider on the shop hotplate and carried two chairs outside to watch the fire.

Stripping a plane and watching the fabric burn was a Druid ritual for us, and we looked forward to it every fall. Misty snow began to fall and patches of yellow light splashed out the windows from the shop lights. After the first bales of fabric burned down we threw on the rest. Immense orange and purple flames climbed for the trees, vaporizing the falling snow into wisps of steam and crackling up to the branches above.

Kern grabbed a stick and drew a rough map of the country in the snow. We hadn't talked about the coast to coast flight very much yet and he was anxious to draw me into his scheme.

"Rinker," he said, "here's the plan."

He made little triangular scratchings for the Allegheny Mountains and a long squiggly line for the Ohio River. Then he drew in the Mississippi and the western plains. He'd been looking at the big world air chart out at the airport. You'd think that to get to Los Angeles all we had to do was take off from New Jersey and point the Cub due west, he said, but actually we'd fly a southwest course for most of the trip, cutting a diagonal across the midwest and the Mississippi Valley before we turned right for the "wide open spaces" of the great west.

Kern was very excited about that, the wide open spaces of the west, especially Texas. He talked about places in mythic Texas—Texarkana, Wichita Falls, El Paso—as if he had already been there. The only thing he couldn't figure out was the Rocky Mountains. They had him stumped, even a little bit afraid.

He was much further along in his thinking than I thought. Still, I wasn't confident about this trip. I didn't see why we had to do it.

Kern stared into the flames, brooding with his hands on his chin. He could sense my reluctance and was frustrated by it. He wanted to get through and explain why he wanted to make the flight, but was afraid of how I would react. Whenever my brother turned sincere on me and revealed a part of himself, I would dig into him for it, and my verbal assaults on him wounded him a lot more than I realized at the time. It wasn't simply the indignity of it. He had this image of what an older brother should be, partly his own expectations, and partly expectations drilled into him by my father. The older boy was supposed to be tough, impervious to insult, such an authority figure that the younger brother wouldn't dare cross him. But that wasn't the case with us and this never stopped bothering Kern.

But I had a lot of admiration for the way he got out what

he had to say that night, while we were outside watching the fabric burn. He knew that I would probably rip him to shreds but he said it anyway.

During the years that we were learning to fly at Basking Ridge, the star of the strip was a young airshow pilot, Eddie Mahler. Eddie was a legend on the east coast airshow circuit, even nationally, the best of a new breed of stunt pilot that was revolutionizing airshow work. Among other astonishing maneuvers, Eddie was credited with inventing the "inverted ribbon pickup." Screaming in over a runway with his open-cockpit biplane rolled upside-down, Eddie plucked a ribbon off a pole with his landing gear and then zoomed back up over the crowd. But most of his airshow work was done in a pearl-white T-6 Texan, virtually identical to my father's. He and my father often flew off for the shows together, buzzing in low over the crowds in their Twin-Texans and doing some formation aerobatics. When they rumbled in with the Texans and threw open their canopies in front of the stands, the show announcers called them Big Eddie and Peg-Leg Buck. Both of us hero-worshiped Eddie and were impressed that my father could fly with him like that, but it wasn't as big a deal for me. It was the sort of crazyass thing that I expected my father to do. But Kern couldn't get over it. He was awed by them both.

Kern looked up from the flames.

"Rink, you're gonna laugh at me for this, but I'm going to say it."

"Kern, I won't laugh."

"Bull, but I want you to know this. Look, I don't want to be this scrawny little teenager nobody ever heard of, okay? I want to be like Big Eddie Mahler. Flying across the country is the most exciting thing we can do with our lives right now. People will notice. It'll be a great thing for aviation. Even guys like Big Eddie will have to respect us. Rink, I want to be *known*, okay? And, you know, I wake up in the morning and remember this trip, and I say to myself, 'Jeez, who the hell came up with this crazy idea?' I mean, I'm afraid of it, Rink, really afraid sometimes, but we have to do it. The only

The great Eddie Mahler (left) was a legend on the airshow circuit, and we hero-worshipped him as boys.

thing I could come up with, the only thing I could think of, was flying coast to coast in the Cub."

This was a moment, I suspected, when my personality could be fatal for my brother. I tried to get the right words out.

"Kern, I can understand that. I mean, I actually do. But don't call yourself scrawny, okay?"

"But I am scrawny."

"Fuck that Kern. We're *both* scrawny."

"But Rink, that's the point! It's easy for you. You're an athlete. You're popular at school. Even when you mooned that old lady everybody loved you for it. All I've got is aviation, and I just want to do this one thing really well. Just one thing Rink. One thing! I need you for this. Just help me fly the Cub to California."

Jesus. I felt I could cry about this. To Kern, everything I did well qualified me as an awful brother. What was I supposed to do? Throw on a pair of dork shorts and play with Louie? Turn myself into an athletic spaz? I wasn't miserable because Kern blamed me for my success. I was miserable because I couldn't understand why he just didn't ignore me.

"Ah shit Kern . . . okay. It's fine. I don't want to fight about this. But there's still one thing I don't understand."

"What's that?"

"Look," I said. "What do you need me for? If I were in your shoes, I'd make this flight alone. You know, screw the younger brother, just leave his ass at home. Then you get to California and you can hog all the credit for yourself."

"Rink, no. You've got to understand this part. It's important. I can't make this trip alone. Jeez, think about it. We'll hit weather. We've got mountains to cross. And the deserts—I think there's eight hundred miles of deserts between here and L.A. It'll be a full-time job for me just handling the plane. We're going to need positive contact with the ground at all times, a navigator, Rink. We can't get lost. I can't do both of those jobs at once."

Most of what he was saying was true, but I wouldn't appreciate it until we got out there. Part of my problem was that I was less experienced at flying, and I didn't understand everything that went into it. My brother had always made it look easy, and I took a lot for granted. But mostly I was stalled by my congenital personality clash with Kern. Everything he said and did burned with earnestness and conviction. It was like atmospheric static out there, cluttering up a radio signal. Now that there was really something to be earnest about, I couldn't hear it.

But I really didn't want to fight with Kern anymore. I felt awful because he always seemed to be jealous of me. I would have to make the effort.

"All right Kern. I'm going to do this thing for you. For the next six months, you own my ass."

"No Rink, no. We're going to do this together, and share everything. I want you to bone up on navigation, study the books, learn the maps. It's something you're good at and we'll need it on the flight. We're a team, Rink. We're going to do this as a team."

Shitbag. A team. I cringed inside when my brother got optimistic and saintly like that, as if we really could reform and become a "team," mostly because I was afraid that we couldn't. But I had to try.

"Okay Kern," I said. "A team. The team approach."

The wind picked up and the snow started falling harder, slanting down in front of our faces and eddying into swirls around our feet. Kern threw on the last bales of fabric and the flames rose again, throwing shadows of the trees against the barn. When the snow started caking on our hair, we went back inside and worked some more on the plane.

We finished sanding the fuselage on Sunday afternoon. Dusting off our old Sears Roebuck paint compressor, we sprayed on the first coat of military-green zinc paint. As Kern swept over the airframe with the spray-gun, I followed behind with a rag to wipe off any drips.

Kern and Louie had wired the barn for sound. When my father updated the radios in his Texan, they rescued the old low-frequency receiver from the corner of the hangar floor and installed it in the tack room adjoining our shop. The Texan radio was a big heavy tube job dating back to World War II, with these immense, clunky dials that made it look like it belonged in a Soviet spacecraft. They cannibalized a set of speakers out of my grandfather's old bullet-nosed Studebaker, which sat abandoned out behind the barn. The result was another Buck family shit-rig, with a nice assist for Louie, but it worked all right for the shop. The speakers were scratchy and throbbed like bassoons on the low notes, and we could only receive a couple of stations. But one high-powered AM signal came in loud and clear.

WABC in New York, 77 on the dial. It was the nation's most antic Top-40 station, and all of the disc jockeys were lunatics; Cousin Brucie, "Big Dan" Ingram, Scott Muny, Ron Lundy, Harry Harrison and, in the morning, the unbeatable Herb Oscar Anderson. Super-dumb, super-cool, ABC was the Golden Age of Pop, and nobody we knew listened to anything else.

So, to the acrid smell of zinc paint and the hiss of the spray nozzle, listening to ABC, we worked until late Sunday night. Kern was very meticulous about the quality of work he would accept and whenever we finished a section, he would go over everything with an inspection light, peering into every corner and weld from a wheeled dolley on the floor. If he found a paint drip or spot of rust that he didn't like, we'd re-sand and paint again. He was whistling all the time, immensely pleased to have his coast-to-coast ship in the barn. Every once and a while he exploded with one of those chirpy thoughts that would occur to him.

"Hey Rink, you know what?"

"No, what?"

"When we're done, this is going to be the cleanest Piper Cub in America. Bar none."

Bar none.

But I was getting a nice high off the paint thinner now, and I liked the pungent, brittle sensation of the zinc chromate congealing to my fingers. The old fighter-plane radio blared, and Kern and I sang along to "Wooly Bully," "Turn! Turn! Turn!," "Hang on Sloopy," and, the best, Barry McGuire's "Eve of Destruction." The long Christmas vacation from school was coming up soon, and it would be fun working out here without anybody else around. Kern and I were monsters for work together, and I was secretly proud of that.

We were on our way. From the sanding, my fingers were blistered and bloody and my back ached. But I liked singing along to the music and shining the airframe gun-metal clean, and once and a while I would silently erupt with some chirpy thought of my own. *Jesus, Kern is really happy out here, working on the plane. And I was happy too.*

CHAPTER 3

THE WINTER THAT WE WORKED ON THE CUB WAS SNOWY AND cold. Arctic blasts from Canada blew down every couple of weeks, loading the barn corners with powdery drifts and the roof gutters with ice. The frozen landscape outside seemed to establish the need for four walls against the world and to lock us inside with the plane. Over the long Christmas recess from school, Kern and I worked on the Cub for ten straight days. After that, we spent nearly every school night and every weekend out in the barn with the plane.

Kern considered the blizzards a godsend. From the moment he came up with the idea for a coast-to-coast flight, his biggest worry was money. My father offered us $500 toward rebuilding the plane, but we knew that this was money he probably couldn't spare, and Kern felt that this really wouldn't be "our plane," "our trip," if most of the funds came from my father. But several times during the storms classes were canceled up at school, and our Willys was equipped with a snow plow and hitch. Kern decided that we should go into the snow-plowing business together to raise our "Cub money."

Kern approached our new trade like a seasoned Junior Achiever. On our first day, as we rumbled out of the drive in the middle of a raging snowstorm, he bubbled over with various ideas about the brilliant "sales techniques" and "pricing strategies" we could try out on our customers. Mostly, however, these were a crock of shit. Our sole sales technique, as it developed, was that I stepped out into the biting wind to shovel and sweep the walk whenever someone agreed to let us plow their place—the "competition wouldn't think of this," Kern said—while he cleared the drive inside the warm cab of the Jeep, listening to Cousin Brucie on WABC.

As a businessman, Kern completely fell apart when it came to customer relations. He was too shy to knock on someone's door to solicit business or collect money. That became my job too. At first I was annoyed about this, and it revived all of my worries about Kern. But over the winter I gradually began to appreciate that Kern and I worked quite well together, a realization so shocking to me I treated it as a major revelation about human character. Vastly different personalities could actually complement each other, backing and filling over their respective deficiencies. This was stunning information, a breakthrough for me. Not despite our differences, but because of them, we were merging into a winning pair, the "team" my brother so desired.

Everyone appreciated the earnest, conscientious way Kern approached a drive. The plowing job had to be perfect. If he couldn't angle the plow close enough to a garage to clear every last inch of powder around the doors, he would send me over to shovel it all out by hand. The flagstone walks had to be immaculately swept. A lot of our customers were these rich old Protestant ladies who lived in the big houses up along Silver Lake. Ever since the Kennedys came along, they had all begun entertaining these ridiculous notions about the wonderful, virtuous things that happened in large Irish-Catholic families like ours. When I stepped up to the door to collect, I would wait for old Mrs. Babcock or Mrs. Hart to start gushing about the "super" job we had done on her drive, and then I would yes-ma'am and no-ma'am her to death before I went in for the kill, charging double and sometimes even triple what Kern told me to ask. Until he got used to it, Kern was indignant every time I came back to the Jeep with the money.

"Rink, you screwed that old lady! Forty bucks. Jeez. I told you to charge $20. You *screwed* her."

"Ah fuck it Kern. That old bag is rolling in it. I should have charged her $50."

So the snow season went. In January, there were a couple of big blows that netted us $150 a day, and by the end of the month we'd already raised $600. We made more than enough with the Willys for all of our Cub fabric and new parts. We were both gloriously happy about it. Kern kept all of our money in a Chock Full O' Nuts coffee can that he hid on a shelf up in his room. On the side of the can, he'd slapped on a piece of masking tape and labeled it with black magic-marker: N.Y To L.A. / 1966. Even after we started buying new parts for the Cub like crazy, way exceeding our original budget, there was always a reserve of $250 or more in the coffee can. It was an enormous morale boost for us. On the theory that he didn't want his sons to have to "struggle" the way he did as a boy, my father actively discouraged us from holding down jobs during the school year, and we were per-petually dependent on him for money. Now we were not only building our own plane, but flush with cash all the time, and our feelings of independence surged. Kern started calling me the Grim Rinker, for the way I bilked all of our customers. For the way he kept track of the cash, counting it up every night and keeping these asinine records in a little account book that he carried around in his pocket, I started calling him First National Kern.

The next big obstacle we faced was my homework, which was a royal pain in the ass and getting in the way of working on the plane. Delbarton set very high academic standards, and I couldn't believe the way the Benedictines piled on the assignments every night. My courses included Latin, biology, geometry, French, English, history, and religion. Four hours of homework a night was pretty standard, and many nights I wasn't done and ready to help Kern with the plane until after ten o'clock.

Kern didn't have this problem. As a senior in good standing, a virtual shoo-in for acceptance to his first choice college, Holy Cross, by long school tradition he was expected to come down with a bad case of "senioritis" and completely goof off in his last year. The monks might assign him homework, but they'd consider him a brown-noser if he actually did it.

So, Kern had plenty of time for the plane. But a lot of repairs required both of us to work at once, and he was frustrated by my inability to help him until very late at night. We started arguing about it as soon as classes resumed after the Christmas vacation. Once, Kern even accused me of lacking "commitment to the project" because I was spending too much time on my homework. One night, while I was studying in front of the woodstove in the tack room adjoining our shop, I arrived at a solution.

"Kern, look," I said. "This is bullshit, the way we're going. You need me to get the plane done. I need you to get my homework done. Why don't we just divvy up my subjects, get everything done in an hour, and then we'll have all night to work on the plane."

Kern thought about that for a moment.

"Nice try Rink. I'm impressed with your thinking. But we can't do it. That would be cheating."

"Kern, that's not cheating," I said. "It's just killing two birds with one stone."

"Rink, it's cheating."

I made a big display of slamming shut my books, stuffing the papers inside, then cradling the whole pile under my arm as I headed for the door of the shop.

"Screw it Kern. I'll finish my homework in the house and see you later."

Kern called out when I got to the door.

"Rink! Wait."

He was standing by the woodstove with his head cocked to one side, averting his eyes, muttering under his breath this mantra he repeated over and over every time he faced a big moral crisis like this. "Jeez . . . Jeez . . . Ah, Jeez."

"Rink," he sighed, "You know what?"

"No, what?"

"Everybody cheats."

"Well Kern that's what I'm saying, exactly. Everybody cheats."

"It's awful," Kern said. "It's wrong. I'm depressed about it, every time I see it at school. But everybody cheats."

"Kern," I said. "Corruption bothers me just as much as it bothers you. But we can't solve the problems of the world all by ourselves. In the meantime, everybody cheats."

"Rink, *everybody* cheats!"

So, that's how we handled it. As soon as we got in from school every night, we built a fire in the woodstove and raced a fast relay through my books. Kern was a Latin and bio whiz, so he did that. Geometry was the only math I ever understood or liked, so that was mine. First year French was a joke because I had lied to Father Sean about my grammar school background, and in fact I had already taken three years of it, so "Frog" usually only took about fifteen minutes. In freshman English we read novels like *Moby Dick*, but Cliffs Notes boiled those nine oceangoing gams down to one page. History I loved and read in the morning on the bus. Religion was total bullshit and we ignored it.

And cheating was beautiful, intellectual nirvana, the only way to get an education. For the two semesters that we worked on the plane, when Kern did most of my homework, I got straight As in all of my courses and my class ranking shot right up into the low teens. Father Adrian, the dean of studies, couldn't get over the way I had "turned the corner" over the Christmas holidays. Most nights we were done with my homework in less than an hour and by seven o'clock Kern and I were cheerfully attacking a new repair on the plane.

Kern was determined to perform a "mint" restoration on our plane, not only because he was Kern and always approached a project that way, meticulously, with precocious attention to detail. He understood a lot better than I did the battering the plane would receive in the brutal desert and mountain flying conditions we faced out west, and he didn't want to leave anything to chance.

Quite beyond this, Kern was in love with Piper Cubs in general and our Cub in particular. By the mid-1960s, Cubs were already considered a classic aircraft, as beloved as the venerable DC-3 cargo-hauler or the Stearman biplane. Cubs were just about the last tailwheel planes available in large numbers to pilots like us, a last living link to the romantic, seat-of-the-pants flying style of the barnstorming era. Our Cub was Piper's PA-11 model, identical to the classic J-3 trainer that dated back to the 1930s except for a slightly larger engine. The registration number, painted on the side of the fuselage in large red letters, was N4971H. Around the Basking Ridge strip, where the Cub had been based for the last ten years, she was affectionately known as "71-Hotel." The Basking Ridge pilots had always considered 71-Hotel a special plane, what was known then as a "hot Cub." The cylinders had been bored out for extra horsepower, the wing struts beefed up, and 71-Hotel had a custom, low-pitch "climb prop." Eddie Mahler had used 71-Hotel for Cub Comedy Acts at airshows early in his career, and she could out-perform any two-seater for miles around, even Super-Cubs with 150-horse engines. All of this meant a lot more to Kern than to me. No expense would be spared toward turning 71-Hotel into "the perfect Cub."

In January, one of the first repairs we made was the shock system on the landing gear. The shocks on a Piper Cub are simple in design. The right and left gear are braced together by an X-shaped steel structure, in the middle of which is a flexible armature wrapped tightly with rubber bungee cords. As the plane rolls over bumps, the bungees expand and retract, giving enough play for rough strips or hard landings.

No flyer we knew bothered to replace bungees on a Cub. The mechanics out at Basking Ridge were even against it. The only thing new bungees did, they said, was make a Cub bounce too high when a student pilot landed hard. On most of the Cubs we'd flown, the bungee shocks were as rancid and lifeless as a dead cat.

Not 71-Hotel, of course. On the day assigned to landing gear, Kern swung our platform-jack underneath the engine-mounts and lifted the Cub wheels off the floor. Our parts source was Van Dusen Aviation Supply in Teterboro. From our first Van Dusen shipment Kern pulled out a package wrapped in manila paper. It was a fresh set of bungees, shiny and black, with the pungent, rubbery smell of a new football.

"Ah Jeez Kern," I said. "New *bungees?*"

"Hey, watch yourself. I told you. This is going to be the cleanest Cub in America. Besides, if we have to go down in the desert somewhere, these bungees could save the plane. Even our lives. I want the landing gear to stay on in rough terrain."

"Ah shit Kern. If we go down in the desert, we'll probably ride a bus the rest of the way to California. What good is a new bungee on a Greyhound?"

"Hey, Rinker, are you listening to me?"

"Yeah, I'm listening."

"Okay then. Suck. We paid for these bungees. We're putting 'em on."

"All right. All right. New bungees then."

With a deep, swift swipe of a matt knife, Kern severed the dusty and oil-soaked old bungees. They released with a pallid twang and spilled onto the floor.

The new bungees—hard and tight—were murderous to get on. They felt strong enough to hold up the landing gear on a Boeing 707. We used a crowbar gripped with an extra length of plumbing pipe for leverage. Grunting and heaving, leaving a fresh deposit of knuckles on the landing gear, we finally secured the bastards. When we screwed down the jack the Cub bounced onto the cement floor, jaunty and a little taller than before.

That was our winter, more or less. With the big Texan radio blaring with Cousin Brucie and WABC, we worked liked the possessed on 71-Hotel. More than fifty different repairs and part replacements had to be made on the airframe—everything from the brakes and carburetor heat baffles to a new trim tab augur in the tail. We ripped out the entire cockpit, from the floorboards to the headliner, and replaced everything with new materials. Parts that weren't available in a catalogue we made ourselves. Kern decided that the old baggage compartment, which was made out of burlap, was substandard and wouldn't hold up in the turbulent conditions we anticipated out west. So we fabricated a new one out of heavy sheet metal that we bought at Sears.

I had always been mechanically inferior to Kern, and was quite self-conscious about it. It annoyed me that I lacked his ability to repair a bike or a tune a car engine, but I never even attempted to apply myself in the shop because that would just turn me into a tool-geek like Kern. I suffered the common affliction of boys who aren't naturally adept at mechanics. I thought that there was something inherently complicated and mysterious about it, when in fact all that is required is a lot of patience. Kern never confronted me on this. It was just something that naturally resolved itself over the course of our long winter of confinement in the barn. After he had assigned me a succession of simpleminded tasks that one of the NASA monkeys could have figured out— changing the bolts on the bungee covers, or putting new rubber grips on the control sticks—he slowly graduated me up to more difficult jobs. By the end of the winter I was rebuilding the carburetor and installing new Plexiglas windows in the cockpit.

I couldn't wait to get into the shop every night. Mostly I was overjoyed about the way I was weasling out of my homework, but I also surged with new feelings of competence and technical knowledge. Kern was pleased too, because he could see that he had converted me into a dedicated tool-geek. I became increasingly fussy about "my own" workspace, insisting that all of the parts and tools I needed for a particular project be neatly segregated in a corner of the shop, away from Kern's parts and tools. With the pride of a mentor, Kern detected these nascent indications of compulsiveness in me and decided to reward them. One Saturday morning, at Sears, he decided to blow some of our Cub money on a new Craftsmen tool box, socket wrenches and a top of the line, rubber-handled set of screwdrivers for me. Back at the shop, he showed me how to etch my initials onto every tool with a soldering gun. "Rink," he said. "You can always tell a good mechanic. He doesn't let *anybody* fuck with his tools."

Bizarre things happen to a boy undergoing profound life

changes like this. One morning in late February I woke just before dawn with a start, deranged by a terrible nightmare. In the dream, I was being chased around a room with no exits by a man who was attempting to poke my eye out with a carburetor-heat cable. The dream was reminiscent of the scene in the three-dimensional *Three Stooges* movie where Moe and Curly are menaced by a doctor with a long syringe. I wiped the sleep from my eyes. The only way my tormentor could have gotten that carb-heat cable off, I figured, was if the bolt assembly on the inlet valve beneath the carburetor was not properly secured. This happened to be the exact part I was working on before I came into bed that night. Shit.

So, I threw on my clothes, tiptoed past my brother's room, and crossed the snowy lawn outside in the romantic gray light of dawn. I pushed through the barn door and threw on the lights to inspect the Cub. Underneath the carburetor, the bolt was properly installed on the inlet valve, and the cable running down from its control in the cockpit was secure. But, sure enough, I'd forgotten to attach the safety nut which kept the whole assembly in place.

I found the nut right where I left it, on top of one of the engine cylinders, and torqued it on with my new socket-wrench.

It was a close call. Every night, as soon as we had finished my homework, Kern inspected everything I'd done the night before. Most of the mistakes he found were minor—I might have used the wrong washers, for example, or the wrong grade of safety wire—and Kern was very patient about that. But the missing nut on the carburetor-heat assembly was serious. It would have earned me a stern lecture from Kern, because you need that carb heat to prevent ice in wet conditions.

"Rink, do you know what would have happened if we hit a rainstorm in Ohio and the carb heat didn't engage?"

"The engine quits, and we wipe out the gear during a forced landing."

"Exactly. Then we don't get to California."

Late in the winter, on a Saturday night, Kern took a rare break from the plane and went up to a dance at school with a date. It was one of those assignations that my sister Macky set up by writing a phone script out for Kern on a yellow legal pad. As soon as I got wind of the deal Macky was setting up for Kern, I bailed out on the dance myself. I still didn't want to be seen socially with my brother.

I was restless at home that night. Three straight months of working every night on the Cub had given me a routine, a mission, and I simply didn't know what to do with myself inside a house any longer. I felt drawn to the plane in the barn outside.

I headed for the front door with my reading book. When I got there, a shipping box from a midwestern aviation supply company was sitting on the hall table. It contained the magneto ignitions for the Cub, which we'd removed from the engine a couple of weeks before and sent out for reconditioning. I stuffed the box of magnetos under my arm to carry out to the barn.

The magnetos. Kern and I were very proud of this step. Most of the pilots we knew—including my father—never bothered to have their magnetos rebuilt until one broke. But Kern and I could afford to go first-class on our ignition system because we'd made so much money plowing drives. It was the kind of precaution we were taking on our coast-to-coast ship. Nothing could fail on our plane, nothing was too good for 71-Hotel.

It was a lovely, moonlit night outside, and I liked being alone with just the sound of my boots crunching on the snow, and the brisk wind chilling my face.

When I got inside and threw on the lights, the engine cowling was off the Cub. On the aluminum firewall, I could see the two spots, bright and shiny, where the old magnetos had been. Out of curiosity, I leafed through Kern's Piper Cub manual and found the pages and diagrams on the magnetos. One thing just lead to another, I guess. Before I knew what I was doing I had pulled the magnetos out of the box and begun installing them on the plane.

Putting magnetos on isn't very complex, no more difficult

than changing the oil filter on a car. I've installed dozens since. But I was excited about my first set, and impressed by the importance of the repair. These were the little dynamos that would fire sparks into our cylinders all the way out to the Pacific.

When I was done, I left the wiring down to the spark-plug harnesses alone. The electrical hookups were too easy to get crossed and Kern would be very particular about that.

I was pleased with myself and didn't want to leave the plane yet, so I made a fire in the tack-room woodstove and sat inside reading, leaving the door to the shop open so I could gaze into the Cub now and then.

It was either that night or a couple of nights later that I came across the passage in Charles Lindbergh's *The Spirit of St. Louis* that simplified our navigation planning. Kern and I still didn't have any idea of where we would cross the Rockies. So I had turned to Lindbergh's book, and the writings of Wiley Post, because both of them had done a great deal of transcontinental flying before they made their famous international flights. On one flight, experiencing engine trouble over the Rockies, Lindbergh had turned "south toward the Mexican border, where the mountains are lower." Post referred to the same area as "the old southern airmail route through El Paso." It took me some time just to *find* El Paso on the map, and I still didn't know what pass to fly, but indeed the peaks down there were a lot lower than up north. I figured that El Paso would be a major waypoint for our trip, the gateway to the far west, and that we should base our navigation planning on that.

It was that kind of night for me, a time for insights and reflection. Mostly, I just enjoyed being alone in the barn with the plane.

The next day Kern and I pulled our usual Sunday morning routine. We put on our best jackets and ties, exited the house through the kitchen so my mother could see us dressed for Mass just the way she liked, and left in the Willys. As soon as we got out of the drive we ripped off our ties, turned left at the intersection instead of right for the church, and drove up to Morristown for breakfast at the Lackawanna Diner.

At the diner, Kern was excited when I told him about El Paso and we began doodling on paper napkins, drawing maps of the country and discussing the various advantages of one route over another. Most of our flight planning was done that way. All winter Kern and I were engaged in a kind of Socratic dialogue about routes—Ohio to Indiana, Indiana to Illinois and so forth—before we reached a consensus on how to cross each state. In stages, we mapped the entire flight on paper napkins at diners and on the back of shipping receipts in our shop.

When we got back to the barn that day, Kern saw the shiny magnetos bolted onto the engine firewall.

"Ah shit Rink. You didn't try to put the mags on, did you?"

"Kern, I followed the drawings. Look. Just look at them."

Kern pored over the mags with the meticulousness of an FAA inspector. Frowning a lot, he looked from the drawings to the engine, then back to the drawings several times, exhaling his mantra of worry, "Jeez . . . Jeez . . . Ah Jeez."

But I could tell that he was pleased, and surprised.

"Gosh Rink. I can't get over this. These mags are perfect. You wanna know something?"

"No, what?"

"Well, I always had you pegged as strictly airframe. But, Jeez, you can do powerplant stuff too!"

"Hey, thanks man," I said. "I really appreciate that."

CHAPTER 4

WHEN THE SPRING THAW ARRIVED, IN MID-MARCH, WE ROLLED the airframe out onto the driveway in front of the barn. It was a bright, sunny Saturday with the fragrance of daffodils and crocuses blooming. My brother was right about the plane. The reconditioned Cub looked factory-fresh, with the tubular steel fuselage sparkling under zinc paint, and the new metal baggage compartment and tail augur gleaming like Cadillac tail fins.

My father was home sick that week. Several times over the winter he was felled with phantom-pain attacks on his leg, and his doctors had ordered bed rest. He wasn't much good at that and he had spent most of his time down in his library, banging out speeches and a book idea on his typewriter. From his library window, he saw us roll out the Cub. He'd kept his promise all winter and left us alone, but he was restless after several days of inactivity and decided to come out and inspect the plane.

From the barn, Kern and I saw him step out to the porte cochere, gaze down the drive, then stop to light his pipe. Gingerly favoring his bad leg, which gave him a funny kind of kangaroo gait, he walked down toward us.

"Rink! It's Dad," Kern said. "He's coming to see the plane."

Kern raced into the tack room and carried a rocking chair out to the Cub.

My father was going through a lot of painful changes that year. For more than a decade politics and charitable causes—AA mostly, but also a lot of fund-raising for Catholic hospitals and schools—had been his lifeblood, defining his identity outside of work and his family. After John Kennedy was assassinated in 1963, he managed a few more political campaigns, but the shooting in Dallas and its aftermath broke his spirit and gradually he lost faith in electoral politics. He was sickened by the escalating war in Vietnam, especially after one of my cousins, Jerry Kernahan, was killed in the conflict. He was always looking for something new to do with himself anyway. By the mid-1960s he had gravitated toward reform movements, first civil rights and then the antiwar effort, and now on weekends he was flying off somewhere to join protest marches, or writing speeches for civil rights leaders, even delivering a few of his own.

It was a fascinating and even a noble soul-searching for a man of my father's background and achievements, and within a few years literally millions of middle-aged men like him would be transformed in the same way by the fabled sixties. But this could only be appreciated with the passage of time. To many of his closest friends in politics and business, civil rights and peace in Vietnam were issues that you paid lip service to, espoused to your children, and then promptly forgot. Successful businessmen with good jobs in New York—at the time, my father was associate publisher of *Look* magazine—weren't supposed to be morally indignant about social causes and exploring activism as a weekend hobby. But that's what my father was doing and he felt unappreciated and lonely. His five oldest children were now all teenagers and developing lives of their own—my oldest sister, Dempsey, had already left home for her first year of college—and we didn't want to join him at protest marches on Saturday afternoons. We were all surprised by the intensity of his focus

Over the winter that we built our plane, my father turned fifty, a big milestone for a man of his youthful outlook, and he seemed to have mellowed a lot.

now—outward to the world, no longer inward to the family— which seemed to be alienating him from everyone. There had always been an undercurrent of unpredictability and instability about him, but now it seemed like a tide.

The changes were evident in the man kangarooing toward us down the drive. He turned fifty that year, a big milestone for a man of his youthful outlook, and as if deliberately anticipating the aging process he had mellowed a lot over the winter. He wasn't rakish any more, just dapper. He dressed the part of a distinguished magazine executive in New York who was emerging in middle age as a writer and social activist. He wore a Dublin-tailored sports jacket, immaculately pressed wool slacks, and he had a cane, a briar pipe, and a tweed cap.

My father's eyes opened wide and danced brightly as he stood lopsided beside the Cub.

"My, my, my, Kernahan," he said, looking at Kern. "This is really sharp. A clean, clean Cub. I'm proud of you. I am just so proud of you."

I was rushed with my old fondness for the man. I could see what the sight of a superbly restored plane was doing for him and it reminded me of the winters we had spent together rebuilding other planes. My father breathed in hard a few times. He was refreshed to be within olfactory range of new zinc paint, hydraulic oil, and rubber bungees.

I loved my father that morning, too, because he was saying just the right thing for Kern. In the past, they had argued a lot over our planes. Kern was fastidious about every repair and my father was an old barnstormer type, impatient and slapdash as a mechanic—"fly 'em and fix 'em again" was his motto—and he and Kern had conducted monumental battles in the barn over how long a project should take. This only made Kern more apprehensive about 71-Hotel; he was terribly dependent on my father's opinion of his work. My father seemed to understand this and he knew what his job was that day. This was Kern's plane, Kern's rebuild. He would lavish praise on his son.

We got some Yoo-Hoo sodas from the refrigerator in the tack room and sat there by the plane doing a post-op on the winter. My father wanted to hear every detail. The control cables, the throttle couplings, the new magnetos.

Sitting in his rocker, my father ran his hands down over the zinc-chromated tubes and ponged the new baggage compartment. Several times he let out a long, low whistle. It was obvious that the workmanship on 71-Hotel was flawless.

"Jeez Kern," he said. "You really went overboard. New bungees."

He reminded Kern that he still owed us $500 for parts. How could we afford to buy all this stuff?

When Kern told him that we still had $400 left over from snow-plowing, and that included paying cash-on-delivery for the fabric and buckets of dope stacked in the corner of the barn, my father was incredulous.

"Well, can't I do something?"

"Just hang on Dad," Kern said. "When we get to planning the routes, you can help us with the maps."

"All right," my father said. "You boys are really something. I guess I'm just ground crew now."

My father's eyes were misty when he said that, but not because he was sad to have reached an age when he was just "ground crew." He was immensely gratified by that mint-condition Piper Cub. It must have been the same kind of melancholy that overtakes parents at graduations and weddings, the feeling of time immutably passing and children moving on. Kern and I didn't need him any more to work on a plane.

My father stood up to leave. He ran his hands down over the airframe once more and ponged the new baggage compartment with his index finger.

"Ah, Dad," Kern said. "Rinker. Rinker did a lot of work on this plane. Fifty percent. Even more than fifty percent."

My father was very glib, recovering from a lapse like that.

"Well, Kern, exactly," he said. "That's what I said, 'You boys.' You did this together. As brothers. Do you know how happy that makes me feel?"

I wished Kern hadn't said that. I stood there red-faced, my heart racing, unable to say anything.

I was inching toward an understanding of my father and I completely sympathized with him at that moment. He was a man engulfed by distractions and the changes of middle age. (And later on, sitting in a lawyer's office in Manhattan, poring over his medical records so my mother could collect his life insurance, I understood a lot more about this period in his life. A great deal of the time, he was so doped up on Demerol and other painkillers it was a miracle he could function at all.) He could only concentrate on one thing at a time, and what he was concentrating on that morning was Kern, Kern's masterful supervision of the Cub rebuild. It was a moment of pleasure for him, a time to get past his preoccupation and worry about his oldest son. Compared to that, I simply didn't rate. I wasn't a factor at all. This was supposed to be Kern's moment.

Besides, I didn't want attention and compliments from my father. It was a lot easier to be ignored, which made it that much easier for me to ignore him, a strategy that was working for both of us right now. My father and I needed a vacation from each other and we both knew it. I couldn't explain this to Kern. He would never understand how, for me, loving my father meant creating as much distance from him as possible. Now Kern had embarrassed me, taking what should have been a carefree, pleasant moment and making it awkward.

My father was chastened by that, and now he seemed intent on addressing us as a pair. Halfway up the drive, he spun on his good leg and leaned on his cane.

"It's a damn fine airplane boys. I'm proud as the blazes of you two."

Whistling some more, he turned and went up the drive, limping with that peculiar gait of his, swinging the cane in his hand like Charlie Chaplin.

In early April, just as we were beginning the laborious, dizzying job of spraying butyrate dope onto the Cub fabric, my sister Macky poked her head through the barn door one night.

"Hi Kern! Hi Rinky! Can I help?"

It was an epic event in our family. A sister had not only ventured into our plane shop, she had offered to help. After adolescence, we had lived completely separate lives from our sisters, a family practice so ordained and seemingly natural that we never thought to question it. The boys and the girls lived in separate wings of the house, attended different high schools, and on weekends my father, Kern, and I religiously disappeared for the airport. I couldn't tell you what my sisters were doing with their lives during those years because I practically never saw them. This was just the way families lived, I thought.

Kern and I were too obsessed about finishing the plane to dwell very long on my sister's reasons for being there. Macky was a lot of fun, a demon for work herself, and she saved the spring for us. Pitching right in on the plane, she worked with us nearly every night until we finished re-covering in May.

Macky was sixteen that year, wedged directly between Kern and me in the family lineup. In a lot of ways she was the most unique child in the family. She had my father's Black-Irish complexion, with olive-tone skin that tanned almost black in the summer, dark brown eyes and a luxuriant mane of unruly brown hair that bounced like surf whenever she said something or laughed. Inquisitive and bright, bubbling over all the time with whatever idea entered her head, she reminded me of a character in *Alice in Wonderland*. The simplest things made her profoundly happy. She was always sampling new people and new experiences, and diving right into a plane re-covering project was the sort of thing she would pursue, just for the novelty of it.

Years later, Macky would tell me that she was bitterly disappointed that Kern and I had not invited her to fly to California too. Everyone just assumed that the boys, especially Kern and I, would enjoy all the adventures in the family. She was confused about that, but the family bias toward boys was too rooted for her to even think about speaking up or even to see her situation very clearly. So, she accepted the next best thing. She could be close to us out in the barn, helping us with the plane.

By the time Macky got to the shop Kern and I had already finished the hardest part of re-covering, cutting and stitching the Grade A Irish linen into sleeves that fit onto the fuselage and wings. These were pasted onto the plane with a milky, sticky airplane glue called nitrate dope. We applied the nitrate with natural-bristle paint brushes, dipping them into coffee cans filled with nitrate. Nitrate is awesome, head-banging stuff, as powerful as angel-dust. When we rebuilt our first three planes, our shop was located in another barn, directly above the horse stable. When we got into the nitrate, all of the horses got sick and keeled over in their stalls. About the only good thing to be said for nitrate is that it expands the sinuses and loosens up the muscles for the milder, sweet-smelling butyrate dope, which is slowly sprayed onto the linen with an air-compressor to tighten and stiffen the fabric.

Butyrate-doping is not a difficult business, just a lot of drudgery. Every time Kern sprayed on a fresh coat of silver primer dope, or later clear finish coats, the entire wing surface and fuselage had to be wet-sanded with fine emory paper and water. The sanding smoothed the surface and removed excess dope that had not penetrated the fabric. Then another coat of dope was sprayed on, dried overnight, and got wet-sanded again. Both sides of each wing and the entire fuselage would get almost twenty sandings. Macky and I assumed complete responsibility for sanding, and this allowed Kern to slip into a more managerial role. Every evening he mixed the dope for the night's work, consulted his records on how many coats he had sprayed on each section, and then told Macky and me which surface to prepare for spraying with the Sears compressor and gun.

Kern was determined to really "cherry out" 71-Hotel with a smooth re-covering and paint job. Every surface Macky and I sanded had to be "baby-butt" smooth, or he'd make us do it over. The chief mechanic out at Basking Ridge, Lee Weber, had showed Kern how to "push" the dope with extra thinner, so the butyrate seeped into the fabric more evenly and deeply and became perfectly recessed.

The more thinner you use, of course, the better the high. Thinner carries quite a punch itself, and thinned dope aspirates into the air in finer particles that go down more easily into the lungs.

All of this was a revelation for Macky. It had never occurred to her that, while doping a plane, you get high on the dope. Sanding was boring, back-breaking work. The dust curling up from the fabric coated our noses and throats and our arms and shoulders ached after an hour. But fortified with butyrate, we could hardly tell we were working. Besides, the warm weather had arrived, Macky and I had ferocious cases of spring fever, and we just wanted to goof off out there and get high. As soon as we got into the shop every night we were clamoring for Kern to start up the compressor and give us our first dose.

"Hey Kern!" I called out. "Give us a hit."

"Ah c'mon Rink," Kern said. "This is an aircraft recovering project. You don't *try* to get high. It's supposed to just happen by mistake."

"Screw that, Kern," I said. "Give us a hit or we don't sand."

Disgusted, Kern kicked on the compressor, reached for the spray gun and gracefully swept the supply hoses behind his back with his free hand. Then he raised the spray-nozzle high over our heads and anointed Macky and me with a long, pungent burst of butyrate.

The nimbus of dope slowly descended from the ceiling and matted onto our shoulders and hair. It was cool and moist, like ocean spray at a beach. We breathed in hard and felt better right away. Butyrate was wonderful stuff.

"Wow Rinky," Macky said. "This is *really* fun. I can feel myself getting high. Kern, hit me again."

After twenty minutes or so we didn't have to beg Kern for a fix. He had started his long, rhythmic sweeps down the fuselage and wings with his spray gun.

Sand and dope, sand and dope, go, go, go. The barn filled with dope fumes. Even on a hot night, we never opened the windows. We had the old Texan radio on loud all the time, and there were some great sanding and doping tunes on WABC then. "Good Vibrations" and "Wooly Bully," "Help Me Rhonda," "You've Lost That Loving Feeling," and "Hanky Panky." Macky and I laughed all night and forgot what we said to each other and sanded the same wing twice, shaking our asses in unison through a wing section and a song.

Every couple of hours, Macky and I took a break from our dope den. We lay outside on the grass, taking in the scent of lilacs and honeysuckle mixing with the butyrate cloud hanging over the barn. It was a good time for Macky and me. Even though we were only eighteen months apart in age, we'd hardly spoken in years, and under the influence of the airplane dope we found it easier to talk. Macky was precociously intuitive about people and closer in age to Kern than I was, and she had a way of analyzing our problems together which relieved me of the guilt I usually felt about Kern. His jealousy of my success and popularity in school was "Kern's hang-up," Macky thought. I shouldn't worry about it because I was never going to change that. Still, I had an obligation to defuse the issue. I only had six more months until he left for college, Macky said, and until then I should humor Kern. This was more or less what my father was telling me, but of course I wouldn't listen to him. But I did listen to Macky.

After a while Kern was overcome by the dope fumes too and came out and joined us. When he got high, Kern was as funny and relaxed as the next kid and we liked having him out there. We were making great progress on the plane and enjoying our spring together.

My mother didn't have any idea about what was going on out there. To her a plane rebuild was just a plane rebuild. My father had always been deliberately vague about our weekend activities together and he pawned off a lot of platitudes to my mother that she seemed to accept. For example, despite all evidence to the contrary, he told her that he was "a very safe pilot," and that he was teaching us to fly the same way. So, he never told her about the airplane dope. Working on an airplane all winter, he told her, "built character in boys," and Kern and I were getting along so much better that year she figured this must be true.

One night in early May my mother looked out through the kitchen window and saw three of her four oldest children prone on the grass beside the barn. We were completely plastered on dope, but she couldn't tell that from a distance. Working that hard on a plane, building all that character, must have been tiring, she thought. Maybe we needed something to eat.

So, she loaded up her wicker tray with cookies and milk and came out across the lawn, quiet as a cat. Suddenly she was there, and I was looking up at her pretty, pert face through the little holes in a wicker tray.

"Oh, hi Mom."

"Are you children all right?"

"Oh we're fine," Kern said. "Just taking a rest from the plane."

"Why are you all lying on the grass?"

"Oh, it's a nice night out I guess."

"Well, maybe you should come in."

"Mommy," Macky said. "You know what?"

"No dear, what?"

"Karl Kincherf wears Davy Crockett underpants."

Karl was a kid who lived in our town and we went to grammar school with him. I'd never heard about his Davy Crockett underpants before, but it sounded like Karl.

"Excuse me Macky?" my mother said, "What did you just say?"

"I said, 'Karl Kincherf wears Davy Crockett underpants.' "

"Macky. Don't say that again. I heard you the first time."

"Mom. You said, 'What did you just say?' And I said, 'Karl Kincherf wears Davy Crockett underpants.' "

"Don't say that!"

"What?"

"That!"

" 'Karl Kincherf wears Davy Crockett underpants?' What's wrong with that?"

"Don't say it!"

Kern and I were just as high as Macky and we didn't see anything wrong with what she was saying. In fact, it made perfect sense. Karl's Davy Crockett underpants was the kind of image that naturally rises to the surface and just pops out while you're doping a plane, and we were grateful for the information, now that it was out.

But my mother was flustered and started looking around for a place to set her tray down.

"Mom," Macky said, "I don't know why you're being so sensitive. All I said was, 'Karl Kincherf wears Davy Crockett underpants.' "

"Oh dear," my mother said. "Macky, you really should come inside now."

"Mom," Kern said. "It's not what you think."

"Oh, not that!" Macky laughed. She had this uproarious, high-octane laugh. "Karl Kincherf wears Davy Crockett underpants. I saw them in Mrs. Kincherf's washing machine when Karl was five."

"Macky, are you *sure* you're all right?"

"Mom. It's not important, okay? Let's drop it. I just wanted you to know."

My mother left the tray of cookies and milk on the grass and decamped for the house.

We never did hear about Karl and his Davy Crockett underwear again. I knew that my mother was confused and suspicious about the conversation, but she didn't want to discuss it. That spring when we doped the plane was one of the times I was grateful about being raised a Catholic. At a certain point the doctrine of silence always took over and protected us from having to say anything about our behavior.

Kern was jubilant. We finished re-covering the Cub by the end of May, which gave us the three-day Memorial Day weekend for the painstaking job of sectioning off the fuselage and wings with masking tape and newspaper for his paint scheme. There would be plenty of time during the week for spraying on the paint.

He decided to paint the Cub red and white, using the paint design for a 1956 Super Cub, his favorite look among all Cubs. When we got to the wings, Kern masked off large, triangular shapes to paint bright red "sunbursts" on the top surface, like all the stunt pilots had on their planes.

"Sunbursts, Kern?" I said. "Why sunbursts?"

"Ah c'mon Rink. Think. Think."

"Kern I'm thinking. But I don't know."

"Look, if we go down in the deserts or the mountains, they'll send search planes out."

"Right. The sunbursts will make it easier to find us from the air."

"Exactly. Rink, this paint job could save our lives."

CHAPTER 5

THE STORIES MY FATHER TOLD US WHEN WE WERE YOUNG WERE full of enchanting accounts about him camping beside his plane at night, falling asleep as the stars lit some distant prairie sky. Kern and I wanted to "rough it" too, sleeping under the wings of the Cub every night, an idea that appealed to us both romantically and financially. By now, the last of our snow-plowing money from the winter had been spent on paint for the plane. One evening we sat down and calculated our expenses for the coast-to-coast flight—fuel, meals, motel rooms on rainy nights—and arrived at a total budget of $300. As soon as school let out in early June we found summer jobs to raise the money, and we went about this in our usual way.

I found a cushy job as an exercise boy at a standard-bred trotter farm across the fields from our house. I was assigned the farm's breeding stock, a couple of stallions and a half-dozen brood mares, each of whom had to be hitched up to an exercise sulky and loped around a large cinder track every couple of days. After the long winter sequestered with the plane, I enjoyed being outside in fresh air and working with horses. I was getting a great tan, and Kern rigged up a holder so I could attach my transistor radio to the sulky and listen to Cousin Brucie on WABC as I circuited the track. The horses could only be run when it was cool, early and late in the day. The rest of the time I took long naps on the tackroom couch.

Kern was miserable at his job. He found work as a cashier at the Acme Supermarket in Bernardsville. The Acme was presided over by a swarthy, pockmarked store manager who strutted the aisles barking out orders and criticizing his employees. Everybody called him Mussolini. Kern and Mussolini took an instant dislike to each other, and practically every shift Kern worked at the Acme was a tragicomedy of labor relations.

Kern was a sensitive, generous kid to begin with, and he naturally sympathized with the female shopper. He had seen what my mother went through several times a week, shopping for all those children. As far as he was concerned, the Acme should treat every customer like "Queen for a Day." That was his philosophy, his "point of view," as he put it. Whenever an old lady or a mother with bawling children appeared at his cash register, Kern would hold up his entire checkout lane to help them stack their groceries in boxes. Then he disappeared for the parking lot to load their car. The line of shoppers in his lane backed all the way up into baked goods.

Mussolini went apeshit every time it happened. Storming out of his manager's booth, he was constantly reprimanding Kern for "not being efficient." But Kern wouldn't give in. It was this obdurate mind-block with him. The customer came first, period. As soon as he thought Mussolini wasn't looking again, he'd help another old lady out to the parking lot. But Mussolini had infallible radar for supermarket gridlock and he'd come racing back out to lambaste Kern.

The whole thing was a farce. My brother was the only teenager in America who could give a shit about Acme customers. But I admired his tenacity and loved hearing about his battles with Mussolini. Finally my older brother was developing into the kind of combative protagonist I had always wanted him to be. But Kern was demoralized about his job. He hated being criticized by the boss every day. When he came in from work, tired and disgusted, he wanted to talk.

"Rink, I'm not giving in to this guy," Kern vowed. "The Acme should be run for the benefit of the customers, not the store manager."

"Right," I said. "It's the principle that counts."

"Yeah. You know what else I don't like about the guy?"

"No, what?"

"Acne. He's got acne. I mean, Mussolini must be at least thirty-five years old. Adult acne is the pits. No way! I'm not kissing *his* ass."

Mussolini retaliated by assigning Kern to the late shift. This was supposed to be onerous punishment, because most of the teenagers who worked at the Acme didn't like working nights. But Kern didn't mind. Mussolini wasn't there at night and now Kern could run the most lethargic checkout lane in the supermarket business. Besides, Kern liked having his days free to work on the Cub.

Kern spent the rest of June contentedly putting the finishing touches on 71-Hotel all day before he went into work. He also went flying quite a bit, to work the winter rust off his arm before we took off for the coast. A friend of ours out at the airport, Jack Sylvester, let Kern use his 65-horse Aeronca Champ.

One morning while I was working at the horsefarm, running the big stallion around the track and singing along with my transistor radio to "You've Lost That Lovin' Feelin'" on WABC, I heard a sudden roar and then an airplane tire went by my face. It was Kern, pulling a buzz job in Sylvester's Champ. I didn't hear him coming because Kern had snuck up quite low and from behind the trees, with the wind on his nose.

Kern kept the ugly yellow Champ on the deck all the way across the farm. His prop blew a rooster-tail of track cinders into my face, and he mowed over a big swath of cattails and bamboo grass when he blasted past the swamp. My heart raced. I loved it when Kern flew like that. His depth-perception and timing were precise and he was just so good already, nimble and hot and cocksure, as good as my father or the great Eddie Mahler.

At the tree-line, Kern pulled the Champ up hard and banked left.

It was a hot, muggy morning. On a day like that, the elevated temperature and humidity cause the air molecules to expand, providing less lift for a wing. And the Champ was a loser, a notorious loser. The fuselage was shaped like a bathtub, and the wings were stubby and fat, about as aerodynamic as an Italian villa. Even on a good day, Champs couldn't climb for shit.

Ah c'mon Kern, I said to myself. Put the nose down and level those wings. You're going to spin the airplane.

At the top of the turn, that's exactly what he did. The nose suddenly pitched up, the high wing stalled and fell to the right, and the plane violently corkscrewed around into a spin.

Spins are aggravated stalls, something that happens when a plane is slowed beyond the point at which it will fly any longer and the wings are banked over or the rudder pushed out. In a standard stall, with the wings level, most planes will recover straight ahead in a few hundred feet. In a spin, the plane cranks over in the direction of the turn and falls into uncontrolled flight. Rotating like a top, the plane plummets with the nose pointed straight at the ground, screaming in the slipstream as it falls wing-over-wing. The increased forces of gravity pull the pilot down into the seat, and the earth gyrating around through the windshield is disorienting and terrifying. Generally a thousand feet or more is lost before the plane builds up enough speed to recover. But most pilots don't recover. Because spins were considered too dangerous, the FAA had phased spin-training out of its curriculum, and most flight schools merely taught pilots how to avoid them. But my father insisted that Kern and I learn to fly the old-fashioned way and gave us spin-training himself.

Still, in a dogmeat design like a Champ, there wasn't much hope. Spins are great killers of pilots, and Kern's was the worst kind—unintended, and low to the ground. At entry he had 800 feet, tops.

I pulled up the horse to watch my brother die.

Kern was doomed, but he did have one advantage that would make this interesting, I thought. He had nerves of steel at the controls of a plane and he wouldn't be spooked by the ground spinning up and trying to swallow the plane. I was willing to bet that he could get the wings level before he cratered into the trees.

My heart pounded. Jabbing out with an imaginary stick, kicking the sulky's footrests for rudders, I talked my brother through the maneuver. Actually, it was my father's voice, yelling forward over the noise of a wailing prop and screaming wings.

Let the spin define itself son. Don't panic and pull out too early.

Good Kern. Close the throttle and keep the stick in your lap. One turn, one and a half, now two. Good. Neutral stick and hard left rudder against the rotation. Goose the stick forward to break the spin.

Jesus. I could hear power coming on. He was recovering. The engine roared and the wings were just coming level as the plane disappeared behind the trees.

The trees blocked my view. I didn't hear a crash or see an impact cloud, but still, I didn't know. Spin-impacts can be deceptively uneventful—the landing gear might take the brunt of the crash, snap off, and then the plane flips over and noiselessly slides out of view into high grass. Pilots aren't killed by the impact, they're killed by the lateral G-forces of slamming against their seat harnesses and flipping over at seventy miles per hour. It could be that, or Kern could have made it out of the fields next door and over the telephone wires by the road. I just didn't know. An agonizing minute went by, then another. All I could do was stare at the trees and wait.

On the other side of James Street, there was a long, low valley of mowed fields that sloped down to Congressman Peter Frelinghuysen's house. There was an extra 100 feet of diving space in there if Kern could rudder across the road and get into the safety of the lower ground.

In fact, that's what he did. Staying low to gather speed, fishtailing across the phone wires into the hay fields, Kern blasted the Champ at full power up over the Congressman's front lawn.

Finally I saw the Champ wallowing up in the haze out over

our house. Kern leveled off at 1,500 feet and flew back over the horse track. He waved the wings to show me that he was all right. I waved back and whipped the horse around the track.

I ran a couple of more horses that morning and pretended to myself that I wasn't upset. Kern had kept his head and brilliantly recovered from a low-level spin, further proof of his exceptional flying skills. Maybe, just to spook me, he had deliberately held the spin until he was on top of the trees. Perhaps I should even be grateful. My father's spin-training had saved Kern.

Fear, however, is a lot more stubborn than that and it doesn't let you off the hook. I trudged home that night exhausted and worried, little twitches of anger flickering through my arms. Ten days before we departed on our dream coast to coast flight, my brother the pilot had missed killing himself by inches. All of my suppressed fears about my family's swashbuckling flying style were revived. Kern's fearlessness in the air wasn't the asset I thought it was. He was going to kill himself someday if he didn't watch it, and he could kill me. Why would I take off for California with a yahoo like this?

Kern was working at the Acme when I got home, so I sulked in the barn for a while and then I sulked in my room. When I heard him come in late from work, I shut off my light and got into bed. I didn't want to face him yet.

Kern quietly undressed in his room. He left his door open and I could hear him in there, sighing his penitential mantra. "Jeez . . . Jeez. . . . ah Jeez." He didn't want to face me either so he spoke through the open door.

"Rink, I know you're awake."

"Yeah."

"Look. I'm sorry. It was incredibly stupid, Rink. I almost killed myself today."

"No kidding."

"Well, I know what you're thinking."

"Oh, great. You even know what I'm thinking."

"Rink, I promise. I'm not going to spin you in the Cub."

"Gee, thanks. I really appreciate that."

"Rink, have a little sympathy, will you? I've been furious with myself all day. I hate myself for this. Daddy keeps telling me that I have to set an example for you. I have to get you to trust me. Now I've done this. Jeez, I *hate* myself."

Shit. The guilt trip. Kern was very effective at that. Now I had to find a way to make him feel better.

"Kern, relax. I'm past it, okay? It could have been me up there, spinning the plane. Everybody's an asshole once in a while and this just happened to be your day."

"Okay Rink. Thanks. But look, don't call me an asshole. Yes, I spun my aircraft. But I knew what to do and I recovered. In fact, it was a classic departure stall-spin, a textbook case. And that's the point, Rink. I was trained for this and I knew exactly what to do. That doesn't make me an asshole."

"Right. The textbook case. Sorry. I promise. I'll never call you an asshole again."

"Thanks. Now look, don't tell Daddy about this, all right?"

"Ah Christ Kern. Why would I tell Daddy? I said you're an asshole. *I'm* not an asshole."

"Jeez . . . Rink, Jeez . . . Okay. But just for the record?"

"Yeah. For the record."

"Champs suck."

A side of me was always glad that Kern spun the Champ. It was a big blunder for him, a big scare for us to get past together. My father never did find out about it and Kern was extremely grateful that I kept his secret. He trusted me now.

A few days later Kern and I pulled our last all-nighter in the barn. All month, Kern had dawdled over minor repairs to the plane, and I was beginning to suspect that his perfectionism masked last-minute jitters about the flight. We planned to depart over the July Fourth weekend, just two weeks away. Now we were racing to finish everything in one night so we could reassemble the plane at the airport over the weekend. Then a licensed mechanic could inspect our work and issue us an airworthiness certificate.

My father was watching the calendar too, and he had lost all patience with Kern. He was constantly peppering Kern with questions about the plane, goading him to finish. He seemed desperate, almost crazed, for us to get the plane out to the airport, and I could see that he was getting emotionally charged about our trip.

After he came in from work that night my father stormed out to the shop. He must have been stewing about it all week, because he didn't start out slowly, the way he usually did with Kern.

"Kern, this plane is perfect!" my father bellowed. "You're not going to hang the thing in the Museum of Modern Art. Get it out of here!"

My father's fury crippled both of us, but it was particularly hard on Kern. He knew that almost anything he said was useless when my father lost control like that. All he could do was stand there with a wrench in his hand and a dejected look on his face.

"Dad, wait! Wait! Let me explain."

"Horseshit! I don't want any explanations. I want this plane at the airport."

Usually I would just let them fight it out. Kern's reticence about confronting my father was his problem, I thought. But I was fed up with my father that night and viewed his visit to the barn as an invasion of our territory. Maybe I could pull him away from Kern by deflecting attention toward me.

"Hey Dad!" I screamed. "It just so happens we're taking this Cub to the airport tomorrow. So pipe down."

"Now goddam it Rinky, you stay out of this. This is be-tween Kern and me."

"Bull. It's between you and nobody. *I've* worked with Kern all winter on this plane."

"Oh, I see. I'm just some old fart you want to push out of the way, is that it?"

"Hey! Your words, Dad. Your words."

Furious, my father fished a pipe out of his pocket and lit it. His position was hopeless and he knew it. For years he'd pumped us full of admonitions about brotherly love, how Kern and I had to stick together to accomplish things, and now I was swinging it back at him like a wrecking ball. He stood there lopsided, looking at us and the plane with this quizzical, pathetic look on his face.

"All right then," he yelled. "Tomorrow! I want this plane at the airport tomorrow!"

He steamed out and left for the house. As he receded into the darkness, the lights from the shop lit his silhouette from behind. When he was angry like that his bad leg jerked up at the knee and gave him a hideous limp, and his head was bent forward with this vacant, hurt look on his face.

We went back to work on the plane. Kern was spraying with the Sears compressor, applying a finish coat of red paint on the wing struts. He looked up when he was done.

"Rink, you know what my damn problem is with Daddy?"

"No, what?"

"I like the guy. I just *like* him. I can never stay mad at him for more than five minutes."

The Rocky Mountains were endlessly alluring to me, a walled labyrinth resisting safe passage in a fragile, low-flying Cub. I knew from my reading and from studying maps that we should cross somewhere south in the range, near El Paso, but I couldn't find the right pass. My father was worried too. He suggested that we seek the advice of an experienced cross-country pilot, Alex Yankaskas, who was the chief pilot for the Ronson Corporation and the father of one of our friends. Yankaskas flew Ronson executives all over the country in twin-engine corporate planes, and he knew the west well. He came over for a visit one Saturday afternoon in late June.

Yankaskas was a quiet, gentle man with all of the advanced pilot ratings, and he didn't have a lot of tolerance for the kind of crazyass barnstorming flying that we did. We could tell from the questions he asked that he was skeptical about two boys flying coast to coast in a Piper Cub without a radio. He gave Kern and me a solemn lecture about the conditions we would face, and he was particularly concerned that we understood the concept of "density altitude." At the high elevations and scorching temperatures we'd be operating in out

The Rocky Mountains were endlessly alluring to me, and I spent hours
up in my attic room studying maps and aviation literature
to find the right pass.

west, the air would provide a lot less lift and the engine
wouldn't run very efficiently. In high density altitude conditions, a plane flying at 6,000 feet actually "feels" as if it is
flying at 8,000 feet. Takeoff and landing distances can double
and even triple and planes dismally wallow in a climb. We
promised Yankaskas that we would bone up on the principle,
but we never did.

It was Yankaskas who showed us the route through the
Rocky Mountains. My heart fluttered as he laid the El Paso
sectional chart flat on the coffee table in our living room,
fishing a pencil out of his pocket to use as a pointer.

The pass. It was the route through the mountains, the gateway to the Pacific. It was a highly mysterious and emotional

place for me. I had always been captivated by the early airmail era in aviation, when brave men flew open cockpit in any weather to get their cargo through, and many of them died doing it. The "southern route" that they pioneered through the Rockies was legendary, and all of the aviation greats—Charles Lindbergh, Amelia Earhart, Wiley Post, Jimmy Doolittle, and Ernest Gann—had flown it at one time or another. Now Kern and I, in a plane no better than the Mailwings and Fairchilds that the airmail pilots flew, would follow the same narrow opening through the great continental wall.

I was passionate about discovering the pass for another reason. My father had never fulfilled his dream of flying himself across the Rockies. His only transcontinental attempt, in 1937, had ended ignominiously in engine failure, just east of the mountains. Kern wanted to fly coast to coast for many reasons, but mostly he was trying to discover himself and find a way to stand out. Over the past year I had gradually realized something important about my own motivation. I wanted to beat my father at something, and beat him good. He had never made it across the mountains himself. If Kern and I beat him there and got through, this would not be something he could question or correct or make us do over—it would be fact. I was fixated on the mountains and the pass as a way to measure myself against my father.

"The pass is right here boys, in the Guadalupe Mountains," Yankaskas said.

He pointed to a narrow ravine between two tall peaks, 8,700 feet high, the twin Guadalupe Peaks. The hard black and gray hatch-markings for the peaks looked ominous and challenging, with swiftly climbing contour lines sweeping up from the deserts of West Texas along a 70-mile wall of even higher peaks. El Paso lay 80 miles due west, and the Rio Grande River curved and eddied along the Mexican border 100 miles to the south. Otherwise, there was nothing but the endless monotony of the deserts marked in beige. We would have to work, just to find the pass.

We would have to work, too, getting over it. The pass was too narrow, and the prevailing "westerlies" whistling through it were too turbulent, to just barrel in between the peaks. We had to *clear* them by well over 1,000 feet, which meant climbing the Cub to well over 10,000 feet. On a hot day in July, this would mean achieving a density altitude of 12,000 or 13,000 feet. It didn't seem possible. The manual for our Cub listed a "maximum altitude" of 10,000 feet, and those published numbers were always notoriously optimistic. We'd be pushing the Cub well past its limits for the whole leg over the mountains.

But that was our mountain, and I was excited just to know its name. Guadalupe. She was the point we'd fly for. I circled the twin peaks in red grease pencil and studied the El Paso and Albuquerque sectionals for nearby airports. Where would we launch for the pass? Even the names sounded romantic— Artesia and Carlsbad in New Mexico, and in west Texas, Pecos and Wink.

Yankaskas gave us another solemn lecture on how to fly the pass. We were to climb for as much altitude as possible and prepare ourselves for brutal leeward turbulence, and then stiff rotors and wind shear on the far side. If the weather reports called for winds greater than fifteen knots, we should wait and try for another day. We shouldn't be afraid to abort, but that decision had to be made at least two miles out. Once we got up near the peaks, there was no turning back. The violent downdrafts and turbulent "ridge effect" could turn us over and plunge us down onto the rocks as soon as we gave up the westerlies on our nose.

Yankaskas put his hands on his knees and stared at us across the coffee table.

"Boys," he said, "This is very serious business. The Rockies are treacherous. Pilots a lot more experienced than you have killed themselves out there. Don't treat this as a lark."

Kern and I nodded attentively, but we weren't really listening. We were young and anxious to be on our way, swelled with the adolescent delusion of invincibility. Fifteen knots of wind didn't sound like very much.

My father embarrassed us that day in front of Yankaskas. After we were done with the maps we all sat in my father's
library and drank Cokes. My father got into yarning and telling flying tales. Mr. Yankaskas fiddled with his fingertips and
his wedding band. Barnstorming blarney was not one of his
pastimes.

One of my father's favorite flying stories was his abortive
transcontinental flight. In 1937 he was paid $85 to ferry an
open-cockpit Travelair from Dothan, Alabama, to San Diego.
In those days pilots flying ships with the old water-cooled
engines carried a ten-gallon waterbag lashed between the
wheels, like the Dust Bowl Okies heading west in their ja-
lopies. Aircraft radiators were notoriously leaky and frequently boiled over on a hot day. When the prop started
throwing too much steam back into his face, a pilot picked a
field or a level road, dead-sticked in, and refilled the radiator
from the waterbag. Cooled for a while, the plane flew out
fine.

In the lower Pecos range in New Mexico, just east of the
Rockies, the Travelair blew its main gasket and my father
was forced down on a deserted farm and ranch road. He
waited there in the shade of his wings for six hours until a
rancher came along in a pickup and gave him a lift to the
nearest town. Thirsty and hot, my father drank from the waterbag and dumped a few ounces of water over his head. As
far as he was concerned, that waterbag saved his life, or at
least it *would* have saved his life, if he had been forced to sit
on the desert floor all night instead of for just six hours.

"And you know what Alex?" my father said.

"No, what, Tom?"

"Kern and Rinker here, they'll be carrying a waterbag for
the deserts. We'll lash 'er right between the wheels of that
Cub."

"Tom, I don't think that's necessary," Yankaskas said. "A
waterbag out there will distort the design and make the Cub
fly poorly. If the boys stay over roads in the deserts, they'll
be fine."

The waterbag was news to us. I think the idea just occurred

to my father on the spot. But once a notion gripped him like that there was no getting rid of it. After Alex Yankaskas left, my father just shrugged his shoulders and pointed his finger at us.

"Boys, find yourself a waterbag. If you can't find one here, I'll check around New York. We need a big job—at least ten gallons. Canvas on the bottom, metal cap on top. Now get cracking. This thing could save your lives."

CHAPTER 6

THE WATERBAG. THAT FREAKING WATERBAG. THE WATERBAG WAS
a curse, retribution, my penance for mooning the old lady in
the Volkswagen and doing too much dope with my sister out
in the barn. My father was obsessed with this mythical vessel
of water. Kern and I could see that it was some kind of tal-
isman for him, a reminder of his own youthful barnstorm
across the prairies, because he kept insisting that we find one
"just like I had in '37." We should have been making other,
more vital preparations for the trip. But we didn't want to
deny my father this one, quaint fantasy—71-Hotel crossing
the high deserts of Texas and Arizona with a Depression-era
waterbag lashed between the wheels.

In the blue Willys, we visited every hardware store and
Army-Navy outlet in three counties, from Dover all the way
down to Princeton. The hardware store men were an American personality type. They wore plastic pocket protectors
with lots of pens and tiny metal rulers, heavy black glasses,
and got annoyed if you asked to see a parts manual, because
they knew every sparkplug and hex-bolt by heart.

"Ah, son, you want a waterbag? This is a hardware store,
not a pharmacy."

"No, not one of those jobs," Kern would say. "An old-fashioned waterbag, like Henry Fonda had on his truck in *Grapes of Wrath.*"

"Well, it's not in the manual. We don't have it."

Kern was easily flustered by rejection. The flinty hardware store men made him feel insecure and he stammered a lot before stalking out of the store. I was annoyed at him for projecting an air of defeat. ("Say, you wouldn't have one of those old waterbags lying around in the cellar, would you?") To put him out of his misery, I volunteered to go into the stores alone while he sat outside in the Willys.

"Sorry son, no waterbags. What are you doing, making a movie?"

The cause was hopeless. It was obvious that waterbags hadn't been manufactured for at least twenty-five years. After a while I didn't even bother asking anymore. While Kern waited in the Jeep, I stepped into the store, looked at the new John Deere lawn tractors for a couple of minutes, and then walked back out, letting the wooden screen door slam with a thwack behind me.

"No dice, Rink?"

"No dice."

It was hot in the Jeep cab and I quickly lost patience with the waterbag chase. I was furious at my father for sending us on this asinine errand, furious at Kern for going along, furious at myself for being related to both of them. It was such a typical regression for us. I had worked hard all year, forging a better relationship with Kern. But something like the waterbag always came along to upset my progress and rekindle my anger at my father and Kern.

Meanwhile, my father was looking in Manhattan. It is a pitiable image to me, still. Here was this poor, phantom-pained man, a victim of his own nostalgia, a top executive with a major American magazine, dragging a heavy wooden leg over the hot tars of Manhattan, searching for a waterbag. At one point he had two secretaries from *Look* and the executive director of the Explorers Club crazed by the project. The Manhattan Yellow Pages were worn thin. Goldberg's Marine down on Chambers Street checked with all of their suppliers. But in Gotham, famous for having at least one of everything, there were no waterbags.

Finally, my father gave up, in his own way. One Friday night he came in looking hot and tired, with his shirt all wrinkled from perspiration, and announced that we could take off from New Jersey without a waterbag. But we were to stop and look as soon as we crossed the Mississippi.

He pointed his finger at us again. "No crossing Texas without a waterbag, you hear?"

A lot of thought had been devoted to the subject and he had identified the problem.

"Boys," my father said, "these hardware-store turkeys here on the East Coast don't know shit from shinola about waterbags. It'll be different as soon as you get out into that Arkansas country. Mark my words. Every damn store out there will have waterbags stacked right up to the ceiling. A dime-a-dozen. You'll see!"

"Dad," I said, "You're absolutely right. Assignment Number One when we hit Arkansas? The waterbag."

Lee Weber, the mechanic out at Basking Ridge, called Kern one morning in late June and told him that 71-Hotel was ready for its test flight. Lee had completed the required annual inspection on the Cub, issued us an airworthiness certificate, and he told Kern that the re-covering job on 71-Hotel was one of the slickest that he'd seen in years. Elated, Kern picked me up at work during my lunch break and we drove over to the strip.

Lee had worked on our planes for years and he and Kern had always been close. He was one of the few people who knew over the winter that we were preparing 71-Hotel for a coast-to-coast flight, and when we got to the airport it was obvious that he had really babied the plane. The controls were perfectly balanced and rigged and Lee had made a number of other fine tunings and adjustments—greasing and calibrating the throttles, justifying the compass for accuracy—that Kern and I had not thought to do. The Cub looked spotless, practically brand new.

As we rolled the plane out of the hangar, Kern was excited when Lee motioned for him to take the seat in the cockpit. Usually Lee or some other older, experienced pilot made the first few flights in a newly rebuilt plane.

"Me, Lee? Me?" Kern said. "You want me to take the first hop?"

"Ah Christ, Kern" Lee said. "Yeah, you. You. You rebuilt the Cub, you test-fly it."

Kern hoisted himself in by the cockpit struts and strapped on his safety belt.

Older, prewar designs like the Cub came stock from the factory without electrical systems, and they didn't have starters. The engine was ignited by manually swinging the propeller, in much the same way an old Ford Model T was pulled through with a hand crank. The starting procedure harked back to the barnstorming era. The copilot or mechanic standing outside and swinging the prop called out an established set of commands, which the pilot responded to as he activated the various controls and switches required for starting. "Switches off" meant that the magneto ignitions had not been engaged, and thus it was safe to pull the propeller through to circulate primer fuel shot into the engine from a metal syringe mounted on the instrument panel. When all was ready, "Contact!" meant that the ignitions were engaged.

"All right, Kern," Lee yelled. "Give me three shots of prime with the switches off."

"Switches off."

Lee threw the prop clockwise three turns, and then gave it a swift, counter-clockwise heave to surge the primer fuel back into the carburetor. A few drops of fuel spilled out of the bottom of the engine cowl and the ramp filled with the smell of 80-octane gas.

"Kern. Brakes."

"Brakes."

"Throttle."

"Throttle."

"Give me Contact."

"Contact!"

She was a dandy old Cub and the cylinders caught on Lee's

first throw. Kern eased the throttle back to idle. From underneath the cowl the valves and rocker-arms evenly clicked
and purred, and the exhaust contentedly blurt-blurted and
coughed white smoke out through the stack. The Continental
sounded perfectly tuned.

Kern knew the test-flight drill, and he S-turned the Cub
down the grass taxiway for the short, north-south runway. He
ran the engine up longer than usual to make sure that everything was working properly, and then he swung onto the runway for a couple of "fast-taxi" runs to check the controls and
the stability of the plane, opening the throttle to half-power
and raising the tail as he sped by us at thirty miles an hour
without lifting the plane off the ground. Fast taxis are treacherous on a bumpy field like Basking Ridge—it's a lot easier
just to "firewall" the throttle to full power and yank the plane
into the air—but Kern didn't seem to notice and handled the
Cub well.

Everything appeared ready and Kern taxied back down for
the runway. At the end of the strip he spiked the throttle,
stood on the right brake, and whipped the plane around in a
tight 360-degree turn on the ground to check for traffic.

I never forgot the picture the Cub made that day, whirling
around on its axis at the end of the strip. 71-Hotel looked
exquisite, pristine. As the wings spun around the light
caught the new sunbursts and they shimmered and merged
as one barn-red swirl, the new windows glinted, and the sun
also illuminated the neat row of ribs underneath the fabric.
All of this was wrapped in the vortices of dust thrown back
by the prop. I felt a possession for the Cub stronger than
anything I had felt all winter, and this was mixed with ap-
preciation for the way my brother handled a plane, which
was so fluid and graceful I couldn't distinguish the end of
one movement he was making with the controls to the beginning of the next.

Kern poured on the coals and dunked the stick forward
coming out of the turn, and the plane lunged onto the runway
with the tail already raised. The Cub vaulted into the air at
the first bump, shivering off some dust. I could see right away
that we had a great plane. As he climbed past the windsock,

Kern was already leaning down with his left hand to crank the trim-control and lower the pitch of the nose. And he was pulling back power too. 71-Hotel just wanted to go. With just one person aboard and not much fuel it was all my brother could do to keep the plane from climbing almost vertically.

I was surprised and even a little annoyed at my reaction as the Cub blew over. I had always prided myself on not being emotional. But my throat was fighting for air and my eyes welled with tears as my brother and the Cub clawed for air. A lot of it had to do with my suppressed affection for my brother, which now I knew that I couldn't deny. And I was proud, as well, to have helped bring him and the plane to this moment. All winter I was worried that we could never possibly finish the Cub on time, and Kern would have been disappointed, shattered by that. Now he was banking the Cub directly over my head, wiggling the wings to show me how well it flew. The sunbursts gleamed, the Continental roared, and 71-Hotel just didn't want to stop climbing. They belonged together, my brother and that plane.

Over the airport, Kern flew straight and level for a while to check the Cub's trim, and then he pulled up for some sharp stalls and tight turns. He descended for the runway in a sweeping, 180-degree turn, side-slipping down over the phone wires and trees before he flared and touched down smoothly on the grass. Pulling up to the ramp, he left the prop turning for Lee.

"Lee, it's perfect," Kern said. "This Cub flies just right. Take her up yourself."

There was none of this trimming down the nose and pulling back the power for Lee. At the end of the runway he pushed the throttle to its stop, raised the tail high, and hauled for air. As he went by us at the gas pumps he was already clearing 500 feet. Kern and I just couldn't believe how that Cub climbed. Lee's strategy of "pushing" the dope with extra thinner had really worked. Not only did we have a great re-covering job that made a smooth, efficient airfoil for lift, but all the extra sanding and thinned dope had made the plane a bit lighter.

Lee banked over sharply for some 360-degree turns, did a

few stalls, and rechecked the trim. Then he dove down over the windsock, pointed the nose at us, and pulled the Cub straight up and over onto its back for a loop. This was the right thing to do, and we were glad that Lee had stretched the wings a bit for us. Nobody at Basking Ridge considered a plane finished until it had been christened by an official Lee Weber loop.

I had to get back to work right away and there wasn't enough time to give me a ride in the Cub. But that didn't seem to matter because Kern was so happy about the plane. All the way back to the horse farm he was jubilant, jabbing out with his free hand at an imaginary stick and kicking around down near the clutch pedal as he told me about how the plane flew. He seemed immensely relieved, carefree, now that we had a finished plane. Maybe this would be the personality I would come to know on the trip.

Kern and I never forgot that date. We test-flew the Cub on June 29, just four days before we took off.

Everything had fallen into place. The night after we test-flew the Cub, Kern and I sat upstairs on his bed and counted the earnings we had stashed in the coffee can. The total came to $326, a comfortable margin over the $300 we had budgeted for the flight. My father called his brother James at his home in Orange County, California, and made arrangements for us to stay with him for a couple of weeks after we reached the west coast. That had been the plan all along, and Kern and I were excited about that. Jimmy had always been our favorite uncle, and we considered him "very California." Casual and relaxed, effortlessly successful in business, Jimmy was notoriously indulgent toward children and didn't lay down a lot of rules for visiting nephews and nieces. Everybody called him Uncle Real Fine, because everything with Jimmy was always "real fine." Jimmy had reservations about our flight, especially when my father told him that we were flying all the way to California without a radio, but he agreed to sit tight and relax until we arrived. He was looking forward to showing us a "real fine time" in California.

Our only remaining obstacle was quitting our jobs. Neither of us had told our employers that we were skipping out early to fly to California, because we wouldn't have been hired in the first place if we weren't planning to work the whole summer. Exiting my job was a cakewalk. The farm manager didn't seem to understand what I was telling him and thought that my brother and I were flying out to L.A. on a commercial airliner, to visit Disneyland and go surfing for a couple of weeks. But he wasn't upset. He liked the way I ran his breeding stock and he told me that my job would be waiting for me when we got back.

Kern, meanwhile, was terrified about breaking the news to Mussolini over at the Acme. During our last week at home, Monday and Tuesday went by, and Kern still hadn't talked to Mussolini. We were planning on taking off at the crack of dawn on Saturday. When Kern came in from his shift Wednesday night, he didn't have the dejected look on his face that always followed a good battle with Mussolini. I was beginning to get worried.

"Hey Kern," I said. "Would you please quit this fucking job? We're taking off for California in less than seventy-two hours."

"Rink, I'm going to do it. Tomorrow," Kern said. "I'm just going to walk right in there, find that snot-nosed jerk, and give him a piece of my mind. He can take the Acme and shove it. Screw you Mussolini! I'm blowing this joint for L.A.!"

"Good Kern. That should do it."

Two more nights went by, but Kern never did talk to Mussolini. At the end of his shift on Friday evening, his last, Kern simply cleared his register, hung up his red Acme apron, punched out his time card, quietly left the store and drove home in the Jeep.

I asked him about it when he got in.

"Hey Kern," I said. "How did it go with Mussolini?"

"Oh! Jeez! My job at the Acme! Gosh darn it all anyway Rink, I mean, God, holy mackerel, shit. Shit! I forgot to tell the Acme! We're taking off for California in the morning and

I've got so many things on my mind I completely forget to tell the Acme. Hilarious, huh Rink?"

"Yeah. It's a fucking stitch."

It didn't take us very long to pack for the trip. The Piper Aircraft Company never imagined that anyone would fly very far in one of its Cubs and the baggage compartment was the size of a milk crate. Once our sleeping bags were stowed in the bottom, there would only be about three inches left for luggage. Kern wanted this to be light—suitcases, even knapsacks, would be too heavy. So we stuffed everything we needed for the coast to coast flight—combs, toothbrushes, a change of Levi's, and some fresh underwear and shirts—into our pillowcases. Our flying maps finished off the load. These we carried in an Acme shopping bag.

As we finished packing, my father yelled up the back stairs and called us down to his library. I knew this was coming and expected the full treatment from him that night: no fights, no buzz jobs, no flying in bad weather and, boys, find that waterbag.

"Ah shit, Kern," I said. "Here we go. The big lecture."

But it wasn't that way at all. My father was very relaxed and gentle that night. He had this avuncular, dreamy-eyed demeanor, intense yet remote, the way the priests up at school got when they were saying goodbye to a favorite senior. There wasn't a thing left to teach us or go over, and he knew it. Kern and I had pored over the maps and our routes a dozen times. Everything it was mechanically possible to do to an aircraft, Kern had done to 71-Hotel. My father had a lot of confidence in us, and he showed it. For years I would remember and miss him for the way he was that night.

Kern and I sat on the couch facing my father in his rocker, drinking Cokes. We talked for a while and my father fed us some pretty good barnstorming blarney about the places we'd see, the Ozarks and Texas mostly. Then he paused, lit his pipe, and pulled a brown paper bag out from behind his typewriter.

He had bought us gifts for the trip. He had even gone to the trouble of wrapping them—actually, I could see from the way they were wrapped that a woman had done it, probably his secretary in New York.

"Boys," he said. "I got you a couple of presents. You know. It's stuff you can use on your flight."

Kern and I both got new Ray-Ban sunglasses. They were the top of the line, Aviator Special model, with the best smoked glass and the pearl-white sweatband running between the lenses. Ray-Ban only made them in adult sizes and they were way too large for us, but my father showed us how to crimp back the holders near the ears with pliers, so they fit snugly. We tried them on and looked at ourselves in the mirror over the fireplace. We looked ridiculous in those big dark shades, like Rocky Raccoon. But the sunlight out west was supposed to be quite harsh and we were glad to have the new eyewear.

Each pair of Ray-Ban aviator goggles came inside a polished leather case, the way they were issued to World War II Air Corps cadets. The case had perforated lines on the back, so it could be attached to a belt and worn military-style on the waist. I didn't like the idea of wearing my Ray-Ban case on my belt, because it made me feel like some dork Eagle Scout running around the Jamboree with a Bowie knife on his hip, but I didn't want to disappoint Kern or my father so I strapped it on. While Kern was putting on his Ray-Ban case, I noticed that he was wearing this godawful purple paisley belt, which looked like something Guy Lombardo would own, and I was hoping like hell that Kern wouldn't wear that thing tomorrow. But then he admired himself in the mirror, hitched up his waist and swiveled around to face us in the room with this proud smile on his face, and I knew that I was screwed in the morning for a flying buddy. Ray-Bans on the purple paisley belt. To Kern, this was tip-top flight gear, the way to travel.

Then, for Kern, my father pulled out of the bag one of his most prized possessions—his old Hamilton aviator's chronograph. The Hamilton was a beautiful, expensive timepiece, with extra sweephands and stop-buttons for timing flight legs, calculating fuel burns and the like. My father had owned it since his Air Corps days during World War II and for years kept it up in the top drawer of his bureau. Now he had had it immaculately restored by a jeweler in New York. The chronograph, with its new leather band, beige face, and luminescent-green sweephands, looked brand new. Kern was thrilled to have it. He strapped it on and it looked great on his tanned arm.

"Gee Dad. Thanks. I never expected you to part with this."

"Ah, it's nothing son," my father said. "You're going to be a big wheel when you finish this flight. I want you to look the part."

My father had another gift for me too. I could tell right away by the way it looked—the thing had been hastily wrapped up in a ball of newspaper—what had happened. At the last minute, my father realized that it would be a terrible display of favoritism to give only Kern a watch, so he'd stopped by a candy store on his way home from work and picked up some total piece of junk for me. He pulled it out of the bag with a flourish.

"And Rinker, good buddy, *this* is for you."

It was a $3.95 Timex. The imitation-alligator wrist-band was plastic, the clunky round body was fake gold, and the hour-numerals on the face were as large and as goofy-looking as the type in a Dr. Seuss book.

In those days Timex was what we called a "dipshit brand." It was on a moral par with Thom McAn shoes, Robert Hall suits, and the Plymouth Valiant sedan. Men who bought anniversary presents for their wives at Sears Roebuck, or neckties at Tie City on Route 46, wore Timex watches.

Everything associated with Timex, in fact, was a profound cultural embarrassment. The tone was set by these klutzy ads that Timex ran on national television, narrated by John Cameron Swayze. In the ads, Acapulco cliff-divers and lunatics in motor boats deliberately beat the living daylights out of their Timex watches, and then handed them over to Swayze for inspection. The watch never failed and Swayze always ended the ad with the same punchline.

"Timex. It takes a lickin', and keeps on tickin'!"

That's the model I got. It was the ugliest watch I had ever seen. I strapped it on and it looked like crap on my tanned arm.

"Gee Dad, thanks," I said. "I never expected you to part with something like this."

"Ah c'mon Rinky," Kern laughed. "That's not fair! Daddy was just trying to be good to both of us. I mean, he forgot about you, but then he remembered and he went right out and got you a watch too."

"Ah shut up Kern," my father said, tears of mirth in his eyes. "You got my Hamilton chronograph. Rinker here, he got shit."

This disparity in gifts was pathetically funny, and we all started to laugh about it, and then we couldn't stop laughing. Just when everybody was recovering I would hold up the Timex on my wrist and we'd all fall off into peals of laughter again. As he roared with laughter my father's eyes welled up with moisture and he kept trying to get his pipe lit but he couldn't, and there was a wonderful self-mockery about him at such moments.

"Ah balls Rinker," my father said. "I'm sorry. Listen, do me a favor tomorrow and deep-six that thing into the Delaware River."

I wasn't upset and I wasn't going to dwell on it. This was the way my father, my brother, and I were, and we could understand and even enjoy it about ourselves, and anyway I was laughing too hard to care.

Tomorrow I would be crossing America with my brother. I was fifteen years old and impatient for experience, annoyed with myself for knowing about life only from books, and now that would change. I'd never been west of the Alleghenies and a whole continent was waiting for me. And it was a beautiful night outside, with crickets screeching, wind swirling through the trees, and the scent of lilac wafting in through the window screens while we laughed and talked in my father's library. We were quiet in the room together for a while and the feelings between my father and my brother over-flowed, and that was enough love in one family for me. All I wanted to do was wake in the morning and light out for the Rockies.

CHAPTER 7

THE ADMIRABLE RESTRAINT MY FATHER HAD DISPLAYED ALL WIN-
ter, leaving us alone to build our plane and plan our trip,
evaporated in stages as our time of departure drew near. It
vanished altogether the day we took off. Later I would think
of that morning as my entire boyhood dispensed in concentrated form. My father's ambitions for us, and the inevitable
bedlam of getting anything done in a large family, combusted
powerfully that day. To begin with, there were delays, maddening delays. Kern and I had resolved to launch as early in
the morning as possible, but sensible planning like this became the first casualty of our trip. We would pay for it dearly
that afternoon.

One night in May, while we were out in the barn painting
the plane, Kern had said to me, "Rink, Day One, we're making Indiana. I can feel Indiana in my bones."

Indiana. Normally I would resist a dreamy notion like that
from Kern. It epitomized his tendency to pluck arbitrary goals
out of thin air and then live for them like someone possessed.
But as soon as he said it I could feel Indiana in my bones
too. Indiana had always seemed vaguely mysterious to us,
probably because we didn't even know where it was before
we began our flight planning. When we checked our maps,

we could see that the Indiana state line was just beyond comfortable range for one day's flying in a Cub—Columbus, Ohio, one hundred miles shy of Indiana, was a much more realistic goal, and thus Indiana was alluring precisely because it was unobtainable. More than anything else, I just liked the way that old frontier state rolled off the tongue, with a romantic, far-off ring. We promised to keep it a secret. Kern was looking forward to calling home when we got there, surprising my father with the news that we'd "made Indiana" on the first day.

On our big day, Kern and I were both awake at dawn, and Kern immediately went down to the kitchen to call the FAA Flight Service Center at Teterboro for a weather briefing. The outlook was not favorable for us. A classic summer low was stalled over much of the east coast and the midwest, and we could expect poor visibility, turbulence, and stratocumulus cloud formations over most of our route as the convection effect built through the day. Worse, the remnants of a Gulf Coast storm, pushing up through the Ohio River Valley, would meet late in the afternoon with a drier, stationary front hanging over the Great Lakes. The systems would collide along the western Pennsylvania border near Pittsburgh and then explode eastward, generating an impenetrable wall of thunderstorms and heavy rain directly in our path. There was one possible advantage in all this. The storm fronts would rocket the muggy low pressure system out to sea, and once they rumbled over, the skies to the west would be clear. To reach Indiana by nightfall, we would have to put in several hours of flying by noon and beat the fronts to western Pennsylvania, then sit out the storms for an hour or two before proceeding on through the midwest.

Chastened, but determined, Kern and I stepped upstairs to wake my parents.

My mother never forgot the scene in their bedroom that morning. "You and Kern just appeared at the foot of our bed at dawn," she recalls. "You stood there quietly with these determined smiles on your faces and those pillowcases filled with your clothes thrown over your shoulders, like hobos waiting for a train. You were both wearing those silly little sunglass cases on your belts. I shook your father and woke him up. 'Daddy,' I said, 'the boys are ready to go.' "

My father, however, wasn't having anything to do with a dawn departure. He pulled on his bathrobe and hopped one-legged over to the window.

"Boys, let's hold off a bit. Look—there's ground fog out there. You need to wait for it to clear. Besides, I told some of the pilots from the strip to meet us out there for your takeoff. Nobody will be there until nine-thirty or ten. Mom, let's get the boys some breakfast."

"Dad, no," Kern said. "We're ready to fly. Now."

"Kern, I'm talking now," my father said. "Mother wants to feed you. Then we'll go."

Kern and I were furious at my father for holding us up, butterflies raged in our stomachs, and the last thing we needed was food. But we knew that we had to humor my father and avoid a fight. Kern's biggest fear all year had been that my father would use some absurd, last-minute pretext to delay or call off the trip, and now he had the best reason of all—bad weather. We were worried all morning that he would ask about it, but it never crossed his mind.

That breakfast was agony. To date, my mother had not expressed the least concern about the wisdom and safety of two teenage boys tackling the Rocky Mountains in a Piper Cub, but she was very concerned about our nutritional intake. When she asked my father about it a couple of weeks before we left, she was horrified to learn that it might take us an entire week to reach California. She knew very well what we'd be up to for those seven days: skip breakfast, wolf down Lance crackers and Yoo-Hoos for lunch, chow down after dark at some awful barbecue joint in Tennessee. Like a lot of northern women, my mother harbored deep, irrational fears about dietary standards elsewhere in the country. It was a well-known fact, for example, that south of the Mason-Dixon line coffee was served to minors. So, she really loaded up the plates that morning. That breakfast had to last us seven days, until we were safely into the nutritional clutches of Aunt Joan in California. Handing us over plates heaped with scrambled eggs, bacon, potatoes, and cottage cheese, she poured herself a cup of tea and sat down to watch us eat. But Kern and I were too excited to eat very well and we picked aimlessly at the food.

My father had the opposite temperament when he was excited. He ate like a horse. Greedily consuming his usual Saturday morning fare—coffee, burnt toast, and a giant bowl of oatmeal—he bantered away.

"God, don't you just love it boys? You stuff your belly full of food, gas up your ship, and fly the bejesus out of the thing until the sun falls at night. Then you sleep under the wings and watch the stars. Christ, when I was your age I would have killed for a trip like this."

Actually, my father was killing us, because he was up to another old stunt that morning. For important family occasions like this—christenings, confirmations, first solos—he loved to make a great show of the family elan. Everybody in America was infected with the Kennedy bug then. The country couldn't get enough of those big, black-and-white spreads in *Life* and *Look*, showing Bobby and Ethel Kennedy, or Sargent and Eunice Shriver, with a dozen Kennedy children in tow, escorting Rose Kennedy to Mass at the little chapel up in Hyannis Port. The model American family was now a clan, doing things en masse. We would have been infected with that bug with or without the Kennedys, but the Kennedys legitimized our behavior. Anyway, that's how my father decided to handle our takeoff for California—it would be managed as an Official Buck Family Event. Every one of our ten brothers and sisters, my father announced at breakfast, would travel out to the airport that morning to wave us off and lend their "moral support."

Shit, I thought. Kern and I didn't want their moral support. Probably even the Kennedy kids were sick and tired of all that moral support by now. But there was no talking my father out of something like this once he was in the mood for chaos, and Kern and I were working hard at avoiding confrontation so he wouldn't have an excuse to pull the plug on our flight.

After breakfast, my father started bellowing up the stairs for my older sisters to put on their best clothes and help my mother get the younger children organized for the day. From the top of the stair landing, all we could hear was doors slamming and my sisters turning their radios on loud.

It was a disaster. My sisters couldn't have cared less, and they didn't like being ambushed with an Official Buck Family Event at 8:30 on a Saturday morning—the beginning of the long July Fourth weekend no less. Dempsey had been away all year at college, and didn't even know that Kern and I were planning on flying coast to coast. Macky was depressed that Kern and I weren't taking her along and wouldn't even get out of bed. Bridget spent her weekend riding horses and detested airplanes, and she wasn't about to interrupt her schedule for this.

Indeed, it seems unimaginable that my father wasn't more sensitive to the immense family rift that had already developed over our flying. Over the past five years, all of my father's time, and virtually all of his spare cash, had been devoted to flying, to Kern and me, and our planes. My sisters weren't openly resentful about this—they were teenagers, and glad to be left alone—but they did feel excluded, ignored. My father never volunteered to blow all of his money on them. Actually, after our trip got underway, both Dempsey and Macky were quite supportive, genuinely excited for us. But they didn't want to be pressured into going out to that "dirty, smelly old airport," as Dempsey put it, to perform the Kennedy routine for us. They didn't need to be reminded all over again how weighted the family was in favor of the two oldest boys.

Dempsey was in a particularly testy mood anyway. She'd had a wonderful time being away at college that first year, learning how to smoke cigarettes and drink coffee and getting away from all those noisy kids at home, and it was miserably depressing to be back in the bosom of her family again. Now my father was yelling up the stairs for her to get dressed and join the family mayhem out at the airport. When he called up the third time, she stormed out to the stair railing and shrieked back down.

"Hey, Daddy," Dempsey yelled. "Airport-Schmairport. I'm not going!"

"Ah c'mon, Dempsey," my father yelled. "You're going to disappoint the boys now."

"Come off it, Daddy," Dempsey yelled back. "They'll be disappointed if I *do* come."

"Now listen here young lady!"

"Daddy, don't give me that listen-here-young-lady stuff. *I'm* not flying to California. Kern and Rinky are flying to California. What am I supposed to do? Go out there and wind up the rubber bands for their little motor?"

My father couldn't roll over my sisters unless my mother backed him up, and she didn't want to have anything to do with it either. Official Buck Family Events were a trial for her, requiring hours of preparation, and this one was unannounced and she wasn't ready for it. Besides, she could see that Kern and I were anxious to take off, and dragging my sisters along would just delay us by hours.

"Dear," my mother said to my father, "leave the girls alone. They don't like the airport."

My father was absolutely brilliant in retreat, an instant victim. When my mother shot him down, he shrugged his shoulders and turned his face up into a scowl. It was the nobody-likes-me-everybody-hates-me-guess-I'll-go-eat-worms approach.

"Boys," my father sighed. "We got skunked. You bust your ass all winter working on a plane, and your own family doesn't even want to see you fly it. That's gratitude for you."

Silently, with dejected looks on our faces, Kern and I pleaded with him to let us leave for the airport.

Somehow, we all got out of the house that morning and departed the drive in Official Buck Family formation. My father led the way in his Oldsmobile with the younger boys, my mother carried the younger girls in her Volkswagen van, and Kern and I brought up the rear in the Willys. At the traffic light up in the village, Kern and I swerved left out of the motorcade and took the back roads through the Great Swamp. We didn't want to be seen dead anywhere near these people.

*In the age of the Kennedys, the model American family was now a clan,
doing things en masse. Kern and I were always posed on either side, the
two oldest boys who framed my father's ambitions for all of us.*

It was madness out at the airport. My father had invited a
number of his friends to watch us take off, and some of the
Basking Ridge pilots brought their wives out to see us off
too, but they were the nonflying wives and none of them
knew squat about aviation. While Kern and I were trying to
ready the plane, there was a crowd milling around the Cub,
and people kept banging their heads into the wing struts,
pestering us with idiotic questions and changing babies' di-
apers back on the tail section. Everybody was astounded by
the simplicity of 71-Hotel. They kept sticking their heads
into the cockpit, wiggling the stick for a second or two and
then staring at us in disbelief, asking one of the pilots if this
really was the plane the Buck boys were flying to California,
or just a toy. On top of this, my father had arranged to have
the soda machine opened up for everyone's use, and my little
brothers and sisters kept spilling root beer and Coke on
Kern's new paint job.

While Kern preflighted and gassed the plane, I stowed our gear. The only way to wedge everything into the baggage compartment, I discovered, was to cram the pillowcases with our clothes at the very bottom, the shopping bag full of our maps in the middle, then the sleeping bags on top. Still, there wasn't enough space. The sleeping bags on top overflowed up past the windows, which would block my view out the back, and we were concerned that the protruding gear would bang up against the fabric headliner and cause it to break apart in heavy turbulence. At the last minute we took everything out again and started jettisoning things from the pillowcases—duplicate tubes of toothpaste, paperback books, extra pants and sneakers. I handed the discarded items over to my mother in a big, messy armful, and stuffed everything back into the baggage compartment. More or less, all we had to wear now were the penny loafers and the Levi's that we already had on.

I jammed the sectional maps we would need that day, and my clipboard for keeping flight notations, into the leather pocket behind Kern's front seat.

The nonexistent waterbag was another royal pain in the ass. My father had told everyone about the waterbag, but of course he forgot to update them when we couldn't find one. Curious onlookers kept coming over to the plane, dipping their head down between the wheels, where the waterbag was supposed to be lashed, and coming back up disappointed. I was civil to the first seven or eight people who asked about the waterbag—maybe it was even a dozen. Then I blew my stack.

"Hey, Rinker, Kern!" my little brother Nicky howled. "Where's the waterbag? Daddy said you can't take off without the waterbag."

"Shut up Nicky," I said. "It's none of your business."

"It is too! Daddy says you have to have a waterbag!"

"Nicky, we don't have it yet. But I'll tell you what. If I do find a waterbag, I'm going to shove it straight up your butt. Now scram!"

Nicky ran off to inform my father that I was threatening to shove a waterbag up his butt.

"Screw this Kern," I said. "Let's fly."

"Yeah. This is a train wreck. Where's Dad?"

Finally, my father bounded over to the plane with an exasperated look on his face, as if this was all our fault.

"Hey, boys, c'mon now! You can't get to California sitting here on the ramp. Hop in. I'll prop you."

Kern strapped himself into the front seat, I took the rear. With a raised hand and a growl, my father cleared the area of kids. Then he leaned into the cockpit for a final chat.

"All right boys," my father said. "Now I'm not going to give you the big lecture or anything. Just pace yourselves, that's all. Six or seven hours of flying a day is plenty. Nobody cares how long it takes you to get out to the coast."

Kern was impatient to go.

"Got it Dad."

"Now another thing," my father said. "We've got a nice crowd here. Everybody came out to watch you take off. Once you get in the air, circle the pattern once, and then come back down the runway for a flyby. A flyby, I said, not a buzz job. There's a difference. Don't get too low. Then just wiggle the wings a little for Mother. Okay?"

Kern wasn't even listening.

"Dad, I think I can get this airplane off this strip, okay? My switches are off, and I'm priming."

I always liked the way my father turned a prop. He had this graceful, muscular way with a propeller in his hands, a jaunty confidence that bespoke years of flying. Embarrassed as I was, sitting there with a crowd watching us, I enjoyed watching him throw the blades.

"All right boys," my father called out. "Make us proud now, and have a great trip. Brakes, Throttle, Contact!"

"Contact!"

The cylinders fired on my father's first throw, blurt-blurting and coughing through the stack, blowing back an aromatic puff of smoke. We waved goodbye to my mother, taxied down to the end of Runway 28, ran up the engine and cleared the controls.

As soon as Kern ruddered onto the strip and firewalled the throttle, I loved that Cub. Despite two passengers, baggage, and a full load of fuel, we only traveled a hundred feet or so down the runway before 71-Hotel popped off the ground and clawed for air. Kern immediately trimmed for some down elevator, to get the nose lower.

He and Lee had rigged the plane well. As we passed the windsock I wiggled my stick in the rear to signal Kern that I wanted to feel the controls, and he wiggled back and gave me the plane. I did a gentle aileron bank to either side, and tapped the rudders. The controls were firm and responsive, not at all like the other old taildraggers we flew, where you moved the controls and then waited a second or two for a response. There was no doubt about it. 71-Hotel was our best restoration yet.

We leveled off downwind of the runway and then Kern banked and dove the Cub to come back in over the crowd. He yelled back to me over the roar of the engine.

"Hey Rink. Did he say a flyby, or a buzz job?"

"Buzz job!"

It was a lie, but I'd had enough of my father at that moment. We were up here, he was down there, and for the next few weeks there would be 2,400 miles of open country between us. Fuck 'im. A buzz job it would be.

Kern gave the runway a close shave. He dove for the grass from 800 feet, pushed the throttle to the stop, and roared past the gas-pump crowd at 120 miles per hour. As we were passing the windsock I looked out the side. My father was kangarooing across the ramp to the edge of the runway in his crazy wooden-legged gait.

Going by the gas pumps, Kern put the right wing over, pulled the sticks back into our laps, and turned up and over the crowd, Eddie Mahler style. Below us, everyone's necks were craned straight up. There was a decent quartering wind on our nose when Kern leveled the wings and hung 71-Hotel on her prop.

We climbed almost vertically over the crowd. As we passed through 700 feet I opened the right window and leaned out into the slipstream, looking back over the tail to my father. When he saw me hanging out the side of the plane my father started waving both of his hands over his head. I took the stick and wiggled the wings in reply and then I washed the rudders back and forth with my feet to fishtail the plane and my father waved some more. He kept waving, waving both arms over his head, growing smaller and smaller as we climbed the plane, and he was waving still as we disappeared over the hills.

I looked back several times at my father as he waved, wiggling the wings for him a couple of more times. Behind and below me, he was framed by the tail section of the plane, as if in a picture. I remember the way the sunlight turned the grass around him a hard green, and the way the image of him was blurred and kept going double from the slipstream beating my hair into my face and whipping up tears in the corners of my eyes. I was filled with an immense sadness and happiness for him at once, and afterward I couldn't understand why that particular vision of him moved me so much, or why it returned so often in my dreams. After a while I just accepted it as a portrait of contentment between us. Maybe we would never say it that way but the truth was that we were happiest watching each other recede in the distance.

There wasn't a lot of time to dwell on that right away. As we climbed through 3,000 feet I could just barely make out through the haze our first navigation checkpoint, the big manmade reservoir at Clinton. The air was choppy already, a bad sign so early in the day, because the turbulence would only build as the sun rose higher. Kern climbed and descended several times, up above 5,000 feet and then back down to 2,500, trying to find a scud-level altitude where the haze thinned out. But it was useless. At any height we were assaulted by the same blinding white glare and low visibility, with the amber sun on our nose burning through the windshield.

Momentarily I lapsed into an old habit, my first navigation chore when we flew west, and decided to tune in the radio frequency for the Flight Service Station at Allentown, Pennsylvania, to check the weather ahead of us. Then I had to laugh at myself. There was no Allentown FSS for us, and there would be no FSS all the way across the country. We didn't have a radio in this plane.

I pulled my seatbelt tight against the turbulence and squinted ahead into the glare. The old Continental roared, the cockpit smelled of burnt oil, and the slipstream rushing in through the open window rifled my shirt and my hair. I was glad to be launched at last. In the seat ahead of me Kern looked back, smiled, and gave me a thumbs-up. I knew that he would push hard to beat the storms ahead, which frightened me, but we were still several hours away from the worst of the weather and there wasn't much point in worrying about what I couldn't yet see. Probably we could find a way through. I knew all along that we'd have to fly like the blazes to make Indiana by nightfall.

CHAPTER 8

As soon as we got out over the Delaware River, barely fifty miles from home, we could see what kind of trouble we were in. Menacing and black anvil-head clouds, their tops silver-bright in the sun, towered up on our right, blocking our planned route to the northwest. To the south, vapory sheets of rain fell to the green fields. In between there was still an open patch of sky. Kern hunched forward over the instrument panel and peered intently through the windshield. Pushing over the rudder and the stick, he steered southwest over the picturesque farmlands of Bucks County, Pennsylvania.

We hadn't expected the weather to develop this quickly. The flight-briefer at Teterboro had forecast these conditions for later in the day, and much further west. But weather is weather and obviously the warring masses of air were pushing trouble eastward faster than predicted.

From the backseat, I leaned over sideways and looked at my brother's face. His mouth was turned up into a grim half-smile. I had never flown alone with him in bad weather but I knew what this expression meant. We were now in a race. He was determined to outfox the advancing edges of the storm and beat the front to Pittsburgh.

I was surprised by Kern's decision to push ahead in the

face of such early signs of adverse weather, and I had to deliberately work at resisting the urge to panic. Kern and I still
didn't know each other very well in the air. His dauntless,
supremely confident attitude in a plane, so different from his
uptight personality on the ground, was a mystery to me. I
couldn't understand where it came from or how one person
could be transformed so dramatically by environment. Kern,
likewise, had no idea of just how frightened I was by turbulence and poor visibility. Fear in the air was something my
father simply wouldn't tolerate, and over the years I had de-
vised a variety of physical and mental stratagems to hide this
weakness—closing my eyes during spins, breaking up cross-
country trips in marginal weather into ten-minute segments,
which made them easier to bear. This was the price I had
paid for inclusion in our weekend flying excursions, and now
I would have to do the same with Kern. I didn't want to
disappoint him this early in the trip, and I vowed not to complain or reveal my fears no matter how much this leg across
Pennsylvania rattled me.

Hitching my seatbelt up another notch, I stuck my head
out into the slipstream for some fresh air, and closed my eyes
for a while and pretended that we weren't surrounded by
angry, jagged walls of clouds and rain falling in several directions.

After Quakertown the air turned rough and the visibility
was constantly changing. Suddenly the clouds on either side
of us would drop low and wedge in sideways, forcing us down
against smudgy barn silos and power-line pylons, and then
we'd come around the gauzy corners of the cloud into open
skies dazzling with rainbows, sparkling fields and tidy, white-
washed Pennsylvania Dutch farms. We were "scud-running,"
trying to get below and between the clouds, and I couldn't
believe we were violating all the lessons of our training during
literally the first hour of our trip.

Kern anxiously looked from side to side as he flew the
plane, jabbing his finger against the map on the magenta sym-
bol of an airport. I could see what he was doing, flying us
from airport to airport in case the weather forced us down.
But after Pottstown there weren't any strips for a long stretch.

As the turbulence became stronger, the compass spun crazily and the plane plunged up and down like a cork bobber. Kern threw back the map and yelled.

"Rink! I've got to concentrate on flying this airplane. Get me to Harrisburg."

Harrisburg. I focused hard on the map, determined to deliver for Kern. I was actually quite prepared for this assignment, but didn't appreciate that about myself yet. The summer before my father had spent nearly two months giving me cross-country flying lessons. I was only fourteen that year and hadn't spent much time in planes equipped with sophisticated radios and instruments, and he could see that I was only comfortable with straight "pilotage" navigation, flying point-to-point by reference to landmarks. But that was fine with an old barnstormer like him, in fact it was preferable. Anybody could scream around in an expensive Bonanza stuffed with all the latest radio-navigation equipment. But what happened when the radio broke or the electrical system failed? Too many pilots couldn't navigate merely by direct reference to the ground. So I had spent several Saturdays and Sundays in a row navigating by rivers, roads, and gravel quarries marked on sectional maps, learning how to pick up a compass course and correct for wind drift when the landmarks ran out. Mapreading and pilotage the old-fashioned way were my father's gift to me, a very simple gift. But that's all that Kern and I needed in 71-Hotel. Simplicity was the only asset we had.

Our original plan called for skirting the north edge of the Allegheny Mountains, where the peaks are lower and there would be less turbulence, following the gently rolling valleys of central Pennsylvania into Youngstown, Ohio. But that course was now obstructed by clouds and the weather had formed a narrow, irregular chute forcing us to divert south through Harrisburg and the lower Susquehanna Valley. This would mean facing the Alleghenies head-on in rough air, but we would have to worry about that when we got there.

On the map I found a rail line just south of Pottstown that meandered west to the Susquehanna, up through Reading and Hershey. If clouds blocked our way there were several intersecting power lines that we could pick up. Wiggling the stick to signal Kern, I ruddered over for the tracks and pointed them out on the map. Throwing open the side windows, I kept my head out in the slipstream to look for landmarks. The ceiling was dropping again and we didn't have a lot of airports in front of us. I didn't have the luxury of guessing at our position and I focused like a gnome on the land and then back to the map.

That's how we flew the first leg, like a pair of old airmailers. While Kern manned the plane and kept us straight and level from the front seat, I hung out the side from the rear, battered by the rain and the slipstream as I concentrated on the terrain. Kern and I seamlessly adjusted to flying this way and barely exchanged a word about it. When the Cub strayed from the rail line I would look ahead to find the tracks again, and then step on the rudder to steer us over and hold our course on the rails while Kern held the plane steady with the stick. In the rougher air we flew like that for three or four minutes at a stretch, sharing the plane and speaking to each other through the feel of the controls. This was immensely comforting to me because I'd always found that my turbulence jitters eased when I could control the plane. Occasionally, the turbulence blowing in through the windows kited the map off my lap, and the map was hard to hang on to because it was slippery with sweat from my hands. Still, I could almost enjoy this adventure now, hanging out the side and peering forward as I ruddered us along the rails.

As we bobbed over the Pennsylvania farmlands, sometimes we could see ahead of us for a good seven or eight miles and sometimes we could barely see a mile or two. But the Continental roared and the floorboards throbbed and the cockpit was filled with the soothing ether of burnt oil. I liked the thunderous, intense propinquity of the two-seat Cub, flying through this black purgatory with my brother. Right there, on the first leg of the trip, I discovered something important about us. Kern's determination and self-confidence were contagious. All I had to do was look forward at his face. He was grinning, enjoying the chase against the weather. He handled the controls maturely, gently managing the stick with just a couple of fingers and softly cupping his left palm over the throttle, not overcontrolling, as most pilots do in rough air. Up here, I was very committed to him; I yearned to please him. Kern was preternaturally gifted as a pilot and so intent on outwitting those clouds that I could almost feel his skill as a physical sensation, and it would have shattered me to disappoint him.

And so, under increasingly inclement skies, we followed the rails into Hershey, crossed the Susquehanna south of Harrisburg, and flew on to the small grass strip at Carlisle, Pennsylvania. It was the last airport where we could refuel before we faced the Alleghenies. The weather was always closing in behind us. We would get past a nice stretch of farms, or over the big Bethlehem Steel blast furnaces along the Susquehanna, and a few minutes later I'd look back over the tail. It was raining where we just had been.

But we'd beat the weather so far, barely. As we entered the traffic pattern at Carlisle, clouds closed in on us from all sides, swirling around and narrowing the clear space of air in front of us like a funnel of water churning down a tub drain. To dodge the clouds, Kern swung the Cub around in a dive and cut off the edge of the pattern, and then quickly cross-controlled, throwing us into a steep, shuddering sideslip to make the field. As we were rolling out on the spongy grass runway, a light rain began pattering onto the windshield and the wing fabric.

We called them the "geezers," the airport geezers. Every little airport in America had one or two, and still does. They're the old-timers in the Dickie pants, the matching Dickie shirt and the broad leather belt, sitting on the gas pump bench. They might be seventy or seventy-five now, not flying much anymore, but geezers aren't envious of the younger pilots, just solicitous. Geezers pour a lot of oil into hot engines and know how to squeak bugs off the windshield without wasting any cleaner. Student pilots on their first solo cross-countrys get to know the geezers quite well. It's the geezer who tells them that they have just landed at the wrong airport, and then talks to them for a while about how easy a mistake that is—all of these little airports look the same from the air—and he steers the young pilot to the right strip. Then the geezer takes the student's logbook, makes an entry for the flight and signs his name. According to him, the kid landed at the correct field.

The airport geezer at Carlisle was a jowl-faced, big-bellied fellow named Wilbur—you never get more than a first name. When he saw us taxi in with the Cub he pulled on a rain slicker and a ball-cap and jogged out to meet us. There was an empty T-hangar by the fuel pumps. We shut down the engine and Wilbur helped us push 71-Hotel out of the rain.

Wilbur was surprised that we were flying around in this kind of weather, in a Cub without a radio no less. But geezers become geezers because they've survived many mistakes themselves and they are not dogmatic in their old age. As we stood in the T-hangar, in gentle tones, Wilbur was slowly backing into the standard lecture on the perils of "Get-There-Itis" when the rain stopped and the skies all around Carlisle cleared. He asked us where we were headed. Kern and I weren't ready yet to tell a stranger that we were flying all the way to California in a Piper Cub so we told him Pittsburgh instead.

The airport manager strolled out and said he was making a run down the road for hamburgers. I was suddenly hungry and I rode off with him. Kern and Wilbur went into the pilots' shack to phone the FAA weather station at Allentown.

When I got back, they were bent over a table in the shack, looking at the Detroit sectional map. The weather situation was still complicated and unfavorable for us. The front we were worried about wasn't due to arrive in Pittsburgh until three-thirty or four in the afternoon, and we could probably beat it there. But ahead of the storm, directly along our route, there were reports of moderate to severe turbulence and scattered rain showers. We had just flown through the advance squall line of that system. It was clearing now around Carlisle, but that didn't mean much. The mountains were only a few miles away and there would be plenty of stratocumulus bangers behind them.

Wilbur had us cased out pretty well. He could see that Kern was determined to get to Pittsburgh, but that I was more tentative, maybe even afraid. A good geezer never tells a transient pilot what to do, especially young ones, because for sure they'll take right off and do the opposite. Instead, geezers anticipate the inevitable fuckup and provide a backup plan. Wilbur suggested that we take off, fly west for fifteen minutes, and see what it was like. In a firm voice he told Kern to turn back if the visibility was poor, the air too rough. Carlisle wasn't going anywhere.

Considering the conditions—a lot of low clouds and poor visibility—following a compass course was unrealistic. Wilbur suggested that we follow the Pennsylvania Turnpike, which ran right by the airport. It wasn't the most direct route over the mountains, but we couldn't get lost if we stayed over the Pike. The windward side turbulence, on the west face of the peaks, would be quite bad. After Shippensburg we would begin passing over the tunnels in the mountains and we'd lose sight of the road for a while, but he told us to just pick a landmark or rock formation up on the high ridge, fly for it, and then we could pick up the Pike again as we came down the other side.

Wilbur advised us to turn southwest after we passed La-trobe. In this kind of weather, with all the pollution from the steel mills ringing Pittsburgh, we wouldn't be able to see anything anyway. Just past the town of Mount Pleasant, the Turnpike would split off for Route 70. Wilbur recommended that we avoid the smog and air traffic around Pittsburgh by following Route 70 into the airport in Washington, Pennsylvania.

It was sparkling and clear outside when we stepped out of the shack. The mowed grass runway was a watery, bright green. The airport sat on a high, broad plateau, commanding a breathtaking prospect of Cumberland County. But it was a deceptive, killer beauty. As I polished off my second hamburger, I felt like the condemned with his last meal. It was going to be a hell of a ride over the mountains.

Wilbur helped us fuel the Cub, checked the oil, and gave us a prop. He acted as if he expected to see us back in Carlisle in twenty minutes, and even offered us a room that night at his house. "The Mrs." would make us a real Pennsylvania Dutch dinner. As we climbed out past the pumps Kern rocked the wings and Wilbur waved.

It was the most murderous corridor of turbulence I have ever experienced. For the next hour and a half I detested my brother. I hated him for catapulting so hard over the mountains, hated my father for letting us make this trip, hated that society of hard, cynical pilots into which we were born and which now obligated me, more or less, to earn my manhood by proving that I could take this abuse. After an hour my knees and my shins, hammered by the turbulence and the shuddering stick against the cockpit walls, ached like scavenged meat.

Bang, bang, bang, bang, across the wretched, washerboard peaks of the Alleghenies we hauled. Kern peered out through the windshield with his chin just above the instrument panel and then looked back, smiling, actually smiling back at me, as our butts and stomachs got walloped by the updrafts and downdrafts. It was maddening, the way he kept flashing me that earnest *Leave It to Beaver* grin of his. It was his way of communicating his apologies for making me sit through all this turbulence, and also showing me that there wasn't anything to worry about, a kind of aerial twenty-third Psalm. Yea though we were flying through the shadow of death, that frigging smile on my brother's face was supposed to comfort me.

He was too good a pilot to pick up a downed wing every time we keeled over in the turbulence. Three seconds later, the back side of the buffet would hit us again and knock us down the other way. I had nothing to do, no task to perform or to distract me, because all we were doing was following the Pennsylvania Turnpike. We couldn't climb and get away from the worst ground effects, because an overcast was starting to drop low. We couldn't descend, and fly the valleys to get some relief from the ridge effect near the peaks, because then we would lose contact with the Turnpike. As it was, we

*Bang, bang, bang, bang, across the wretched, washerboard peaks of the
Alleghenies we hauled. It was the most murderous corridor
of turbulence I have ever experienced.*

were skirting over the tops of the ridges with just a few hundred feet of clearance, and every one of those damn ridge
lines packed a ferocious wallop for us.

Turnpike, tunnel, Turnpike, tunnel, bounce-jolt-bounce.
The Alleghenies are bleak, featureless terrain, and there
wasn't a single farm or a town to break the monotony of the
range. The mountains were flinty and hard, gray and black
as they ran to the narrow horizons, with endless hardwood
stands and pine barrens on top. Perhaps seven or eight

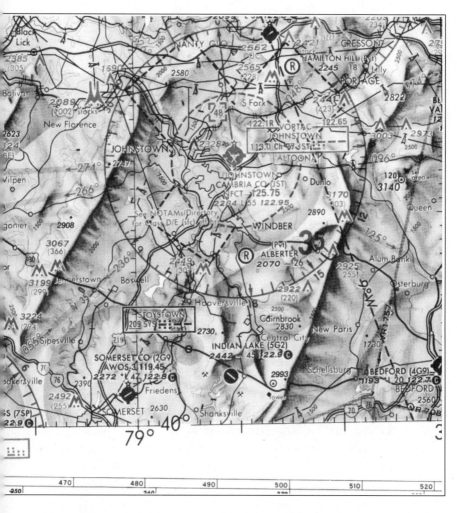

seconds passed between turbulent buffets, and it was very rough turbulence, enough to jiggle the throttle and force Kern to constantly adjust it. I shook all over, trembling from the cold blasts of air coming in through the windows, which made my perspiring hands and chest shiver. But Kern wouldn't throttle back and slow the plane down to make the ride a little easier. He was determined to make it to Washington County Airport and refuel before the front came through. Indiana. If this was the price I had to pay to get there, I wanted out. It was the worst spell of flying in my life.

After the town of Ligonier the mountains thinned out and

the turbulence was milder. But the storm seemed to resent our progress over the mountains and pushed forward new artillery. Mean, snarling black clouds were popping up everywhere, and we were just flying in a maze, poking around for white patches of sky ahead. The headwinds were even stronger than before, a good sign, in a way. We were getting close to the center of the front and it was obvious that it was blowing through quite hard and wasn't going to get stalled. Behind it there would be clear skies and beautiful conditions across Ohio and Indiana.

But where to go? We couldn't turn southwest at Latrobe as Wilbur advised, because the city was socked in by rain. Diverting north instead, we lost the Pike for a while, then picked it back up later. But we had missed the turnoff for Route 70. Now we were almost upon Pittsburgh itself. In this weather, there was no way, legally or safely, to proceed due west over the city. Our destination at Washington was still fifty miles to the southwest, behind a solid wall of gray and black clouds.

Then I just had this lucky little run of memory and map reading.

Barnstorming blarney. I had reached the age of weariness concerning my father's fabulous talk. He was an Olympic-class bullshitter and everyone loved him for it, but not me. By the age of ten I knew every one of his yarns by heart and after that they were maddening, starting to come around for the fourth or fifth time. It never occurred to me, however, that barnstorming blarney might someday prove useful to me, that it was in fact an education, a ground-school course in geography and aerial escape routes, another one of my father's cryptic gifts to me.

But it occurred to me right there, because now we were in trouble over Pittsburgh. My father had always spoken affectionately of this city on the western frontier of Pennsylvania, which he regarded as an industrial utopia. It was his kind of town, big-shouldered and loud, full of beefy, fun-loving steelworkers and insane millionaires. Toward the end of World War II, before his big crash, my father had a friend who flew military cargo out of the North Philadelphia Airport in twin-

engine Lockheeds. My father was working for *Life* then, but
he liked the Lockheed and he often flew along on weekends
as a copilot, to get some free stick time. They landed at Pittsburgh a lot, at the old Allegheny County Airport on the western side of the Monongahela River, and loved to carouse at
night in the waterfront bars. Pittsburgh had always been legendary among pilots for its miserable weather. The big
weather systems pouring out of the Great Lakes condensed
near the junction of the Ohio and the Monongahela rivers
with the smoke from the giant U. S. Steel mills, smothering
the terrain all the way to West Virginia with a dense blanket
of smog.

"Pittsburgh," my father used to say to us. "You know what
they call it? 'Hell with the lid taken off.' It's awful there, but
we always got through. What we did, see, was stay out over
the rivers, between the mills, and then we'd fly the steel
plants stack-to-stack."

Stack-to-stack. Ahead of us, flashing pinkish red in the
haze, was the beacon on a tall obstruction. I stared at the
map. We were quite lost at the moment but I quickly scrolled
through all the possibilities, eliminating other nearby obstructions by poking my head out into the air and squinting down
at the obvious landmarks, the rail junctions and roads. The
tower ahead of us was the first tall one east of the Monongahela, which had to be the big U.S. Steel blast furnace at
Braddock, clearly marked on the sectional map as a "Stack"
with a flashing red beacon.

I wanted to be positive—we couldn't risk a navigation error
at this point, because the weather behind us was closed off.
I gave myself an extra fifteen seconds, peering around for
other beacons, and then checking the location of the stack
against the city below. I was as certain as I could be. That
stack was Braddock.

"Kern!"

"Yo."

"I want this airplane over that stack."

"Done. Rink, are you sure you know what you're doing?"

"I know what I'm doing."

Whoa! Elevator going up. There was quite a strong updraft

rocketing out of that stack. It hadn't occurred to either of us that the blast furnace exhaust churning up through a U.S. Steel stack was just about the strongest thermal you could find. We launched straight up toward the clouds, with the altimeter winding around like a second hand.

As the smell of sulfur and molten steel swirled through the cockpit, Kern closed the throttle, downed the left wing and cross-controlled to slip sideways and spill off lift, and pointed the nose down. It was awesome and harshly beautiful, slipping sideways at a 45-degree bank in the effluent of a steel mill.

But I was jubilant and swelling with pride as we boomeranged through that blast furnace exhaust. There, on the immense roof of the mill, in white block letters, I could read: BRADDOCK.

Stack-to-stack, that's how we flew it. From Braddock we crossed the Monongahela to Duquesne, from Duquesne we flew to McKeesport, from McKeesport to Clairton, and then we flew down over the glorious, giant oxbow in the mighty Mon and south to Monessen.

It was a lovely stretch of flying down through the American Ruhr. Now and then the sky opened up and the sun poked through, shimmering off the river and the ceramic-tile exterior of the stacks. Below us spread a busy industrial setting. The steel mills on either side of the river belched out smoke, the rail lines were full of cars, and barges eased under picturesque steel bridges, which glared softly in the haze. Down along the waterfront the buildings and mills were made of brick and hard granite. Up on the ridgelines, row upon row of white wooden houses perched on the slopes, with terraced gardens thrown out in every direction from the back yards. And the churches. There were so many churches in the Mon Valley. Every town hugging the river—McKeesport and Duquesne, Clairton, Dravosburg, Donora, and Charleroi—had a bright cluster of cathedrals and brick parishes in its midst, immaculate and brimming with wide green lawns in the back. Shiny onion domes and Cyrillic crosses from the church steeples reached up to us in the plane, jewels in the necklace formed by the course of the broad river.

I was very confident of our position now, and I could have flown those industrial landmarks forever. After the bleak, turbulent agony of the mountains, the Mon Valley was a joy to fly. Now we were approaching the last oxbow on the river and our first full state—Pennsylvania—would be behind us. My heart had always belonged to Pennsylvania anyway, because that is where my father's family came from and those were the stories I loved best. Now Kern and I had flown it all and been delivered to this magical western edge.

But there wasn't a lot of time for appreciating the beauty of the steel country after we picked up Route 70 at Monessen. The storm raging out of Ohio still meant to defeat us. The stretch of country west of the Mon Valley is wooded and lonely, and we flew on for fifteen minutes in nasty turbulence and spitting rain. Finally we could make out the hangars of the Washington County airport. The sky above them was twisting up a dragon's tail of angry gray and black clouds. As we firewalled for the field everything ahead of us turned a solid wall of black. We weren't beating the front any longer. We had met it.

Kern kept the Cub high to avoid any obstructions beneath us and punched through some yellowish, bumpy clouds. The runway ahead of us was obscured by rain. When I threw open the side door to stare down and see where we were, the propwash from the propeller sprayed my face and shoulders with rain. But I could see our position on the highway now and then I pulled back into the cockpit to look at the map. The runway ran due east and west, at a slight angle to the highway.

"Kern! Fly 270 degrees, now! Start your descent."

"Rink, where's the wind? We don't know the wind."

"Fuck the wind Kern! We've got plenty of room. It's a 5,000-foot, paved runway."

The wind wasn't consistent anyway. By looking straight down at the tree branches, I could see that it was kiting all over the place, gusting hard and presenting us with a 25-degree crosswind from either side. But that was the great thing about Kern—I knew that he could sideslip or crab through anything, a freaking gale if he had to. We were weathervaning all over the place as we descended on final approach, but Kern was holding my 270 degrees pretty well.

Finally, through the vortices of rain and cloud ahead of us, we could see the white centerline of the runway. Kern closed the throttle and slipped hard to make the pavement.

We were fast and pushed both sideways and from behind, by gusts that couldn't decide whether they were a crosswind or a tailwind. The Cub took up a lot of runway, jackassing down the wet tar. Kern would think he had the wings stalled, then a gust would balloon us up again, he'd slip and stall us again, and then we bounced some more. The wheels skittered all over the place, hydroplaning on the wet runway, and Kern didn't dare touch the brakes. But finally we were stalled hard and the wheels felt solid in the puddles, and the tail would stay down.

As he turned off for a taxiway, Kern reached back and squeezed my knee, which I could never forget because my knee was tender to the touch from banging against the cockpit walls in the turbulence.

"Jesus, Rink. Way to go. That was aces—all day."

I was happy about that compliment from my brother, and relieved to be on the ground. The raging stratocumulus couldn't hurt us now. The front was right on top of the airport and all we had to do was wait an hour or two for it to cleanse the skies ahead of us, and then we'd crop the bejesus out of 71-Hotel that evening to make Indiana.

But it was more than beating the weather that thrilled me. I was enchanted with this journey now, in love with my brother and myself. Everything about us had led to this moment. My brother's fortitude and skill with a plane had been outstanding. I had listened inside me and found a use for barnstorming blarney. Understanding navigation, enjoying it, seemed a divine gift now. And I had to admit that even my father's kick-ass style of flying, my long education in being afraid in planes, had helped me across the Alleghenies. These forces had merged as one and delivered us through the storms. River to river we'd flown Pennsylvania in the most awful weather imaginable, and I was confident that the rest of the country couldn't throw anything worse at us.

The wings echoed like timpani drums as we taxied in. Torrential sheets of rain were falling now. Water came through the seals on the windshield, beaded up on the ceiling, and fell on our heads. Drenched, our loafers and socks filling up to our ankles, we tied down the Cub and ran across the tarmac in the rain to the pilots' shack. We were laughing and elated as we pushed through the door.

I was exhausted. Collapsing onto the couch in the pilots' shack, I slept soundly for two hours. Kern woke me after the front passed through. I could see as soon as I rose off the couch that it was beautiful outside and I felt refreshed, expectant. We had earned this—clear, open skies across Ohio and into Indiana. Slumber had cleared my head. Already, we'd made the longest cross-country flight of our lives, and that hateful ride across the Alleghenies seemed like it happened a year ago.

I don't recall what I dreamed about on that couch and I don't remember thinking about it much, but not again on that trip, not for the rest of my life, did I fear flying with my brother.

CHAPTER 9

KERN AND I CROSSED INTO OHIO AT SIX-THIRTY THAT EVENING, pointing the Cub west into an orange disc of sun. Now we were racing across another state, this time to reach Indiana before nightfall. In the wake of the storm the evening was clear and cool, and our wings rested on still air. The green immensity of Ohio opened before us, a moist, intense vista of ponds freshened by the rains and silver-domed silos drawing us west.

Kern dove the Cub low, swooping down across the interstate highway and making big, sweeping S-turns as the big semis and station wagons loaded with vacationing families crawled by underneath. We threw open the windows and opened the throttle wide, beginning a kind of insect night-feeding, darting from pond to pond along our route. At the first pond we squawked up a flight of Canada geese, then hauled up over their heads to clear some high tension lines. In the opal light ahead of us two boys were playing catch with a softball beside an oxbow creek. The wind must have been ahead of us as we bore down on them, because they never heard us coming. One of the boys tossed up the softball, a graceful, arching high fly that greased right up between our wheels. The catcher reached up and—astounded—saw us at the last second, lost his footing, and went tumbling assfirst into the creek. Splash.

Further along, east of Columbus, a farmer had driven his tractor out across the fields to a spillway dam. He was running a pump off his power-takeoff to feed his cattle. He sat on his tractor seat, smoking a cigarette, taking in his fields and the falling light. His two boys, shirtless, lounged on the orange wheel fenders. They wore red ball caps. As we droned by they calmly reached up and waved, big, neighborly, midwestern farmers' waves. They were expecting us, it seemed, as if we passed by that way every night.

I liked the midwest. The roads ran straight to the horizon, easy to follow, winding here and there around creek beds and stands of trees. The towns were orderly and compact, with clusters of white churches, spotless Greek Revival façades along Main Street, and listless clouds of dust rising from the Dairy Queen parking lots out along the edges. You could see life down there, just as it was lived, and the flat geography of the plains was open and explicit. Every town along our way announced itself with large block letters painted on top of the water tower or the grain elevators. HEBRON. Good. Just another forty miles to Columbus. Who needed a radio, or a gyro compass, in a land as sensible as this?

But all of this sightseeing was done in a hurry. Kern had the engine opened up to 2,400 rpm to make extra speed, but that was also consuming more fuel. Ohio is more than two hundred miles across, just about the range of our Cub, and we would have to stop for fuel. As we passed Newark I measured the distance we had flown from Pittsburgh with my route-plotter and leaned up over my brother's shoulder to show him my calculations. Columbus, almost exactly in the middle of the state, was a logical refueling stop, and the smaller airport southwest of town was uncontrolled and we could get in there without a radio.

As soon as we found Columbus Southwest, Kern firewalled for the airport and steeply banked the Cub around to land. He wheeled onto the runway with the tail raised, fast-taxied to the pumps, and called back as he threw off the ignition switches.

"Rink, it's almost eight o'clock. This is just a pit stop."

"Affirmative."

I raced for the ladder, he went for the fuel hose. We only needed ten gallons in the wing tank to make it to Indiana. A geezer came out and offered to check the oil and clean the windshield, but we told him not to bother. We pumped the fuel as quickly as we could, and the tab came to $3.96. Sorry Geezer, no time for you tonight, here's $5 for the gas, forget the change. Skip the Brakes, Throttle, Contact! jive and just throw the prop. I dove into the backseat on the run as Kern dashed for the runway.

I felt sorry for the geezer, who seemed like a nice fellow. We left him standing in a cloud of dust thrown back by our prop, scratching his head and feeling quite useless. Kern opened up the throttle 30 feet from the runway. We skidded onto the centerline, popped into the air and turned west at 200 feet, hauling ass for Indiana. It was the swiftest aircraft refueling in history. We were in and out of Columbus in eight minutes.

We leveled off relatively high, at 5,000 feet, to get as long a view of the country beneath us as we could in the receding light. Maybe, just barely, we could make Indiana.

Indiana. It was a completely fabricated goal and, considering everything, especially the weather we had battled all day, quite pointless. We'd already made impressive progress for one day and passed our original target, Columbus. But to Kern a personal goal was a commandment, and I knew that he wasn't going to spare an ounce of horsepower until we were hard down on Indiana soil. All I could do was laugh about it, chortling in the rear seat as I watched the pretty Ohio towns go by.

From the front seat, with those immense sunglasses still on, Kern looked back with that earnest grin of his. Beaver Cleaver in Ray-Bans. He knew what I was laughing about.

"Rink, you can shit on me all you want, but we're making Indiana tonight."

"Kern. Why don't we just land at the next airport, call home, and *tell* them its Indiana? Nobody will know the difference."

"Nope. It's gotta be Indiana. I'm not going to lie about this."

I was having too much fun to worry about it. Ohio is a flyer's paradise, with a grass landing strip every twenty miles or so, alongside nearly every town. Some of them were just long fairways that the airport operator shared with the local golf course, but we'd been into a lot worse and Kern could put us down almost anywhere. When it got too dark to see ahead of us, we could swing around and land at one of those.

So, we were relaxed and laughing in our small cockpit, soothed by the pastel twilight. I loosened my seatbelt and leaned forward from the rear seat, holding the map on my brother's knee. If we still had half-an-hour's light when we got abeam of the big air base at Dayton, I told him, Indiana was ours. The paved municipal field just over the Indiana line at Richmond was probably already out of reach, but I'd found on the map a small grass strip at East Richmond, fifteen miles closer.

At dusk, we passed out of Ohio along the forested, western edge of Preble County, just beyond the hamlet of New Paris. The sky was slate-gray as we crossed the state line into Indiana. But we could make out the rotating beacon at Richmond off to the south and, navigating off that, we found the little field at East Richmond. As Kern descended and banked for the runway, the last of the sun fell behind the horizon and it was almost pitch-black. But there was a full moon that night, a great, merciful disc of light planted midway above the horizon right where we needed it. Kern expertly nursed the Cub down through the dark, probing for the grass with the stick.

As we taxied in over the rutted grass, we noticed a long line of ragged yellow biplanes parked by the hangar.

"Rink," Kern called back, "those are Stearmans. This is a duster strip."

We were excited about that, and couldn't believe our good luck in choosing a place to remain overnight. My father and all of the old barnstormer types that we knew at Basking Ridge had always referred to this part of the country as Stearman Land. They were very sentimental about it, and to pilots of their generation the cropdusting region west of the Ohio River was revered as a flyer's nirvana. During World War II, more than ten thousand open-cockpit Boeing Stearmans had been produced for the Air Corps training fields out west, and tailwheel pilots like us regarded the Stearman as the most majestic, noble plane ever built. After the war ex-military pilots, or just farmers with a love of flying, had snapped the Yellow Perils up at government auctions and converted them for cropdusting use, installing huge, 450-horsepower and even 600-horsepower Pratt & Whitney radial engines, gutting the front cockpit for a one-ton hopper, and welding sprayer bars to the wings. Many pilots of the postwar generation had built up their time as cropdusters before they joined the military or the airlines. There were still huge fleets of yellow Stearmans roaming the west, following the crops all summer the same way that the big wheat-combine crews moved north across the plains with the national grain harvest.

The lore of Stearmans, the wild flying and living that the young duster crews enjoy, acted powerfully on pilots. All flyers are wanderers at heart and harbor Walter Mitty fantasies. If they could only shuck their jobs and the lives they know, they would leave the local airport far behind and spend a season flying bush planes in Alaska, or get a job dropping mail along the sheep-station routes of Queensland and New South Wales. Of course, they never did it, but that just made the dream more alluring. No flying fantasy, however, quite surpassed a long summer tour of the cropdusting strips of the American west. That's where barnstorming still lived. My father was very excited about this aspect of our trip, and he thought that we were leaving at just the right time—early July is the height of the dusting season. We would love the "Stearman men of the west," he said, and find them very hospitable and entertaining. In Arkansas or Oklahoma, when it was time to find the waterbag, all we would have to do is ask a good old Stearman man about it.

As we taxied in, the dusting operation was still busy. The hangar was lit, and a mechanic with a helmet on was welding inside, throwing off a nimbus of orange and blue sparks. The place was a classic American dump, with the stench of pesticides and nitrogen fertilizer hanging along the taxiways and rusting one hundred-gallon drums holding up the pilots' shack. This didn't seem like an airport that handled a lot of transient traffic, and no one came out and directed us to a parking spot. So we just wheeled around behind a large gathering of parked Stearmans and shut the engine down.

A couple of the crop-dusting pilots had been working late, readying their loads for the next day. They wandered over as we climbed out of the Cub. They were wondrous specimens of the breed, big, tall hulking guys with brown pegs for teeth, western drawls, and sunburnt scars on their arms and hands. They certainly weren't geezers, but they were helpful. They had watched us land in the dark and told us we were honorary dusters now, young fuckups, they said, who could snatch a landing from the jaws of a crash. They helped us tie down and fuel the Cub and we would launch with them at dawn.

There was an old Pullman-style diner on the other side of the interstate, out across a railroad line. We had to climb a wire fence on either side of the railroad tracks to get there. Before we went into the restaurant we called my father collect from the phone booth outside, cupping our ears together on the receiver. No way, we agreed, would we tell him about the Pennsylvania weather, or about landing at an unlit strip after dark.

My father must have been sitting all evening with the phone in his lap. We didn't even get off a full ring before he picked it up. When he heard it was us, we could hear the tension and worry going out of his voice.

"Boys! How are you?"

"Fine, Dad. Just fine."

"Where are you?"

"Indiana. East Richmond, Indiana."

"Oh Jesus boys that's just great. Jesus, Indiana. Mom, they made Indiana."

My older sisters were there. I could hear them talking in the background. I guess they were now excited about our trip. Years later they would still talk about that week in July, when everyone would sit around the large family room adjacent to our kitchen every night, waiting for us to call.

1st Day

LEG	TIME	MILES	GAL. GAS	# GAS	G/H
NYT – HARRIS	2:02	142	9.3	3.72	4.6
HARRIS – POTTS (WASH co.)	2:11	175	10.7	4.28 $5.00 spent?	4.7
PITT – Colum.	2:01	165	10.1	3.96	5.1
Colum – Rich (Indiana)	1:00	71	6.7	{Free Gas}	6.7

2nd Day

RICH TO INDY	1:05	76	9	{Free gas from jerk}	
INDY – FULTON (Dead Apt.)					
EV. Stuart	2:25	189	11.9	4.64	
COKES				50 cents	
EV. Stu. to BLYTHE.	1:55	163	8.2	3.23	
FOOD				2.58	
BLYTHE – BRINK	1:25	87	7.1	2.80	
MOTEL {"CHEAP"}				3.00	

CANADA DRY
or BETTER MIXING
BEFORE STRIKING

Third

BRINK TO HAZEN	35 min.			{Dead Apt. free oil}	
HAZ – ARK.	1:35	98	9.3	3.62	
BKFAST				1.21	
ARK – Nash (Dead Apt) → Free Gas-no one there					
– EAKER	4:05	186	14.3	5.60	
EAK – Decatur {Dead Apt.}			Oil ·	50 cents	
(Texas)	1:30				
Dec. – Taylor (Albany)		168	13.3	# 5.20	
Dinner + Cowboy HAT				7.23	

In 1966, a gallon of aviation fuel cost just thirty-nine cents. But we were worried about running out of money and kept meticulous records.

"Indiana! Wow. Indiana. Isn't that far? Dad, how many miles is that?"

My younger brothers and sisters had stayed awake in all the excitement. Now, as we spoke with my father, they were marching around the kitchen table together in their pajamas, letting out banshee whoops and singing a chorus of "Indiana, Indiana, Indiana." My mother got on and we lied to her about what a great day we'd had, the beautiful weather all the way out and what a swell country America was, how well the plane flew. Before we hung up, we promised to call again the next night.

I was surprised by how relaxed my father was during that first call home. We didn't say another word to him that night. For months, he had been secretly obsessed with this trip, painstakingly examining our maps, discussing the difficult desert and mountain crossings, egging us to finish the plane on time and hectoring us about the waterbag. Now the details of our flight didn't seem to interest him at all. I suppose he just figured that he had worked us well all those years, and now we were down and safe in Indiana on the first night and that proved to all the skeptics, friends of his who had wondered why he was letting us make this trip, that his boys could do it. The details were now out of his hands.

Several years later, when he was struck with a bad phantom pain attack, I drove my father to the hospital for his Demerol shots. On the ride home in the car, before he fell asleep, he droned on and on about the night that Kern and I called from Indiana. He was so happy for us that night, he said, happy and relieved, that after we hung up he climbed the stairs to his room, took off his wooden leg, and cried in bed.

The waitresses at the diner were bright-faced and coltish, with long shiny legs, hairnets, and lacey bras showing up beneath the transparent restaurant uniforms girls wore in those days. The place wasn't busy at all and we must have blown in at just the right time, relieving the Edward Hopper loneliness along the counter. The waitresses dawdled and flirted with us and I liked them a lot. They wore more makeup than eastern girls and moved between the tables and the kitchen with languid sexuality, and they didn't have any pretensions.

The special that night was all-you-can-eat Southern-fried chicken for $1.99. We wolfed it down with mashed potatoes, green beans, and iced tea. While we were eating our dessert the waitresses asked us where we were from, and we told them New Jersey. Boy, they said, that's a lot of flying for one day. They made it sound as if New Jersey was a whole continent away, and actually I felt that way myself. Already, it felt as if we'd been gone for weeks. We swaggered out of there a foot taller, with toothpicks angled out of our mouths and our Ray-Bans sticking out of the top of our shirt pockets, the way we'd seen the big-time airshow pilots do it at home.

It was a cool, clear night, with an immense panorama of stars overhead, and we couldn't believe how open the sky was out here. We walked the long way back to the airport, to avoid climbing over the fences. The air smelled of new-cut hay and manure spread on the fields. We didn't say much as we walked along but Kern did thank me for one thing.

"Rink, you made a huge difference today. Really. I never would have made it to Indiana by myself."

"Yeah. Thanks. The funny thing is, I agree with you."

It was a moment of pure knowledge and pure satisfaction. I didn't feel particularly elated about making a big difference all day, I just knew that it was true. I knew, as well, that I never would have believed this before we left home—I didn't expect to contribute that much to the flying effort. During that walk in the dark a new welter of feelings that would build throughout the trip began overtaking me. First of all, time seemed unbelievably stretched—hours became days and days became weeks, even months. Distance, too, seemed implausibly and romantically grand. Here in Indiana, we were still close enough to Ohio to spit back across the state line. But the short distance we'd traveled to "make Indiana" and land in the state seemed oceanic, as if we'd flown all the way to Montana. And with the stretching of time and contentment every other muscle and pore in my body was relaxed. It seemed easy, all of a sudden, being at peace with Kern. All we had to do now was live moment to moment for this flight we were making together.

Back at the airport, we rolled our sleeping bags out beneath the wing. We used the Cub's seat cushions for pillows. We lay there for a while, lazy from our meal and drugged by the nitrogen pall of the duster strip, chatting, staring up at the stars. Kern was pleased with himself and our hard day of flying and I was happy about that. Except for the distant hum of the interstate, Indiana seemed real quiet. At a little before eleven a lone locomotive roared through on the tracks and then we dozed off, still laughing inside about the little ones back home, marching "Indiana" around the table.

CHAPTER 10

THE COUGHING OF FOUR STEARMAN ENGINES WOKE US AT DAWN the next morning. The sky was still all flinty gray, with a ribbon of cobalt and pink glowing on the eastern horizon. The duster pilots at East Richmond had arrived for their morning flying and were firing up the yellow biplanes parked in front of us, to warm the engines before they flew. Kern and I were cold and stiff from sleeping on the ground and our sleeping bags were wet with dew. Sand and pebbles thrown back by the props raked our faces, and the stack exhaust was a velvety bit of warmth.

It was a morning ritual, and we grew used to it as we followed the cropdusting strips west. As the first streams of sun warmed the country, the Stearman pilots were the first to wake. The still hours just after dawn are the best time of day for cropdusting. Before it was light Kern and I would hear the sound of boots crossing gravel, the rattle of tie-down chains, the telltale whine of starter-clutches engaging. The pilots left the biplanes idling on the ramp while they went in for coffee. Kern and I would roll up our sleeping bags and follow them into the shack. In the half-light behind us, the big Pratt & Whitneys radials played a morning hymn. The gear boxes clicked, the throaty manifolds hummed, the air from the props whistled through the sprayer bars. The sound seemed to urge us west. In the baritone rumble I could hear the crescendo of a hundred more cropduster radials coughing to life down through Arkansas and Texas, a vast American symphony tracking the sun across the Rockies to Bakersfield and Salinas.

We rolled out of our sleeping bags and stowed them in the baggage compartment. One of the pilots we had met the night before jumped off his wing and strolled over to the Cub. He was older than the other dusters, forty-five perhaps, tall and bony in a faded jumpsuit, with a face so burned and wrinkled by the sun that it looked like driftwood. He lit a cigarette and took a deep drag, smiling as he watched us wiggle into our pants and pull on our shoes.

His name was Hank, Hank the Stearman man. Hank was the chief pilot and owner of the duster operation at East Richmond. He introduced himself and seemed curious about us, amused that we had dropped in the night before and then camped under the wing. Raunchy duster-strips like East Richmond didn't get a lot of transient traffic, certainly not a pair of scrawny kids in Levi's and penny loafers who spent the night sleeping under the wing of their plane.

Hank ran his hands over his face to wipe off some sleep, stretched his arms high and cracked his knuckles, and then ran the hand with the lit cigarette through his hair.

"Where you boys from?" he asked.

"New Jersey!" Kern piped.

"New Jersey. Hmmm. All the way from New Jersey. How long did that take you?"

"One day. We took off just yesterday."

"Jeez. Pretty good. All the way from Jersey in a day. Where you headed in such a rush?"

I prayed inside that Kern would just say something innocuous, like Indianapolis, so we could prop and get out of there fast without a lot of fuss and bother. But Kern flashed him his best *Leave It to Beaver* smile and gave Hank the whole nine yards.

"Ah, Hank, we're flying this Cub to California," Kern said.

Hank paused a lot between words and never showed much

surprise, which I took to be the midwestern manner of speaking.

"California. You bet . . . Hmmmm . . . okay. Let's just look at that. What'd'ya got here anyway, the 85-horse?"

"Yeah. It's a PA-11."

"Yeah, good . . . lights. I mean, you got lights? You landed after dark last night."

"Well, Hank, see, we were just trying to . . ."

"Nah, nah, nah, hold on. I'm not saying nothing or anything, you know? Lights? Who needs lights? Hell's bells, we're landing Stearmans in the dark around here all the time. Who's got lights? I don't have any lights."

"Yeah," Kern said. "We don't do that all the time, Hank."

"Who said that? Did I say that? . . . Exactly. Just when it's forced on you, you know? Ah, what about radios? You're going all the way to the coast. I bet you put in something real nice."

"It's the standard Cub, Hank," Kern said. "No radio."

"No radio! Hey, who's got radios? I ferried a 450-Stearman all the way to Panhandle, Texas, last year. No radio."

Kern spread his hands wide and lifted them toward his shoulders, palms up.

"You don't need it!"

"Exactly! You don't need it!" Hank said. "Fuck 'em. All these guys flying around in Bonanzas and shit. They're such hot stuff because they got a panel full of radios. And then, you know, they crash, and the FAA inspectors come. Everybody's standing 'round the wreck scratching their heads. How'd they crash with all them radios in the panel? Nobody gets it. You don't need radios."

"Yeah. Well, for us, we just couldn't afford a radio, that's all."

"Okay . . . great. Let me just run this by once more, so I get it right, okay?"

"Sure Hank."

"We got two kids from New Jersey."

"Yeah."

"Names? You got names?"

"Yeah. I'm Kern," my brother said, reaching over to shake Hank's hand.

"*Kern?*"

My brother smiled sheepishly. He was always self-conscious when people got stalled on his name.

"Yeah, Kern," he said. "It's short for Kernahan."

"Fernahan. Jesus."

"No, Kernahan. That's the name my parents gave me."

"Some parents. Ferdinand. Whatever. And what about the sidekick here? Is this a brother?"

"That's me," I said, stepping over to shake Hank's hand, which was so weathered and rough it felt like a cedar fence-post. "I'm Rinker."

"Rinker?" Hank said. "That's the name? Rinker?"

"That's the name."

"You bet. Ah . . . okay, we got a last name here? Go on now, just do it to me. I'm ready for this one. Hit me with that last name."

Kern and I said it together.

"Buck."

"Buck! Whoa. Buck! Good. Good-good-good. All of a sudden, situation normal. I mean, I just like this all over here. Ferdinand and Rinkle—what is it again?"

"Rinker. R-I-N-K-E-R. And Kern. Buck."

"I copy that. Romeo-India-November-Kilo-Echo-Romeo. Rinker. I like it. It's catchy."

"Yeah. Thanks Hank."

"All right then. Here we go. We got the standard Piper Cub with nothing on it—just seats, two sticks, and the 85-horse Continental. No lights, no radio, no nothing. And we got Ferdinand and Rinker Buck. And this whole frigging hootenany is flying coast to coast."

"That's it Hank," Kern said.

"Hey, what the fuck? I'm not saying nothing or anything! I mean, stick with aviation long enough? You'll see everything."

Kern didn't like the insinuation. He was very sensitive to criticism anyway, and he didn't consider what we were doing to be the least bit abnormal.

"Ah, Hank, I've just got my private now, and a little over one hundred hours," Kern said. "But I need cross-country time for the commercial. So, this is what we're doing. You have to use the equipment you got."

"Exactly," Hank said. "Look at all these shithouse Stearmans here. That's the equipment I got. But listen, how are you going to get this Cub over the Rockies?"

"Well Hank, we're going to do the Guadalupe Pass near El Paso. It's just a little over 9,000 feet."

"What's your surface ceiling on this Cub?"

"10,000."

"Shit. Okay. I'm not saying nothing, all right? But I mean, you won't make your service ceiling on a hot day. Nobody makes their service ceiling period. "

"No. Hank. That's what the book says. But we've got a climb prop, and the cylinders are bored out. The mechanics back home say this Cub delivers over 100-horsepower, as good as the Continental 108."

Hank scratched his head and crushed his cigarette on the ramp under his scuffed boot.

"The climb prop, huh? I'm not saying. Maybe you can try it, I don't know. I mean, I've done all kinds of shit in airplanes, myself."

"Everybody's done stuff in airplanes."

"Exactly! That's what I'm saying . . . try it. It could just happen."

"Okay," Kern said. "But listen, we owe you for gas from last night. We filled up."

"No you don't! No way," Hank said. "The fuel's on me boys. I'm into this thing now, okay? Coast to coast in a stock Cub? Shit. I'm into it. You guys are all right. Now look, I'm ferrying Stearmans down to Texas all the time. Come on into the shack, let's call weather, and, Ferdinand, I'll show you all the routes."

"Kern."

"Kern! You bet. Whatever, Kern, Fern, Schmern, it's just a problem you got with that name. But let's do it."

Kern was smiling now. It wasn't light enough to fly anyway, and we could use the help.

"Thanks!" Kern said. "Great."

I pulled our bag of maps out of the baggage compartment.

Hank motioned with an outstretched arm toward his run-down shack.

"We'll give you some coffee too. You like coffee?"

"Oh yeah. We'll have some coffee."

"I mean, you know, hot chocolate or some shit for Rinkler here. Whatever we got."

The pilots' shack was dingy and cluttered, with old airplane parts and welding rods spilling off the shelves and a Stearman center section wedged up in the rafters. The other pilots and the hopper-crew were in there, smoking, warming their hands over a kerosene stove. A Coleman lantern hissed from the ceiling.

Hank handed us some coffee in tin cups, a dark, crude-oil brew fortified by a thick bottom of rounds. It was the first coffee of our lives, and probably the worst. We stood there in the smoky room pretending we liked it and bravely sipped it down, taming it as best we could with sugar and powdered milk.

Hank and Kern stepped over to the phone and called the FAA weather station in Indianapolis. The situation was similar to the one we faced the day before. Another large, moist warm front, the remnants of a Gulf Coast storm, was moving north up the Mississippi River Valley, and it would spill clouds down low over the Cumberland Plateau of Kentucky and Tennessee and the Ozarks to the west. Our route across Indiana and southern Illinois would be clear, but we'd probably hit the weather around noon, after we made our planned turn southwest to head through Arkansas and Oklahoma to reach Texas. The bad weather would probably meet us down near Cairo, Illinois.

Hank took the phone away from Kern and meticulously queried the weather briefer about the conditions forecast for western Kentucky and Tennessee. He lit another cigarette and took a long, thoughtful drag.

Hank swiped away the oil cans and wrenches from a workbench and laid down our maps. He showed us the best route across to Indianapolis and then south to Vincennes, after which we could follow the great river valleys opening up to the south—the meandering Wabash River to the Ohio, then the Ohio to the Mississippi. That's where we'd run into trouble, but Hank had flown that country dozens of times against the Gulf fronts and he was confident that one route would remain clear.

The weather front, Hank explained, would probably remain high, bunching up along the Ozarks and the Cumberlands on either side of the northern Mississippi River Valley. The high ground on the outer rim of the valley would be obscured. But he'd found that he could usually get through if he stayed down low through the middle area, flying something he called the Kentucky Swale. This was a section of low, interconnected ravines west of the Cumberland Plateau, a natural basin of creek beds and tributaries falling toward the Mississippi. The low ground began just south of the confluence of the Wabash and the Ohio rivers and ran down through Paducah, Kentucky. On days like this there was usually a clear tunnel of air down through the swale.

"It's right here," Hank said, jabbing his finger on a spot near the middle of the St. Louis sectional, near Morganfield, Kentucky. "This is the Kentucky Swale."

He pointed to a rail line that we could pick up at Paducah and follow south as far as Dyersburg, Tennessee, and marked it with my red grease pencil.

"It's real pretty country too," Hank said. "The hill country to the east might be obscured but you just keep down in that swale, over the rail line, and you'll get through. You can turn for the Mississippi as soon as the weather clears to the west, at either Blytheville or Memphis."

We would be flying quite low, and Hank told us to expect a lot of turbulence and ground effect until we hit the river. But the weather system should pass by mid-afternoon and our reward would be a nice evening run through the pine barrens of Arkansas. Navigating across that featureless timber country was difficult, and Hank suggested that we follow a freight line that began at Osceola, Arkansas and would eventually deliver us into Brinkley. He marked that on the map for us too. There was a big Stearman strip at Brinkley where he had often spent the night. We'd like all the duster crews in there, Hank said. The government issued big forestry spraying contracts out of Brinkley all summer, and the strip teemed with itinerant cropdusting crews. It was a wild place.

A brick-colored sun rose on the horizon. The pilots began filing out to their rumbling Stearmans, pulling on their white crash helmets and goggles. They were annoyed with Hank for dawdling with us in the shack and they started racing their engines and inching up on the ramp. We were anxious to get off too, now that we had a route through the weather and across the Mississippi.

But Hank seemed to want to linger and we dawdled in the shack with him for a while longer. Finally, he pulled on his crash helmet and stood at the door. We folded our maps, thanked him, and turned to go.

"Ah, say there Ferdinand," Hank said. "Have you ever flown that Cub in formation?"

"Oh sure Hank," Kern lied.

"Good."

Hank and his pilots were dusting that morning over by Spring Grove. It was along our way. He told Kern just to taxi out and line up on the runway behind the Number Three Stearman. When he saw the prop in front of him whirl to full power, Kern was to stay with that plane. Hank would slide in behind us in Number Four. We could tag along with the Stearman formation as long as we liked, and Hank thought that we might enjoy watching them spray the fields.

We raced out to the Cub, propped, and fell in line behind the Number Three plane. Hank strapped into his Stearman and crossed the ramp behind us. We bounced out the taxiway with a noisy Stearman fore and aft of us, gunning our engine with the formation over the bumps.

Nobody else used the strip so we just braked in formation out on the grass runway and ran up our engines. As the pilot in the first plane advanced his throttle, the trembling Pratt & Whitneys roared, and we raced down the strip.

Whahhh-Whahhhh-Whahhh-Whahhh. It was a magnificent climbout surrounded by those gargantuan props and yellow wings, an ovation of noise and lift. Two thousand horses thundered around us. Kern did a nice job of flying, jockeying the throttle back and forth on takeoff to stay in line with the heavily loaded biplanes, fish-tailing with the rudders to stay out of their heavy propwash. And he flew it tight, too, just 30 feet off the rudder and slightly to the left of Number Three, with Hank sidling in to us in the same position.

Climbing away from the field, we hit a little early-morning turbulence—it wasn't much, just a few bubbles in the air where the first rays of the sun hit the cool air over the ponds—and the wings of all the Stearmans around us rocked and swayed out, and I was worried at first that we'd slide into another plane. But formation work was another trick of flying that Kern seemed to be able to get right the first time. We'd flown tight formations before, with the Basking Ridge flyers back home on the way to air shows, but usually with my father flying our plane. A lot of the pilots from our home strip were crazy and they were always looping and rolling right beside us, and then my father would join them in aerobatics, and I was scared most of the time and this had always made me leery of formation work. But it just felt right that morning over Indiana, surrounded by the steady, throaty roar that the Stearmans threw off, with Hank on our side grinning and giving us the thumbs up from his open-cockpit. Everything I'd been though with Kern yesterday seemed to prepare me for this. We were just meant to be up there, climbing out with all those Stearmans.

The formation leveled off and throttled back at 400 feet. Pristine farmlands, shimmering with morning dew, stretched out beneath us. The air was crisp and cool and cottony patches of ground fog coiled up from the ponds and the creeks. We hedgehopped over some tree lines and corn fields, swinging wide around the farmhouses. But everything was heard and seen as if in a dream. The thunderous Stearman formation enveloped us in white noise.

On our right, Hank skidded in closer, grinning wide beneath his goggles. He kept nudging us closer and closer to the Number Three plane on our left, cocking his head with encouragement and giving Kern a thumbs-up. Older, high-time pilots can tell things right away about another pilot. Kern was flying well with the formation. Hank nudged us in again.

At Spring Grove, the Number One plane peeled away and dove for a soy bean field. The field was long and had a line of phone wires on the near end and a tree line on the other. The pilots would have their hands full covering the ends. Number Two waited about ten seconds and began his run, then Number Three. We looked over to Hank. He was pointing down, motioning for Kern to follow Number Three. Kern closed the throttle and banked over so hard that we were pulled down in our seats.

Kern followed the formation down to the field, pushing past one hundred miles per hour as we screamed over the telephone wires. Ahead of us three Stearmans were diagonally spread across the soy bean rows, wingtip-to-wingtip, and flying so low that their props spit up a juicy green blur from the crop leaves. The sprayer bars churned out a chalky cloud of pesticide. It was a wonderful sensation, buzzing with our wheels right down in the furrows with three Stearmans roaring ahead of us, Hank diving down over the wires behind us, and the field, the sky, and the tree line ahead blurred by the misty, putrid vortices of crop spray.

At the trees, the forward planes zoomed back up. Hammerheading over, they dove back in from the opposite direction for another run. Kern ruddered right to avoid them, firewalled and climbed straight up. We turned and crossed the field diagonally, watching the formation make another run.

Kern pointed the Cub west for Indianapolis. Hank left the other Stearmans and flew with us for a few miles, pulling in tight on our left wing. He was grinning again, waving both arms over his head like a boxer saluting a crowd, a happy, playful Stearman man, clowning around in his open cockpit. He was reluctant to let us go.

Then he waved once more and turned away, wagging his wings as he plunged back down for his fields.

For the next ten miles we could see plumes of dust rising as Hank and his pilots worked that field. Another duster crew was operating immediately to the south and indeed all morning, until we left the agricultural plains behind for the narrow ravines of Kentucky, we saw white clouds of pesticide rising below us in every direction as the big yellow Stearmans and white Piper Pawnees worked the fields.

As we pushed on to Indianapolis, strange emotions gripped me. I was often overwhelmed by loneliness early in the morning in the air, especially when the weather was as clear as this and the navigation was easy. Even counting the air time, we hadn't spent more than an hour with Hank, but I liked him and I missed him already. I guess this would be a trip of instant friendships and quick partings. I didn't realize yet how fortunate we were to have met him. We faced another rough patch of flying at noon, when we met the next storm front. Without Hank's help we never would have made it past the Wabash.

CHAPTER 11

"TWO KIDS FLYING TO CALIFORNIA IN A PIPER CUB?" THE GAS jockey in Indianapolis asked. "You bet. That's a story, see, a *story*. I can smell a hot tip as good as the next guy."

Now that we had shared the details of our flight with Hank back in East Richmond, and received such fulsome encouragement from a real live Stearman man, Kern felt that we could tell almost everyone. When we stopped to refuel at the Sky Harbor Airport in Indianapolis at a little past seven that morning, the gas jockey pumping fuel up on the wing asked where we were headed. Kern spilled everything in his best eager-beaver style. The man nearly fell off his ladder with excitement. I was beginning to understand that a lot of people saw in this flight things that we had not seen ourselves.

Neither of us liked that bonehead gas jockey very much. He was a short, fussy man with a pencil-point moustache, a starched Texaco uniform, and all of these ridiculous little three-in-one tools attached to his belt. Pumping gas at the Indianapolis airport was a very important job, maybe one of the most important jobs in all of Indiana, he wanted us to know. Sooner or later, everybody had to pass through an airport, and you wouldn't believe the people he met, the gas jockey said. Rock stars and movie actresses, visiting politicians, famous trial attorneys who flew their own planes—they were always dropping into "Indy" unannounced and he was the first to know. Newspaper reporters, who the gas jockey seemed to feel had the second most important job in Indiana, relied on him for a steady stream of "hot tips." Now, *we* were the hot tip.

The gas jockey begged us to wait on the ground for a few minutes so he could call one of his "closest friends," a reporter from the *The Indianapolis Star*. In return, he'd give us our gas for free.

Kern wasn't agreeable at first. He wanted to push on south immediately and beat the storms to the Mississippi. Newspaper publicity had never been a part of our plan, and Kern didn't want any delays this early in the trip. Kern didn't like to confront strangers with bad news, and he tried to be polite about it.

"Sir, that's a very generous offer," he said. "We'd really enjoy a newspaper interview. But we've got to push on."

The gas jockey held up a $5 bill.

"Look, let me just call my friend," he pleaded. "Breakfast? You want breakfast? I'll throw that in too. There's a coffee shop right across the ramp."

Now we had a real problem on our hands, because I was starving. This was a major division between Kern and me, our vastly different metabolisms. At fifteen I required a minimum of five square meals a day, at least two of them with steaks, and I still went to bed every night feeling famished. Kern ate like a camel and could subsist from dawn to dusk on a single candy bar. I started to cave right away. I could rationalize stopping for breakfast not simply because I was hungry, but it was still quite early in our trip, and we didn't really know whether our $300 could get us to California and back. On that score, we seemed to be on a roll, and I felt greedy about it. In East Richmond, Hank had given us a free tank of gas, now we were inching up on our second, with breakfast thrown in to boot. At this rate the whole state of Indiana was going by virtually gratis. Considering everything, it would be downright irresponsible, unsafe even, to tackle the weather ahead on an empty stomach.

"Ah, Kern," I said. "Can I just say one thing? Money. Don't forget money. This guy's talking a free breakfast."

"Ah Jeez Rink. It's only seven in the morning. How can you be hungry already?"

"Kern, I'm not hungry. Who says I'm hungry? But look, for five bucks, we can both get steaks."

"See?" The gas jockey said, waving his $5 bill around. "Your brother's hungry. Just what I thought. We're talking twenty minutes here. My friend will run right out."

"Ah Jeez Rink," Kern said.

I flashed my new Timex up in front of Kern's face, with those big, goofy Dr. Seuss numbers all over the watch face.

"Kern. It's seven-thirty in the morning. We've got bags of time."

"See? Your brother wants to do it!" the gas jockey said.

Kern was annoyed now, and that usually made him more assertive.

"All right!" he snapped, taking the $5 and pointing his finger at the gas jockey. "But we're taking the free tank of gas and the breakfast no matter what. That reporter better be here in twenty minutes, as soon as we're finished eating, or we're taking off."

"Deal! I'm calling him right now."

Great. I was getting breakfast after all, but the best part about it was listening to Kern dig his spurs into that asinine gas jockey. Now that we'd made Indiana in a day and flown formation with those Stearmans, his ground-borne ego had come up a notch.

By the time the reporter arrived, with an *Indianapolis Star* photographer in tow, we were more relaxed. Over breakfast we went over our maps. We saw that we could easily get across the Mississippi in just four or five hours of flying, even if we did have to sit out some storms at noon. Reaching the Mississippi was an important milestone for us, and we hadn't realized that the river was so close to the bottom of Indiana. We didn't care if we made it all the way down to the Stearman strip at Brinkley that night. Anywhere in Arkansas would be fine, because it was across the Mississippi. "Making Indiana" our first day had had a profound psychological effect on us. We weren't judging distances by miles any longer, but instead by sound—how a state rolled off the tongue. Indiana to Arkansas sounded like a great distance to fly on our second day, an impressive amount of territory to report.

"Rink, when we call home tonight, Daddy's just going to shit," Kern said. " 'Hey Dad, we're across the Mississippi already.' He won't believe it."

The reporter from the *Star* was a roly-poly man with a pressed, open-neck blue shirt, tousled gray hair and an easy, familiar manner. Like most of the reporters we had met over the years, he didn't know a thing about aviation, and he couldn't understand how we could find our way around the country without radios and an autopilot. But he seemed genuinely interested in us and made us feel as if we were important. His face turned bright and he furiously began taking notes when Kern answered his question about what my father thought about this trip.

"My father?" Kern said. "Well, he's the one who taught us to fly. When he was our age, he did the same thing, flying out across the country and working his way through the Depression as a pilot. So, my father knows what it's like to do this. He's excited for us."

"Kinda like reliving your father's youth, in other words," the reporter said.

Kern shrugged his shoulders and said yeah.

This part of our story, the reporter said, was "great color." Everybody would enjoy reading about two boys barnstorming across the country, reliving their father's Depression-era youth.

Neither of us had considered this angle before. As far as we were concerned, we were flying to California to get away from my father for a few weeks. But as soon as the reporter said it, we both recognized that there was an element of truth to it, perhaps more than we even wanted to admit to ourselves. The irony of this surprised us both. For years we had sat up late at night, listening to my father's fabulous barnstorming blarney, and this had virtually defined our image of him. It never occurred to us that those tales had also formed the expectations we had for ourselves, but that seemed patently obvious as soon as the reporter said it. Now that we were old enough to get away ourselves, we had reconstructed virtually an identical adventure. But of course we hadn't perceived that about ourselves earlier because a father's influence is taken for granted, it takes years to surface and, besides, the last person a teenager will admit to emulating is a parent.

But we didn't give a second thought to the interview with *The Star*. Probably the newspaper would bury the article back in the features section, and this would just be another zany human interest story for the readers of Indianapolis. Who cared about two kids from New Jersey flying coast to coast in a Piper Cub?

We finished the interview with the reporter out by the plane, and the photographer posed us for pictures up by the propeller. The gas jockey came back out and seemed quite pleased with himself, proud of his association with the reporter. He made a great show of propping the Cub for us, so the reporter could see that he was an experienced hand around airplanes.

Cheerfully we waved goodbye and roared down the macadam at Indianapolis, flying south over the luminous, green farmlands of central Indiana, down past Martinsville, Bloomfield, and Vincennes. Two hours later we crossed into southern Illinois and picked up the Wabash. Storm clouds were gathering to the south and we tightened our safety belts against the first belts of turbulence of the advancing front.

I was a little heartsick, watching Indiana recede off the left wing. We had dreamed about the state for weeks and flown hard to get there, and now Indiana, romantic, far-off Indiana, was behind us already, before noon on the second day.

But I wasn't completely sentimental about it. As we followed the twisting, muddy oxbows of the Wabash into southern Illinois, I checked the notebook I was keeping on our fuel and living expenses. Despite consuming almost $20 worth of food and fuel in Indiana, there was only one entry for the entire state—$4.02 for dinner in East Richmond last night. And we'd pulled a fast one on that dumbass gas jockey too. The *Star* reporter picked up our breakfast tab, so we just pocketed the $5 the gas jockey had given us and never told him about it. Crossing Indiana, we'd made a *profit* of 98 cents.

These Hoosiers were outstanding. All you had to do in Indiana was land somewhere and spoon-feed everybody a bunch of bullshit about flying coast to coast, and then they actually paid you to cross their state.

Hank had opened up for us a magic stretch of land.

Near the bottom of Illinois the Wabash emptied into the Ohio and we followed that for an hour, crossing south over the banks when we reached Paducah, Kentucky. The rail line that Hank had circled in red grease pencil was easy enough to find, we picked it up, and the country below us changed quickly after that. For the next hour and a half the twin rails, alternately shimmering in the sun or bathed in deep shadows, hypnotically drew us down through the craggy hill country of western Kentucky and Tennessee.

The weather pushing up from the Gulf had developed more or less as predicted. To the east, a thick wall of gray cloud draped the foothills of the Cumberlands, and to the west the sky over the Mississippi Valley was an opaque black. But it was still clear down through Hank's swale, underneath a low overcast pressing us down to the iron ridges. We were amazed that he could divine, just from early-morning weather reports, this narrow tunnel of clear visibility—the only one for a hundred miles in either direction. But we were forced to fly quite low to remain within it, and after the open, green fields of the midwest, the elimination of color and spatial distance was disorienting. The landscape skirting beneath our wheels was harshly beautiful, lonely and rugged, with occasional clumps of log cabins and small crop fields hacked atop the narrow plateaus. Whitewater creeks flashed in the shadowy ravines.

Frequently, low clouds forced us down to just a few hundred feet above the ridge lines. My field of vision was restricted in the backseat, and often I could see only straight down. My vertical view had a disorienting *Alice in Wonderland* quality to it, as if I were tumbling head over heels down onto the land instead of flying over it. As Kern followed the serpentine terrain, the rail line, the river rapids, and the two sides of the ravine merged together and sped by underneath, one image at the bottom of a funnel. Rails, water, and ravine dizzily swirled sideways as Kern turned to follow the tracks around the next bend.

Then he'd find a patch of clear air above and climb, skimming the ridge-tops. Traces of habitation suddenly appeared up on the plateaus. Beside dilapidated log cabins and sheds, women in bright bandanas and men in straw hats leaned on hoes in their gardens, or sat in groups on their broken down porches, gaping up at us as we swept over their heads. They were the only signs of life we saw in more than two hours of flying. The eerie, primitive landscape racing by intensified my romantic excitement about the time we were making and the distance we had already traveled.

Just north of Wingo, Kentucky, the tracks disappeared into a mountain tunnel. We climbed over the summit and wedged in under the clouds. As we dove back down the other side of the mountain in turbulence and picked up the tracks, a diesel locomotive, silvery and sleek, was exiting the southern portal of the tunnel. A long string of freight cars snaked out of the tunnel behind it.

We raced the train to the state line at Fulton. While we battled stiff headwinds above, the locomotive and cars gathered momentum downslope and slowly outdistanced us. Kern powered up and dove as hard as he could for the railed platform on the back of the caboose.

At the big bends in the track, where the train had to slow to make the turns, we caught up again, billowing 500 feet above the caboose in the brisk headwind. A railroader in bib overalls came out on the platform, lit his pipe and looked up, doffing his cap and waving. Two more trainmen stepped out to the platform and waved their caps, urging us on. When the ravines opened up and it was safe to go low, we dove below the mountain walls and out of the headwind, roaring at full power just above our waving audience on the caboose. The trainmen laughed and elbowed each other as they looked up. Then the ravines narrowed again and we were forced back up, ballooning motionless in the headwind. Once more the train pulled away.

The race with the train was maddening and hilarious at once. We were deep into Kentucky already, bobbing up and down through this moody, Appalachian swale of Hank's, within striking distance of the Mississippi. We were making great time, a lot farther along than we expected to be by the middle of the second day, and the throb of the engine and the smell of burnt oil was strangely soothing as the exotic, hardtack beauty of Kentucky flashed by beneath our struts. I felt very far away from home now. Still, in a race with a train, a long, fifty-car freighter at that, we were losing.

At Fulton the rail lines descended on a long, downhill straightaway. Kern poured on the coals and goosed the stick forward to give the Cub everything she had. The airspeed indicator was showing almost the red line of 120 miles per hour, but we still couldn't make much headway over the ground and catch the train—the headwinds were that fierce. The wings were bucking and kicking in the turbulence and even with the nose pointed almost straight down we were ballooned up by the winds and the Cub wanted to climb. Finally Kern had to throttle way back to keep us from billowing up into the clouds.

"Rink, this is great!" Kern yelled back.

I wondered what was great about it. Any moment now my stomach was going to hurl the steak and eggs I had for breakfast.

"Oh yeah?"

"Yeah! These are trailing edge winds. We've passed the center of the front."

Up ahead, the caboose raced off and slowly disappeared. One of the trainmen fetched a signal lantern from inside and pointed it back at us from the platform, flashing goodbye. DASH. DASH. DASH. Kern wiggled our wings in reply.

After that roller-coaster race with the train, I was desperate to get my hands on the controls. The ground effect here in the Kentucky swale was almost as bad as the turbulence over the Alleghenies, and I decided that I just wasn't going to be uncomfortable like that again. I didn't care what Kern thought about me now. It was a compulsion for me. I had to fly the plane for a spell.

Until I read about it nearly twenty years later, in a book about instrument flying, I didn't realize that I suffered throughout our flight from something called copilot vertigo. The phenomenon is especially severe in tandem-seat designs like Cubs, where visibility over the pilot in front is limited. Bounced around by the gusts, unable to see a clear horizon because of the clouds, the pilot in the backseat suffers from the loss of eye coordination with the movement of the plane over land. The sensation and panic of spatial disorientation can occur after just a few minutes of flying, and the copilot longs to battle the turbulence himself and restore his sense of control.

And I was panicked. The harrowing, nauseating effects of vertigo were overwhelming me. The nose cowling and the instruments on the panel in front of Kern were spinning wildly around in a circle before my eyes and I was shivering all over. It didn't help to close my eyes. As soon as I opened them again, the plane seemed inverted. Finally I couldn't take it any longer and I threw the map forward and shook my stick in the rear.

"Kern! I'm going to puke if you don't give me this airplane. She's mine!"

Kern immediately threw his hands in the air.

"It's your airplane Rink. Why didn't you tell me sooner?"

The relief was almost instantaneous. I felt restored to balance, with a clear left and right and the ground where it should be, as soon as I could feel the plane through the stick.

Shortly after I took the controls we were hit by a hard buffet from the right, and I stepped on the rudder all the way to the stop, cross-controlled hard with the stick and even goosed the throttle some to bore through the patch of rough air. This wasn't the way to do it—I was overcontrolling the plane—but I didn't care how many Gs I had to pull to keep the Cub straight and level. The body movement and the adrenaline rush of throwing the plane around the sky helped restore my senses.

Kern grabbed the crash strut over his head with one hand and reached over and retarded the throttle with the other. Flying that hard in turbulence risked overstressing the plane, and he wanted to slow us down. But he was laughing as he turned to face me and yell back.

"Rink! Whoa! You're overcontrolling the plane. Take it easy."

"I hate this fucking turbulence, Kern. *You* sit there and take it for a while."

"It's okay! I understand. Just watch your airspeed."

I was glad to reach that moment. I didn't have to hide my fears and my turbulence jitters any longer and apparently Kern didn't care. I had been foolish to worry about it in the first place.

During that leg of the trip I contrived another small fix which made my position in the rear seat a lot more bearable. Grabbing one of the sleeping bags from the baggage compartment, I folded it flat on top of my seat cushion so that I could see out over Kern's shoulders and past the windshield. My forward visibility was greatly improved and I had extra cushioning against the nonstop turbulence. There wasn't enough head clearance from the crash struts in the front seat for Kern to do this, and by the end of the trip his ass was so sore from flying through turbulence that he walked stiffly and had to sleep on his stomach every night.

We flew that way for the rest of the day, switching off and trading the map and the stick, and I could see that Kern was enjoying himself. Once in a while he shook the stick or reached back and squeezed my knee, giving me a hand signal to fly the tracks or the terrain differently. But most of the time while I was flying he sat contentedly up front, following along on the map and staring out to the sky, brooding about the weather and how we could outfox it to speed our progress.

I always remembered that leg through Kentucky for another reason. Kern was very pleased with my flying and impressed with the way that I doggedly held my altitude and course, deviating only when we had clouds or an obstruction ahead to dodge. This was deeply satisfying to me and I knew exactly where that discipline came from. During my cross-country training, my father had been merciless with me about maintaining my altitude and heading. Even in rough air, he held me to strict Air Corps standards—plus or minus 50 feet on the altimeter, no more than three or four degrees of variation on the compass, and there was hell to pay if I buried my head in the map too long and let the plane wander. "Altitude, goddamnit," my father would bark into my ear. I wasn't bitter about that and even enjoyed the hard work, but I did regret that we never just kicked back and enjoyed ourselves up there. There were no displays of affection either. The problem carried over on the ground. After an afternoon of flying with my father, I was so gun-shy and tense around him I could barely speak to him for a week.

But I could enjoy myself with Kern. He didn't care about enforcing Air Corps standards, even though I was flying up to that for him. And he was very open about his feelings and would express whatever was on his mind at the moment.

"Rink, you're doing great!" he yelled back over the noise of the engine. "I can't get over how well you handle this Cub."

The turbulence I was battling, the feelings I experienced, swirled around inside me with a vertigo of their own. When Kern said things like that I would suffer these momentary, intense bouts of anxiety and loneliness for my father. I couldn't understand it. All winter, I had looked forward to getting away from my father. Whenever I thought about him and planes, I thought of drudgery and hard work, a man who treated me as if he were still a hardass Stearman instructor preparing air cadets for war. Now that we were finally out here enjoying our adventure, I missed him—plaintively, even passionately sometimes. Of course, I didn't understand yet that emotions are dealt in pairs, subject to laws of association. I loved the man I hated for making me fly the way he did, but this was confusing and the turbulence was so bad I couldn't thoughtfully sort all this out.

Every twenty minutes or so, weary of these thoughts, my

arms stiff from battling the turbulence, I shook the stick and gave the plane back to Kern.

So, we banged down through the bottom of Hank's swale. The air was rough and the face of the land below was desolate and unfamiliar, but every time I got the map back I could see that we were making good progress. Kentucky was a brutal stretch of flying, but I enjoyed the responsibility of spelling Kern at the controls and I knew that I was proving to be worth a lot more to him than either of us had expected.

I played a nice trick on Kern as we approached the Mississippi. He was flying up front, following the last couple of ravines out of the swale, and hadn't asked to see the map for a while. I called forward that there was a large obstruction ahead and that he should turn due west and climb to 3,000 feet. As we turned, I picked up the Deer Creek below. Over the next ten miles, as it fell to the river, the creek passed from the rocky, hardwood foothills of Tennessee to the spongy, effluvial plain of the Mississippi River.

I told Kern to expedite the climb so that he couldn't see out over the nose. Vacantly he stared up over the prop to the sky, grateful that we finally had enough clear air ahead of us for some altitude. Through the side windows, though, I could see the river shimmering out of the landscape, immense and brown and undulating from horizon to horizon.

Leveling off at 3,000 feet, Kern throttled back, checked his engine instruments and looked aimlessly ahead. Then he raised his left hand and called back. The wings gently rocked and the rudder pedals danced. The bolt of excitement passed from him through to the controls, and then to the plane and me.

"Rink! That's it! Look. The Mississippi."

It was the most glorious and impressive piece of landscape I ever hoped to see.

The river filled the sky. To the north the oxbows eddied out and looped back on themselves, a twisting congeries of brown water and sandy banks disappearing into Missouri, and to the south the flow straightened out and spilled broad as a lake, emptying out into vast wetlands beyond the banks. The Mississippi was a whole continent of water, an inland ocean, bisecting the land. We couldn't believe the amount of water moving past us, and how broad the river was, bank to bank. The banks were immense washes of sand, as big themselves as the rivers we knew back home, curving out where the river turned into huge, open deserts, blinding under the sun. Nothing I'd read or seen about the Mississippi had prepared me for this, a body of water so large. The prospect from 3,000 feet in clear air, taking in thirty or forty miles of river, was staggering. It was a majesty of water and banks, an abstraction, too grand to take in.

We flew ourselves drunk on that river. We actually crossed the banks three times, by cutting diagonally across the huge oxbow near Blytheville, Arkansas. At the first loop of the river we dove down low over the sandy edges and then ran flat out across the water. The wind rifled up the water into white-caps. We were amazed at the flotsam carried downstream by the flow. There were immense trees and logs grounded on the sand bars, their spoked roots and branches crowning out of the water, bearded with aquatic weeds and sand. At treetop level we crossed the swampy, piney land in the middle of the river and pointed the nose toward a tugboat pulling a string of barges around the muddy shoals of the oxbow. When we reached the tug, Kern drew sharply back with the stick and we pulled straight up. Just before we stalled he threw in all of his left aileron and rudder and we spilled over on our wingtip for a "hammerhead" turn, and then we screamed back down over the smoky stack of the tug, choking from the filmy diesel exhaust. A couple of crewmen came out and watched us from the stern rails and then the cook from the galley, who was wearing this ridiculous looking white chef's hat, stuck his head out onto the deck and waved. Kern banked the wings right over their heads and we headed for the far shore. We were reluctant to leave the river behind but we were low on fuel and were forced to turn due west again, to drop down for the big macadam runway at Blytheville, Arkansas.

Kern turned for the traffic pattern and pulled the throttle back to descend. As we dropped below the horizon of pines we both stared back at the river.

"Rink, I can't get over this. It's two o'clock on our second day, and we're across the Mississippi already."

For some crazyass reason that we never did figure out, there was a funeral director sitting in his Cadillac hearse in the airport parking lot, lethargically watching the student pilots taking off and landing in their shitwreck yellow Champs. He strolled over and chatted with the geezer while we fueled the plane. It was scorching hot here in Arkansas, but the undertaker wore a heavy, dark suit, a starched shirt and tie, and a black Stetson. He had the lugubrious but pleasant demeanor of all undertakers.

I was hungry again but Kern didn't mind. We were across the Mississippi already and it didn't matter whether we flew another leg today or not. The funeral director offered to drive us into town for lunch and we all piled into the front seat of the hearse. He spoke in a deep southern drawl that we could hardly understand, prattling all the way into town about this and that, mostly the local industry and sights. It was hot in the front seat of the hearse and I was exhausted from flying, and my ears were still ringing from the throbbing engine of the plane. Halfway into town, lulled by the saccharine, indecipherable drawl of the funeral director, I fell asleep against the passenger-side door, which was an odd sensation, because I was in a hearse, and I felt like we'd flown hard all day just so I could die and go to heaven in Arkansas.

One thing about the citizenry of Arkansas amazed us. They were obsessed with the Kennedys. Everybody kept telling us that we looked "jest like" the Kennedy brothers. The geezer at the airport had said it, and now, as he dropped us off in town, the funeral director said the same thing.

"Lawd," he said. "You boys es jest doubles for dose Ken'dee men. Know that pitcher of young Jack on his PT boat? Well, you thar, ya look jest like 'im."

The funeral director had elbowed Kern when he said that.

"Hey Rink," Kern said, stepping out of the hearse. "Do you think it's true?"

"What?"

"Me. Looking like Jack Kennedy."

"Ah, Kern. Who gives a shit? Let's eat."

The funeral director dropped us off at a cavernous, country-style cafe built underneath the bleachers of a horse track in Blytheville, which overflowed with a Sunday afternoon crowd. We were amazed at the gaudy hairdos and extravagant makeup of the waitresses, and how much fried chicken you could buy for a dollar in Arkansas. I couldn't believe how they piled up the plates—people in Arkansas seemed to be world-class eaters. In addition to wonderfully flaky but moist Southern-fried chicken, we got collard greens cooked in ham bones, corn, okra, all kinds of jellies and sauces, mashed potatoes and noodles with gravy, homemade bread and pecan pie for desert.

The waitresses kept coming by and refilling our iced tea glasses, whether we asked for it or not. And you couldn't refuse either.

"Mo? Sure, honey."

When they heard our accents, everyone in the cafe wanted to know where we were from.

"Nu Jursa! Whoa, Nu Jursa! Hey evry'baddy, dese boys 'ere es all de way from Nu Jursa!"

And the damn Kennedy thing. Arkansas was bonkers over the Kennedys. Everybody in the restaurant was just awed by this, our likeness to the Ken'dee brothers. They kept scratching their heads, looking at us, then hee-hawing with laughter about it. "Fer sur," these boys from Nu Jursa were the spit'n image of Jack and little Bobby.

It was the funniest "thang," one of the waitresses said.

"Evra dern Yanka I meet looks jes like them Ken'dees. I mean, dis one har, with dem big eyes? Gawd, ain't he JFK? And you! Look at you with dat pur-fek kirly 'air. Ya're Bobby! Jes a reglar little Bobby-socks, fer sur."

Kern enjoyed all the attention and broke out into smiles and blushed every time someone told him he looked like old Jack, which just made him look more like Jack.

"See Rink?" Kern said. "Jack. Jack Kennedy. Everybody thinks I look just like JFK."

Myself, I didn't mind being Bobby that much. I got used to it. All through Arkansas, and then down through Oklahoma and into east Texas, every time we landed, the Ken'dee routine started all over again. "You thar, golly-gee, she-it, ain't that Jack tho? And Bobby! Jes look at that little Bobby, wil'ya?" Maybe they were pulling our legs, and every Yankee in penny loafers and paisley shirts got this treatment, but there was something about it that felt natural too. Not only because my father worked on the Kennedy campaigns, but because everyone seemed to be, we were obsessed with the Kennedys as children. We named horses and dogs after various members of the first clan and in the spring of 1961, after John Kennedy had been in office for a while, Kern and I rode up into town with pictures of the President in our pockets, so the barber could give us the same "Princeton" haircut that Jack wore. Growing up, we had always been painfully aware that we were considered odd as a family, this big, crazyass Irish brood that made a lot of noise and caused a commotion wherever we went. Also, we were Democrats in a strictly Republican voting district. Then the Kennedys came along and saved our social asses. Even the way my father drilled us with achievement and togetherness from dawn to dusk seemed legitimate for the times. Now that Kern and I were out in the country, doing something with ourselves, we practically expected to be taken for an imitation Bobby and Jack.

Besides, everybody down south was fun-loving and hospitable, and I liked the bumptious, talkative atmosphere in the southern and western cafes. Indeed, it was practically nirvana down there, because the food was so outrageously inexpensive and good. In Arkansas, I discovered the most delectable method of preparing protein known to man, chicken-fried steak, and I ordered one almost every night after that. Give me one of those, with a hefty pile of okra and mashed potatoes on the side, and you can call me Bobby all you want.

When we stepped out of the cafe, the funeral director had swung around with his hearse to run us back to the airport.

At the airport, it was still quite hot, and we were too tired and woozy to fly. Arkansas, and in particular Arkansas food, was a drug that slowed us down. We found a large shade tree behind the operations shack, rolled out our sleeping bags, and slept off our lunch. When we woke, around six, the sun was low, the sky crystal clear, and a light breeze was freshening off the river. We felt revived, ready to fly again, greedy for more miles behind us.

We propped the Cub, taxied down for the active runway, and pushed off southwest for the big Stearman strip at Brinkley that Hank had told us about. The pattern of our days was emerging. Every morning we took off at dawn and flew hard for seven or eight hours, broke at some little town for a late lunch and some sightseeing, and then raced the sun another 250 miles before we tied down for the night.

We flew the oxbows of the Mississippi down to Osceola and found the rail line running southwest. I didn't want to leave the river yet so I stowed the map and shook the stick, yelling forward to Kern.

"Yo, Jack! Mind if I take the controls?"

"It's your airplane Bobby."

I curled down for the river holding lots of power, found a tug pulling a string of barges, and gave it a nice buzz job. Hammerheading up, I dive-bombed the pilot house a couple of times until the crew came out and waved.

What a country it was, I thought, what a journey we were having. Hank in the morning, drawls and a hearse ride in the afternoon. It didn't seem possible that such differences in terrain and speech could be contained in one day. The shadowy, desolate ravines of western Kentucky had separated morning from afternoon, warping distance and time. It felt as if we'd been gone for a year.

So, lazy and content, feeling queerly detached, we dove down for one last sweep of the river. Then we picked up the rails and had a nice evening run over the monotonously flat and green pine barrens of central Arkansas. The forest seemed to stretch forever and there wasn't anything to look at but the tracks. But a pink, gauzy sun was dropping low in the west, bathing our faces in warmth, and the air was still, and once more we could forget the hell earlier in the day and enjoy the luxury of flying into pastel light.

CHAPTER 12

THE SKY WAS DENSE WITH STEARMANS WHEN WE GOT TO BRINK-
ley. It was a spectacularly clear evening and we could see far
across the vast stands of pine. From several directions groups
of battered, yellow cropdusters darted over the treetops as
they returned from their evening runs. When the planes got
close to the field they all dove for the runway at once, twisting and snarling around each other and landing in pods of
two or three. It was a dogfight down there.

Greenhorns that we were, we politely entered the pattern
according to procedure, inserting ourselves into the maddening flow of planes from a downwind leg. While Kern was busy
avoiding one flock of dusters, I was calling out traffic to the
left and right, and then some lone yahoo in a big orange
Stearman plowed down from over the top of us in a tight
turn, practically inverted. We could feel the wash from his
prop as he growled past our nose.

So we powered up and went around the field and tried
again. But it was useless. Biplanes kept cutting us off. Kern
threw up his hands.

"Forget it Rink! I'm just going to fly like these guys."

I was happy about it. I was drowsy from the long run over
the pine barrens and had been fighting sleep for the last forty-

five minutes. I hated nodding off in a plane like that. Now I was wide awake, with big monster biplanes growling all around us, trying to figure out this crazy Stearman strip called Brinkley. It looked exciting down there on the ground, with all those yellow biplanes crawling around like Caterpillar tractors and blowing dust back from their tails. This was our second night in a row at a Stearman strip and probably we'd have some fun here.

Besides, I always liked it when my brother got annoyed like that, declared himself, and took command of a situation. That was the brother I wanted and I knew, too, that he would give me a good spot of flying now.

Kern shifted his shoulders, grit his teeth, firewalled, and cranked the Cub around 180 degrees. There was a mangy pair of Stearmans just below us, descending wing-to-wing for the runway. Kern kicked out his right rudder to the stop, cross-controlled very hard with the stick and plunged the nose forward, shuddering us in a steep diving slip down to the Stearmans. He parked our nose about 30 feet from the Stearman tails and walked the rudders vigorously to keep us there and fight their wash, and we followed their wake turbulence down to the ground.

It was just bizarre, this Brinkley. Even as we were flaring and Kern was fighting the Cub to get it stalled in the prop-wake of those big Stearmans ahead of us, another yellow monster behind us stalled and bounced onto the strip, and the son of a bitch just rolled right for us without braking. If Kern hadn't ruddered out of his way, the guy would have tractored right over us. This wasn't an airport. It was the chariot-race in *Ben-Hur*.

Brinkley was a hole. The carcasses of wrecked planes and abandoned engines, festooned with vines and weeds, lay in piles along the edges of the runway and the taxiways. Behind the main staging area for the duster crews ran a Tobacco Road of hangars and bunkhouses, all of it covered by the gray, putrid film of pesticide and dust. No one came out to direct us to an operations shack or gas pump, so we just followed the two planes ahead of us past the hangars. Meanwhile, more Stearmans were landing on the runway, backing up in a line behind us. The pilots raced their engines and waved their arms at us to move out of the way.

I could tell right away that we'd landed at the wrong place. As we taxied by, the duster crews stood in knots, leaning against their wings and kicking at the dust, either ignoring us or waving us to taxi clear of their area. They didn't want to be bothered with two kids in a shiny Piper Cub. All we could do was continue taxiing along this one-lane tie-down area, until there weren't any more duster crews or pilots waving us away. Finally, our path was blocked by a rutted hill. Kern powered up and scrambled the Cub to the top, swinging us around to a stop with the brakes.

Now we sat abandoned on a hill above the whole works. Below, the quilt of yellow biplane wings parked at all angles, the gaggles of men, and the haphazard collection of sprayer tanks, hoses, and orange tractors looked like some poorly disciplined guerilla air force. The sun was sinking behind the trees and it was too late to fly on to the next airport.

Our heads were still back in Indiana. There would be a Hank down there to sort this out for us. While I pulled our gear from the plane, Kern walked down the hill to ask about gas and a tiedown. When I heard laughter down by the planes and Kern's voice rising, I ran down the hill.

Kern was talking to a roughneck who had stepped out from one of the duster crews. He was trying to explain that we'd flown all day from Indiana and that we were headed for California, and that all we needed was some gas and a tie-down spot. Then we'd sleep under the wings and stay out of everybody's way.

When I got a good look at the fellow, I could see that Kern was talking to the wrong guy. The man's jeans and shirt were layered with what looked like a week's worth of pesticides and grease, and he hadn't shaved in several days. A plug of tobacco dilated his cheek. He sneered at Kern as if he were the dumbest kid he'd ever seen.

"Well whoopee!" the man said. "Prettyboy here is flying his little Piper Cub all the way to California! Me? I'm sprayin' gypsy moths in M'nro County."

Peals of laughter howled around us in the dwindling light.

For some reason, the duster crew thought that this was the funniest thing they'd heard all year.

They just stood there in the weak light rednecking us, laughing at our penny loafers and paisley shirts, asking us whether our Mamma knew we were out after dark, wondering whether or not we were planning on getting laid, right here in Brinkley, or whether we'd wait until we got to the coast and found some "California snatch." If we were so smart, flying a little Cub all the way to California, they wanted to know, why the fuck had we landed at a pisshole like Brinkley? It was beginning to look as though old Hank had really screwed the pooch for us on this one.

We turned away for the Cub. As we walked back up the hill the duster crew continued yelling out insults. We were both upset by it. We didn't know whether we were really in for trouble here, or whether we could get everyone to ignore us by just disappearing behind our plane. Dark, frightening images invaded my thoughts. Our impression of the deep south in those days was formed by the black and white television footage we'd seen of civil rights marches, and the beatings and murders of the freedom riders in Mississippi and Alabama. These buckaroos here in Brinkley could pummel us and leave us half-dead under a wing somewhere, and no one would care. No one would even find us. We sat up by the Cub wondering what to do.

Gradually the men below dispersed, scattering into town in their pickups. In the splashy pools of light provided by running tractors, mechanics and a couple of hopper crews worked on the planes.

Kern and I decided to brave the yahoos again, and we strolled back down below.

Walking from one group to the next, we eventually found a man who identified himself as the operations manager of the strip. He grudgingly agreed to run his gas truck up the hill to fuel us. But he wasn't glad to see us and he told us that we'd made a mistake landing at Brinkley. This was a duster strip, he told us, for "dusters only," and they didn't welcome transient traffic. He didn't want us to sleep on the airport either. When the duster crews came back from town they'd all be drunk and rowdy, and he didn't want to be "responsible" for what might happen to us.

But the fellow had half a heart and he could see that we were upset by the way we had been treated. He told us not to mind the duster crews. Most of those pilots, he explained, were "lifers," veteran cropdusters who flew the fields and the timber every summer and then eked out a precarious living on unemployment insurance all winter. They didn't like outsiders, especially "prettyboy pilots" for whom aviation was just a hobby. A lot of these duster pilots, the man said, were also "rejects," a class of flyer we had heard about. Either because of accident histories, violations on their licenses, or medical limitations, they would never be hired by the military or the airlines. No respectable airport wanted them as flight instructors either. So they were stuck, dusting for a living because that's the only kind of flying they could do. So much for the fraternity of cropdusters, my father's vaunted "Stearman men of the west."

Kern was concerned about leaving 71-Hotel overnight on the strip, but the fellow told us not to worry. It was a clear night and there wouldn't be much wind, and he threw some chocks under the wheels for us. He promised to keep an eye on the plane himself, but not because he was eager to do us a favor. He just wanted us off the strip for the night, and airborne first thing in the morning, so he didn't have to worry about us anymore.

We thanked him and left, carrying our pillowcases and sleeping bags under our arms, and walked out to the highway. Out on the road, a pink neon sign flickered a half mile away. MOTEL CHEAP.

It was dusty and pitch-black along the gravel shoulder of the highway. Dirt devils and spent cigarette packs, kicked up by the passing cars, swirled around our legs. As the passing headlights flared onto the pines lining the road, spectral, hideous stick figures jumped from the branches.

I have always thought of that walk with my brother to the MOTEL CHEAP as a portrait of our divergent personalities. Kern was dejected, humiliated by our redneck drubbing at the duster strip. In Indiana, and again at Blytheville, the day

had been such a high. Back on the Mississippi delta, everybody joked with us and made us the Arkansas Ken'dees.
Here, in the heart of Arkansas darkness, we were just trash
to be kicked. Kern's personality was trusting and euphoric,
and the world generally saw that in him and liked it, returning
it with a loving surplus. But when events or people turned
against him, he became lost in a maze. All he could do was
stumble around inside and bump into things, mostly himself,
trapped by confusion and anger.

Meanwhile, now that we were safely off the Stearman strip,
I was whistling past the graveyard. I fancied myself a grown,
experienced boy, full of the dark melodrama of life. I loved
the spooky shadows and evil fever lurking in these Arkansas
badlands. I was wordy then, quite wordy, a pretension I'd
picked up as a result of collecting high grades in English and
creative writing. I was always searching for that big, $15 word
that described my present situation with what I considered
to be suitable erudition. As it happened, the word "malevolence" was one of my favorites that year. I liked malevolence,
the way the word sounded, and what it meant. The world
was just chock full of malevolence, I thought, and it took a
dedicated malevolence-fighter like me to survive this cruel
life. And here was a place where the locals truly wallowed in
malevolence. Me, frightened by a little malevolence? Never.
Come to think of it, there were a lot of other M words that
aptly described our predicament just now. Someday I would
have great barnstorming blarney tales of my own about central Arkansas, full of alliteration, of course. I couldn't wait to
get home and boast to everyone about my noble forbearance
in the face of these monstrous, malignant, malicious, malin-
gering, malfeasant, mendacious, meretricious, and malevolent
morons of miserable Arkansas. And they were all malodorous
too!

But I couldn't bother with all that vocabulary right now
because I had to cheer my brother up. I didn't like it when
Kern was upset like this because he'd brood all night. I felt
responsible for him at such moments. Except for my mother,
nobody understood his sensitive nature quite the way I did,
and I enjoyed the way I could pull him out of a black mood.

That was one thing about Kern that I did know. I could always make him laugh.

Along the highway to the MOTEL CHEAP, I let him sink to his lowest point before I spoke up.

"Hey Kern."

"Yeah?"

"The Stearman men of the west."

"Ah Jeez Rink. Don't start on me now."

I dropped my bags to the ground and threw my hand out for the imaginary stick, assuming the grandiloquent barnstorming blarney pose of my father.

"The *great* Stearman men of the west."

Kern was laughing now. He shifted his load to one arm and held his stomach.

"Ah Jeez Rink, can you believe it? They're *assholes* down here. White trash in a cockpit."

"Boys," I continued, sweeping out my arm for emphasis, "You'll never meet a better group of pilots than the Stearman men of the west."

Kern was howling, bending over to laugh.

"God Rink," Kern said. "The Stearman men of the west. What crap. Daddy's so full of shit sometimes I could scream."

Paydirt. This was good, very good, I thought. When Kern got cynical about my father, seeing him the way I saw him, I always considered it progress. Anyway, he was happier now. Our situation was pathetic, and we'd really blown it landing at Brinkley. But, what the hell. You couldn't let these malevolent morons get you down. We were determined to laugh our way through this one and have a sense of humor about ourselves.

Dawdling and howling at our own jokes, we walked up toward the motel.

The MOTEL CHEAP was pretty much as advertised. It was a gray, cinder block affair with hollow-core doors, a broken ice machine, and polyester blankets so worn in the middle we could see right through to the semiwhite sheets. We checked in at the rancid front desk, and were delighted to learn that a room with two beds cost just $3. For some reason that we couldn't understand, the clerk was surprised that we wanted to keep the room all night. Inside the room, in the drawer of the nightstand, we found a Gideon Bible and a six-pack of condoms. All night, doors kept opening and shutting in the rooms down the line, and drunken caterwauls and heavy sexual moaning reached us through the thin walls. We weren't familiar with those sounds yet and I just figured that people down here required lots of talk and physical activity to get to sleep. It took me a while to sort out the MOTEL CHEAP, but eventually I realized the truth. The youngest aviators ever to fly America coast to coast spent their second night away from home at an Arkansas whorehouse.

There was a truck stop and diner across the highway. Before we went in for dinner, we walked down past the diesel pumps to a pay phone mounted on an aluminum pole.

We were in a fine mood as we dialed home for the Arkansas gam. Recovering from the rednecks at the strip felt like an injection of courage, and it was a tonic for our companionship. We were almost defiant about it. We could tackle anything now.

My father would be elated to hear that we were across the Mississippi, within striking distance of Texas. At home, by his library phone, he was keeping track of our progress on a large aeronautic planning chart of the continental United States, precisely marking in red pencil the routes we described to him every night. He had bought the chart at a map store in Rockefeller Center in New York just before we left. He was immensely enjoying this exercise, and we welcomed it too, because it kept him busy with something at home and out of our hair. He kept the chart, his pencils, and a route-plotter by the phone every night, so everything would be ready when we called.

"Across the Mississippi!" my father barked into the phone. "*Beyond* the Mississippi. Boys, this is great, just great. Now, let me see. Brinkley. Brinkley, Arkansas. Hell, I remember Brinkley."

That was bullshit, probably, but who cared? Slowly, we were developing an effective strategy for managing him at long distance. Be prepared for lots of barnstorming blarney, and always be upbeat. The only news he would hear was good news.

Kern fed him just the right diet. He told my father that we'd enjoyed beautiful flying all day, that geezers kept buying us food and fuel, and that we'd met a lot of great Stearman men. 71-Hotel was holding up well. Kern ran him through our routes—East Richmond to Indy, the Wabash to the Ohio, the rail line from Paducah, then Blytheville to Brinkley. He gave me a thumbs up from the phone. My father was swallowing all of it and he was extravagantly pleased.

He was happy about another development, though he wouldn't share it with us for two more days. Reporters from all over the country had begun calling. The *Indianapolis Star* story was moved that afternoon on the wires of the Associated Press, setting off a mad media scramble to locate us. Newspaper editors from Little Rock to Oklahoma City read the AP copy, checked a map, and were excited about the possibility that we would be passing through their area within the next twenty-four hours, a great local angle for their Independence Day weekend coverage. We'd never even considered that angle, it was just something we backed into by mistake. But two teenage boys, flying coast to coast in a Piper Cub over the July Fourth weekend, was irresistible to a lot of newspapers, and now they were frantic to find us and do a piece. Everyone just assumed that my father would know where we were and that they could track us down through him.

But until we called home at night, my father was as mystified as everyone else about our whereabouts. He'd spent a good part of the day poring over his map at home and calling the FAA weather briefers, convinced that he could accurately track our flight path. But my father didn't know about the advice we had received from Hank about flying the Kentucky swale, and it completely stymied him. The weather briefers told him that it was virtually impossible for us to traverse the Mississippi River valley that day. He reasoned that we had either swung north above the storms, into Missouri and Oklahoma, or crossed on the eastern face of the Cumberlands, down through Lexington and Nashville.

So, my father told all of the reporters to look along those hypothetical routes, which were hundreds of miles north and east of our actual position. They all came up dry. Every little grass strip for hundreds of miles around St. Louis and Tulsa, and down through central Kentucky and Tennessee, had been harassed by exasperated reporters all evening. Now their deadlines had passed and they were all disappointed and annoyed with my father. Half the newspapers in the south and midwest had been sent on a wild goose chase.

My father was too embarrassed about it to mention the reporters that night. Also, he didn't want to rattle Kern and overload him with another detail just yet. He had already decided that he wouldn't crank up his publicity machine until we were safely across the Rockies.

But Kern could sense that something was up. My father wasn't reacting in the right way to what he was telling him. As Kern described our flight legs over the phone, my father sighed a lot and kept making these little clucking noises with his tongue.

"Oh!" my father said. "So that's where you went. Good. Good! . . . Ah shit."

"Hey Dad, c'mon!" Kern exclaimed into the phone. "We made great progress today. We're a whole leg beyond the Mississippi already."

"Oh I know, son. I know! It's just, well, I can't figure out how you got through Kentucky in that weather."

Kern didn't flinch.

"Oh c'mon Dad, get with it. There's one thing I've learned on this trip. The weather reports can be wrong."

"Right!" my father said. "Right. I copy that."

Jesus, this was great, a lot better than I expected. Kern was really learning to throw the shit.

They changed the subject. At this point Kern frowned and started stammering on the phone. He didn't seem to know what to do. He snatched the pencil out of my shirt pocket and wrote out a note in large block letters on the back of the local phonebook.

RINK: THE WATERBAG.

Balls. The waterbag. That damn thing was coming around

again. Kern and I had assumed that my father would forget about it by now—we certainly had.

I wasn't going to let Kern handle this. He could bullshit my father once in a night, but not twice. Out of sympathy and loyalty to my father, Kern might get backed into promising to find a waterbag. No way, I thought. We'd never get to California if we stopped to look for that freaking thing. We'd have to stonewall. I'd found over the years that I could always do that by smothering my father with a lot of detail and senseless lingo, and of course it never hurt to ass-kiss him to death.

I grabbed the phone from Kern.

"Hey Dad!" I said. "It's great to hear your voice."

"Rinker! Ditto. Kern tells me that you're doing all the navigating. That's great! I can't believe the time you guys are making."

"Dad, it's a beautiful country. Just like you said."

"Good. Now listen," my father said. "Kern doesn't seem to think you can find the waterbag."

"Nah, nah, Dad. Not to worry. Kern was too busy gassing up the plane tonight, and I forgot to tell him. You see, I met this great Stearman man out here in Brinkley tonight."

"Yeah? What's he flying?"

"Oh Jeez Dad you should see it. It's the monster Stearman. He's got the big 600 P&W up front, just like your Texan, the three-blade Ham Standard prop, slaved ailerons, and big leading edge spoilers. What an airplane."

"Ah shit. I wish I could see that. You must be meeting all these great Stearman men. Good chaps, are they?"

"Oh the best Dad, the best. Great guys. Just like you told us. The Stearman men of the west."

"Ah great. That's great. Now look. About the waterbag."

"Dad it's okay! We're covered. It's just like you said it would be. This Stearman guy, see, he says that every hardware store down here has tons of waterbags. They're stacked right up to the ceiling."

"See? See? What'd I tell you?"

"Oh yeah Dad. You were right. This is waterbag country down here."

"Great. Tell Kern. Now look . . ."

"Dad, relax. I'm on top of it. First thing in the morning, see, this ole Stearman man is driving us into town for breakfast, and he's going to show us the store with the waterbags. He's even going to help us lash the thing between the wheels."

"Good work Rink," my father said. "Cripes, this thing is going just like clockwork. Today, you crossed the Mississippi. Tomorrow, you get the waterbag."

He sounded very chipper, hanging up. A thousand miles away, I could almost here him whistling to himself by the phone.

I always felt great about myself, the perfect son, when I could buffalo my father like that. The truth didn't matter here. The situation was impervious to truth. I was pretty sure by now that there wasn't a waterbag in all of America, so how could I truthfully promise to find one? To hell with the truth. My job was keeping the old boy back home happy, so Kern and I could avoid dicking around for a waterbag and get to California. My father would never know the difference anyway.

Inside the diner, over chicken-fried steak, Kern wasn't so sure. He was working through his real feelings about the waterbag. I could see that he wanted to please my father, but he was also exasperated by his intrusiveness, his obdurate, private obsession with the waterbag. Finally Kern stabbed his fork into a pile of mashed potatoes and blurted out his thoughts.

"Rink, you know what I think? You know how I really feel?"

"No, what?"

"Fuck the waterbag! Just fuck that damn thing. We've flown our asses off for two days and done well. We already looked for one back home. Daddy's been a real pain in the ass on this one and we don't need a waterbag."

Uh-oh. Kern might occasionally express feelings this strong, but later he would doubt them. I would have to psyche him out. I needed to show some reluctance, put up a little resistance, to harden his anger into a decision. Besides, if I agreed with him too easily, he'd worry that we were ganging up on my father.

"Well, Kern, gee, I don't know," I said. "This waterbag thing could be important, you know."

"No, fuck it Rink. I'm pissed at Daddy right now. This is my trip—sorry, our trip. He's got no right to tell us we need a waterbag to cross the deserts. I'm the pilot-in-command and it's *my* decision."

"Right. And I'm the copilot. It's my job to follow orders. So, if you really think this is right. . . ."

"Rink, stop! I'm not talking about this anymore. I've made up my mind. Fuck the waterbag. Now, do you copy that?"

"Roger. Loud and clear. Foxtrot-Uncle-Charlie-Kilo the waterbag."

We rose at dawn and trudged back down the piney highway to the cropduster strip. There were already a lot of planes running, their big Pratt & Whitneys rumbling while the tall landing gears of the Stearmans trembled and strained against wooden chocks. Gangs of cropdusters and hopper crews leaned against the wings, grinning like hyenas and smoking, and there was another group drinking coffee around a shiny canteen truck. Stone-faced, we walked down past the malevolent morons and the droning line of planes. Nobody seemed to want to bother us this early in the day. We quickly pre-flighted and propped the Cub, coasted down the hill, and firewalled the throttle as soon as we hit the runway. We never looked back and we never wanted to hear of Brinkley, Arkansas, again.

A lonely stretch of flying lay before us. There was still another sixty or seventy miles of timber barrens to the southwest, as featureless and broad as an ocean, with barely a trace of habitation or a checkpoint to look at. Occasionally there was a bubble in the air from cold moisture rising off a lake, and white tracings of ground fog exposed the outlines of creeks and swamps. But mostly all we could do was follow the rails toward Arkadelphia. Kern and I droned along with the throbbing plane, saying nothing to each other. Finally the pine barrens thinned and were broken by shimmering swamplands that gradually gave way to harder soil, rolling beige and red grasslands.

After Arkadelphia, we entered the pretty, undulating farm country along the Little River. I always loved the sight of agricultural activity from the air. Below us, men on tractors were towing huge agricultural sprayers, and wagons loaded with irrigation pipe, out to the fields. Herds of Hereford and Whiteface were bunched up in the brown-green landscape, massing at feed pens. In the soft, morning light, with the lakes up by Hot Springs glittering like new silver, and the Ouachita Mountains to the northwest glowing purple and black, the Little River was mystical. The far corner of Arkansas is tidy and fenced in, but still it is more western than southern, suggestive of open prairie. It was some of the loveliest country we saw.

Out over the Little River, throbbing along in the Cub, the simplest thought suddenly occurred to me. I wished that my father could see this exquisite piece of country with me. It was a pity not to share it with him.

I was often prone to early-morning bouts of loneliness like this in the air. Still, I couldn't understand why I missed my father so. Certainly I was still boiling inside about the water-bag, and in the full light of day I felt guilty about lying to my father about it last night. But my concerns about him were much greater than that and in fact were buried deeply in medical trauma. That spring, quite by accident, I had begun facing that. All through our coast to coast flight I was brooding through a sense of foreboding about him without quite realizing it.

In late May, just before Kern and I finished the Cub, I was injured pretty badly in a track accident. I was running the mile in the All-County meet on the old cinder track up in Morristown when a runner ahead of me stumbled and took down the pack. Vaulting over the tangled, cursing mass of bodies in front of me, I felt a sharp stab of pain in my left knee and then I tumbled hard onto the cinders. I had been spiked by another runner, and a two-inch gash was opened in my knee.

As I stumbled off the track, blood and cinders gushed down my leg. When I looked down, I could see bone at the bottom of the wound, and my entire knee was stuffed like a fruitcake with cinders.

I was rushed to the hospital. It was a Saturday, my father was called, and he drove right over. I was angry at myself for blowing the race and I was in a lot of pain. Of course I was glad to see my father beside me in the emergency room, but for reasons that even then I knew to be strange.

Because of my father's frequent phantom-pain attacks, hospital emergency rooms had been a permanent fixture of my childhood. My father's attacks often arrived late at night, and Kern and I usually went along to the hospital with my mother to help him in and out of the car. I always felt guilty that I couldn't do more for my father during these excruciating, mysterious attacks. In the hospital emergency room, he often asked to hold my hand, so that he could squeeze it when a particularly bad spasm began and thus distract himself from the pain. It was a rather compelling shared agony, because my father was quite strong and unavoidably hurt my hand when he squeezed. But he was otherwise very stoic about those terrible phantoms and I was intimidated by that, because I knew that I could never live up to a man as brave as he and endure pain the way he could.

But it was always easy for me to forget those hospital visits as soon as they were over. My father experienced immediate relief from his phantoms once he received a Demerol shot, and then he dozed contentedly on the car seat during the ride home. The next day he gingerly hobbled around on crutches or on a special, lightweight peg leg that he had bought for recovery periods like this, but otherwise he seemed miraculously restored. We didn't have much to worry about until the next attack arrived, and that could be many weeks away, sometimes even months.

As hard as I tried, however, I was never able to forget the first phantom attack I witnessed, when I was eight. My father, Kern, and I were working that day down in our lower field, removing tree stumps with a team of horses from a section of newly cleared meadow. Overexerting himself on a stump, my father keeled over onto the ground and began writhing in agony from his phantoms, his bad leg twitching and jolting into the air. My mother called the police and the officer who arrived decided not to wait for an ambulance but to take my father to the hospital right away in his squad car. The three of us lifted my father into the rear seat of the car, a distance of only ten or twelve yards, but afterward it seemed the longest mile of my life. On the count of three Kern and the police officer lifted my father by his armpits, while I brought up the rear with his legs. As soon as I placed my father's legs on my shoulders and stood to carry him, his phantomed leg began twitching and banging spasmodically on my shoulder, which set the other leg off, and by the force of those big, immense limbs I was alternately driven into the ground or lifted into the air, but my father called out that I *had* to hang on and get him to the car. I gripped harder with my arms to restrain his legs, which caused him considerably more pain. But I didn't have a choice and all I could do was hang on for dear life and stumble along until we deposited him in a heap into the car.

My father congratulated me heartily for that, but I didn't feel any better about it. Collapsed in the rear seat of the car with his shoulders resting against the door, still twitching all over, his face was as white as marble and his eyes were bulging out of their sockets. For years, I was haunted by that memory and that vision of him. An older boy, or maybe just a stronger one, I thought, could have cradled those legs in his arms more gently and delivered my father to the car with less pain. To get him to the safety of the car, and thus to the hospital, I had caused him immeasurable suffering.

These real-life medical dramas had a parallel existence in my dreams. I not only dreamed frequently about my father dying, hardly surprising under the circumstances, but I dreamed a lot about becoming a victim myself. In my dreams, I was forever waking up in recovery rooms from spectacular airplane and car wrecks, usually to find my father sitting beside me and complimenting me on my relaxed composure. I suppose I was meant to conclude that I could handle injury as well as he could. I considered myself crazy and obsessed for having such dreams and never told anyone about them.

There was nothing dreamlike about my visit to the emergency room after I was spiked. As a plastic surgeon probed the wound on my knee, I was holding my father's hand, or at least the three fingers that I could get mine around, to squeeze against the pain. The surgeon explained that there was no way of flushing all those cinders out of my knee. They would work out through the surface over time. It took two separate layers of sutures to close the wound. But because of all the cinders compacted in my knee, the local anesthetic couldn't reach the nerve ends and wasn't very effective.

The surgeon worked on me for about forty-five minutes and I was in agony, feeling every millimeter of the needle and string as they ground over the cinders. I winced a lot, squeezed my father's fingers, and tears welled in the corners of my eyes. Toward the end I trembled in a cold sweat and my father stroked my back beneath my running jersey.

I was pleased with myself, however, for taking all those stitches without complaining. My father was watching and complimenting me, which was important enough to me, but I also felt that I had proven something to myself. There wasn't anything particularly mysterious or mythic about enduring physical pain. When you had to, you just did it.

At an emotional moment like this, my father's storytelling prowess was an asset. He could always pull the right story from his vast trove of tales. Moved by what he saw me go through that day, I guess, he decided to share with me the details of his big crash in 1946. Instead of returning directly home, he took me to a restaurant in Bernardsville for a late lunch, and as soon as we sat down he began to tell me about his crash. I was immensely relieved, and curious, because his accident had always been shrouded in mystery, and it was the one flying story he never told. Finally I would learn the truth about the accident that continued to blight all of our lives.

The accident occurred in June 1946 outside Wilmington, Delaware, while my father was on a business trip with a young salesman he was training for Time Inc. The big mistake he made that day was allowing his traveling companion, who had been trained to fly by the Navy during World War II, to take the controls of the plane. He was unfamiliar with the highly unusual design of the plane that my father owned, an experimental Skyfarer, which among other eccentricities had unorthodox rudders. When the engine failed on takeoff, the young salesmen tried to squeeze the plane into a small field for an emergency landing. They brushed a tree going in and damaged the right wing. Just before they touched down the engine roared back to life. My father took the controls and managed to climb back up to 2,000 feet. As he maneuvered to return to the airport in Wilmington, the damaged wing came off at the root and disappeared off the side. They spun down for the trees in a terrifying maple-leaf spin.

My father never really knew what happened after impact, and he would spend the rest of his life trying to resolve two versions of the same event that he dimly recalled. Either he was thrown clear of the wreck on impact and went back to the plane to save his friend, or he was struggling to extricate both of them from the seats after the plane caught fire. In either case, the flames spread quickly and reached the fuel tanks in the wings, which were full. My father was thrown clear by the explosion. The engine blew off in the same direction, landing on my father's leg and pinning him against a tree. His back was broken and he couldn't move, his leg was on fire, and all he could do was lay there helpless as his plane and passenger burned.

My father's life was saved by a young nurse. Because of the postwar housing shortage, she was living in a lakeside bungalow near the remote spot where the plane went in. She rushed through the woods, somehow managed to free my father's mangled leg from underneath the hissing engine, and pulled him to safety away from the burning plane. Several acres of dry pine were ignited by the flaming wreckage. Working around the fire, a logging crew spent almost three hours cutting a path to my father so he could be evacuated by ambulance. While my father waited in the forest within sight of his smoking plane, a rescue squad of medics and nurses hiked in to begin treating him.

My father was particularly passionate about one detail that he shared with me that day. In fact, I had never seen him so emotional.

While he was still in the forest, resting on a stretcher among charred trees, it was obvious that he had lost an immense amount of blood. A tall black medic knelt down on the pine needles beside my father, held up a plastic container of sterile blood plasma, and found a vein in his arm for the needle. While he held up the bag with one hand, letting the plasma trickle down, the medic wiped my father's forehead with a clean bandage and stroked his cheek.

It was odd, my father thought, the sensations he could remember. He was sure that he was dying, and the forest smelled of burnt pine needles and bark. There were birds singing in the trees all around him. He could hear the grunt and heave of the logging crew approaching as they cut a makeshift ambulance road. All the while the medic stroked his cheek and spoke with him in a deep southern accent.

"Now listen here Mister Pilot," the medic said, "God doesn't want you yet. You're my responsibility now. I'm not allow'n you to die, you hear?"

He spent the entire summer recovering in the hospital in Wilmington, and wasn't released until September. In addition to his broken back and crushed leg, all of his ribs were fractured and he had severe internal injuries. The surgeons found a large section of his scalp inside his shirt. Several times, his condition was grave enough to warrant the Last Rites of the church. "I got so sick of that damn priest," my father said, "I threw him out of the room."

Many of the nurses and the orderlies at the hospital were also black, and my father believed that they saved his life. It was a spiritual experience for him, perhaps the most intense of his life. When he described this to me, my father had that dreamy, far-off look he would get when something meant a lot to him.

"Rinker, I went down in my Skyfarer as big a racist as any other jerk out of Scranton, Pennsylvania. My parents didn't deliberately raise me to hate blacks. I was simply taught to avoid them and think of them as inferior. But I couldn't feel that way after my wreck. Every one of those blacks in the hospital was so gentle and kind to me. They did things for me they didn't have to. It's pathetic. It's a statement on human nature. But I had to go through an experience like that, so much pain, losing a leg, a crash that practically destroyed my life and career, just to feel the right way about a group of people I never should have judged in the first place. I never got over it. It's still something that divides me from my brothers. They don't understand this about me. But it's as simple as that. I *love* the black race. They are the best people on earth."

Listening to my father say that was a revelation for me. I was confused at the time, embarrassed even, about my father's growing radicalism over civil rights. I was desperate for a normal life and a normal father—it would have been a lot easier on me if he was just some run-of-the-mill suburban chucklehead, playing golf on Saturday afternoon. It was painful, watching him go through these crusades. Most of the time he seemed blindly furious at the world—at the Roman Catholic Church, for failing to integrate its schools, and for not wholeheartedly supporting the civil rights movement, at friends from work who still told racist jokes— and I couldn't understand such anger when outwardly his life seemed so successful, and should have been so easy for him. Kern and I were both aware that my father was changing quickly on us, but we didn't know why. Now I realized that there was a strong personal basis for my father's activism.

At the restaurant, I was exhausted and my knee was pounding, but we talked for a while more and I enjoyed it. Actually, my father talked and I listened. Once he began revealing himself to me, he didn't seem able to stop. Perhaps it had something to do with his background in AA. The long confessional monologue, encouraged in twelve-step programs, was a habit for him by now. He said something else that day that stayed with me for years.

"You know, I always thought I'd be satisfied just to see Kern solo. Then he had to get his private. Now, you're planning this coast to coast flight. Hell, this is great for me. After Kern was born, I was hospitalized a lot, and then I went through my amputation. I was drinking right up until you were born, Rinker. There were times, lots of times, when I didn't think I'd live to see you boys grown."

The realization slowly dawned on me after that. My father wasn't going to be with us forever. Maybe, his years were already numbered. But I wasn't ready to face that yet so I tried to think of other things.

Out along the Little River, while Kern flew the plane, I enjoyed the agrarian scenery going by. Red and black splashed on green where the cattle herded, the sun glinted off metal barn roofs, and gang-harrows, pulled by mammoth tractors, churned up dust. And I missed my father. Arkansas meant a lot of things to me but that is what I remembered most.

At noon that day we reached the Red River and dashed across the hard, beige plains along the southeastern corner of Oklahoma.

It was our first view of the "real west." Kern and I were awed by the absence of trees and fence lines, and the endless, breathtaking expanse of prairie vista. The colors were very different here. The sky ran horizon-to-horizon a hard azure blue, and from the recent rains wildflowers and scrub heather bloomed yellow and terra-cotta. We refueled at Durant, Oklahoma, wolfed down some lunch, and climbed back out into the scorching heat, pointing 71-Hotel due southwest. The first turbulent buffets of the day were boiling up off the prairie floor, but we were glad to have put so much terrain behind us and to have entered such new land.

Texas, mythic Texas, the Shangri-la of barnstorming blarney, was just an hour away. Up front, Kern was grinning again, dreaming up something.

"Rink!"

"Yo!"

"First thing in Texas, you know what?"

"No, what?"

"Hats. Tonight, we're buying cowboy hats."

CHAPTER 13

WE ENTERED TEXAS OVER LAKE TEXOMA, A LARGE INLAND BODY
of water along the Oklahoma border where the Red River
was dammed, just north of Denison. On the Dallas–Fort
Worth sectional map, I could see that we would cross the
state border in the middle of the lake. I leaned forward and
yelled over the roar of the engine.

"Kern. We're here. It's Texas."

"Ah Jeez Rink. Texas. We've made Texas."

From the southern edge of the lake the vast tabletop prairie opened out before us. The plains were an irregular quilt-
work of beige and red clay, with occasional clumps of green
where the grasses and cottonwood trees congregated at the
watery draws. To the west the Red River snaked through a
maze of deep canyons toward Wichita Falls. The rivers here
were preternaturally blue for inland water, a brilliant green-
blue, more aquamarine than an artist would ever paint an
ocean. The water got that color by flowing through cliffs that
were a sandy mosaic of hard beiges, grays and quarry-tile red,
so that the river contrasted sharply with its banks and threw
up a more concentrated pigment. The expanse of the prairie,
and the more dramatic canyon country to the west, was intensified by low-lying clouds. Banks of broken cumulus raked

underneath our wings, their bases no more than 2,000 feet, stretching out over the prairie as far as we could see.

Kern dropped the Cub beneath the clouds and the visibility in every direction was flawless. The low ceiling forced the eye to take in an immense horizon of land, the way a long, low porch ceiling stretches the depth of field out a window. We had heard about this kind of cloud formation, from my father's barnstorming blarney, in fact. It was the fabled Texas sky. The clouds were formed by concentric flows of moist air pushing up from the Gulf of Mexico, then running out of steam when the winds died in the middle of the day. The heat scorching up from the surface of the prairie condensed the stalled moisture into low, cottony puffs.

Geography became spiritual. The panorama of cloud, prairie, and river was transcendent, and it seemed to me that we had entered entirely new light. Horizons as open as this were a visual baptism for an eastern boy. Even more powerfully than before I felt the distance we had traveled, and Texas was the real Continental Divide for me. Texas *was* different. Unshackled from the fence-lines and confining horizons of the east, we were free, completely free, perpetually united and animated in an element of sky that seemed to stretch forever.

Out over the prairie, Kern "flew the cotton," an old barnstorming term that we had heard and now, of course, being in Texas, we just had to try. He picked a narrow space between two clouds and honked back on the stick. We climbed vertically up through the wispy edges of cloud, passed the tops, and then went weightless as the Cub stalled with a sigh of sprung control cables and flexed fabric. Kern put the wing over for a hammerhead and we dove back down through the same hole. He found another hole, and then another.

Whooping and yelling to each other, we hammerheaded up some more. That is how we arrived in Texas. Prairie, cloud, the weightless sigh of our wings, and then the prairie racing up at us again as we dove through the holes of a perfect Texas sky.

I liked the isolation of Texas. After Denison we didn't see a town for more than an hour, and the terrain below was just one, long scrub prairie, mile after indistinguishable mile, with the shadowy badlands of the gulch country rising off our right wing. We weren't in the hard desert yet so there was no reason to remain over highways and, besides, there weren't any roads going our way. We struck out southwest over open country.

As soon as Denison disappeared I realized that I faced a new navigational challenge. With no landmarks to steer by, and hundreds of square miles of featureless country separating the towns, we could easily bypass or miss our destination airport with a compass error of just a few degrees. Our single tank of gas gave us too limited a range to search for alternates. I would have to dead-reckon carefully, establishing our position by precisely timing our flight legs and keeping an exact record of our compass heading. I took out a pencil and pad and went to work. Every ten minutes I recorded compass readings and then, with my route-plotter, hazarded a guess on our position.

At least once an hour, we'd cross a two-lane road or a particularly dramatic canyon draw marked on the map, and maybe we'd get lucky and there was a power line or a creek intersecting at the same place, and then we had a reliable fix to supplement my dead reckoning. But most of the way across Texas all we had was a compass course and my time-elapsed calculations. The prairie winds were fickle and constantly changing direction—at the low altitudes we were flying, winds-aloft reports weren't very reliable—and I had to correct a lot for drift. After an hour or two of flying we'd see the sun glinting off rooftops on the horizon, steer for it, and hope that when we got there that it was Sweetwater or Lamesa. Most of the time I was right, and sometimes I was off by a town or two, but we never wandered off course more than twenty or thirty miles.

Several times, in the distance off our beam, we saw a windmill and fences, beckoning us with reflections of the sun. We flew over for a look. They were ranches, and it was branding season. We circled low and waved to the cowboys on their horses.

Those branding paddocks were a nice moment for us, especially for Kern. Over the winter, while we worked on the Cub in the barn, he had spoken in breathless terms of reaching the wide open west.

"Rink, wait'll we hit Texas. There's still real live cowboys out there. They have cattle-drives and roundups, just like you see on *Bonanza* and *Rawhide*."

"Ah Kern, come off it," I would say. "Why do you believe that shit on TV? They herd cattle today with helicopters and pickups."

"No way Rink. I'm telling you. They do it still with quarter horses. Purebred quarter horses, with a little mustang thrown in."

That was another problem with Kern, I thought. He was a sucker for quarter horses, and western-style riding. When we were young, my father had built us a rodeo corral in our lower field, replete with audience bleachers, a steer chute, and a barrel-course. Then he went overboard and bought us a quarter horse gelding trained for roping. On Sunday afternoons, we'd all go down to the "Buck Corral" and my father would pull these mangy Black Angus calves that he was raising out of the barn, whip them through the chute, and Kern and I would take turns racing around the corral on the roping horse, lassoing the calves, and then jumping off and wrestling those bawling, farting runts to the ground. It was a lot of crap, I thought. Usually it took us a full ten minutes to rope a calf, and by then the miserable little bovine was so tired it laid down on the ground and practically begged us to tie it up. But Kern loved this stuff. During our "Rodeo Days," he wore a cowboy hat and imitation-leather chaps all afternoon. Our roping horse was named, of all things, Texas. As far as I was concerned, Kern was living in the past, and he was expecting far too much from our trip.

Well, shit. I had to be wrong about something. We were both excited as we circled the paddocks in the Cub. Below, real-live cow-punchers, on quarter horses, were chasing Hereford and longhorn crosses around a dusty corral. My knees felt weak, just watching them, and I was humming "Home on the Range."

"Rink! Get a load of that guy, right there! Doesn't he look just like Michael Landon in *Bonanza*?"

By gum, it was Little Joe. The painted pony galloped ahead of the rest, all silver saddle buckles and foamy breast collar. The rider was classically handsome and lithe, with brown leather chaps, matching vest, spurs, and a curled-up Stetson.

"Jesus Kern. Look at this! You think it's fake maybe? A dude ranch or something?"

"Nah, nah, nah Rink. Dude ranches are in Montana. This is real! These are cowboys. Would you please get this into your thick skull? We're in Texas!"

We just couldn't get over it. Real live cowboys, in real live Texas. Life had never seemed as direct and as romantic as this.

From 500 feet, it was like viewing a performance, a thing of equestrian beauty. The cutting horses, leaning over hard and digging in their hindquarters, piled into the herd of cows. Then we'd see a pretty chestnut or a buckskin with a black mane cut a calf out from its mother, and the rider threw his rope. The calf flipped over in a cloud of dust. The horses were excellently trained. While the calf was still in mid-air, the horse lunged back to bring tight the rope, looking back to the saddle to make sure the cowboy was ready for his back-trot. Swirling the rope home on the pommel, the cowboy spurred the pony and they galloped off, dragging the calf by its leg or neck. At the branding fire, when they put the hot iron to the steer's rump, we could see a puff of smoke curl up from the sizzling flesh.

Could the country really be like this, just as my brother imagined it? Sometimes it didn't feel as if we were flying at all, or navigating, or worrying about fuel. We were crossing a dream space. Up ahead, we'd see another cloud of dust, which meant another branding corral, and we'd fly for it. We crossed the prairie that way, lighting from paddock to paddock.

Denton went by, then Decatur, Paradise, and Perrin. We

decided that we would try and make Abilene that night. Abilene, we knew, was a mythic cow-town, the kind of place where we belonged right now. On *Rawhide*, Clint Eastwood was always telling the boys to "Head 'em up, and move 'em out," so they could make Abilene before the gulches ran dry. Country and western music wasn't popular on the east coast then, but there was one hit tune that we knew, "Abilene." "Abilene, Oh Abilene," the singer wailed. So, we would fly for Abilene and stay there for the night.

It wasn't all beauty and barnstorming rhapsody though. In our feathery Cub, the turbulence was brutal. This was different, hard stuff out here. The buffets were long, powerful drafts that hauled the plane up and down, sometimes at more than 1,000 feet a minute on our vertical speed indicator. The wallops hit us a lot of times in clear air; they were not associated with mountainous terrain or clouds. It was too much, even for Kern. He throttled back to under 2,000 rpm, to slow the plane through the rough air, picking the speed back up by diving a little when an updraft finally gave up on us and dropped us weightless under a cloud. But, mostly, it was just a game of waiting for the next malevolent monster to hit.

All that rough flying through Texas—for that matter, throughout the west—was really our own fault, a product of our naïveté and inexperience. Kern and I had both studied the aviation bible, William K. Kershner's *The Private Pilot's Flight Manual*, but we'd never bothered to prepare for our flight by reading Kershner's *Instrument Flight Manual*, or the many volumes available on aviation weather and desert and mountain flying. If we had, we would have known the cardinal rule of western flying: never take off in the heat of midday. As it climbs toward its meridian the sun generates huge, bone-rattling thermals directly off the prairie floor. The thermals remain active until four or five in the afternoon. Nobody ever bothered to tell us this either, and no flyer we knew would have thought to, because we were surrounded by romantics, not scientific pilots.

Kern and I both managed to survive the hellish turbulence

of the west, for quite different reasons. It was another study in our divergent personalities. He was virtually immune to discomfort in the air, and in any case was too determined to reach California to sit out the rough air on the ground. I was miserable a lot of the time but felt intellectually committed to bearing up in the turbulence.

I was a lot more bookish than Kern, and I had read and reread all the aviation greats—Antoine de Saint Exupéry, Ernest K. Gann, Nevil Shute. (Anne Morrow Lindbergh's *North to the Orient*, I thought, was the best flying memoir of all.) This self-education in aviation literature had steeled me for our flight. To adventurers like St. Ex and Gann, physical discomfort and hazard weren't an unfortunate byproduct of flying, but instead an existential challenge, practically the whole point. My favorite essay, and one I had practically memorized, was Exupéry's brilliant ode to turbulence in *Wind, Sand and Stars*, "The Elements," a description of his encounter with the tail end of a typhoon while flying the mails in Patagonia. In *Fate is the Hunter*, Gann battles killer turbulence from Presque Isle to Natal. They wrote about the hell of rough-air flying the same way Joseph Conrad or Herman Melville wrote about rough seas. These were perils to be reflected on later, experiences that they turned into finely wrought homilies on courage, perseverance and faith. They never pretended to be fearless, but they weren't deterred either. There was always another range, the next Andean or Himalayan peak, to conquer. Flying was like that, I thought. The seatbelt was already as tight as it could be, and still you gave it one more yank against the murderous chop and flew on. I finally appreciated all the reading I had done once we got out over Texas and were bounced all over the prairie sky. St. Ex and Gann had given me strength. I never stopped hating turbulence and I was frightened by it, but I did find a way simply to endure.

As the day wore on, I became more physically hardened. Actually, it was the accumulation of days that helped. The night before, undressing at the MOTEL CHEAP, Kern and I were both surprised by the black and blue marks on our bellies and hips. Flying the rough air of Kentucky, the constant jostling of our bodies against the seat belts had bruised and opened up our blood capillaries. As we continued west in turbulence, the black and blue marks merged into a continuous ring around our waists, so that in bathing suits we looked liked zebras with a single stripe. The bruises didn't hurt that much, except at the beginning and the end of the day, and we found that we could relieve the pain by taking a hot shower or jumping into a motel pool.

Kern didn't seem to mind his own rough-air welts that much. But he was taken aback when he saw mine. He knew how much I hated flying in turbulence. As soon as we hit the first patch of bad air in Texas, he shook the controls so I could fly awhile myself, and we also elected to fly shorter hops, remaining in the air for two hours or less. This only helped a little, but Kern's sympathetic attitude made it easier to bear the hours until the turbulence abated in the late afternoon.

Nobody told us about prairie dogs either. We didn't even know what they were at first, and had to ask at the next airport. We encountered our first colony about fifteen minutes out of Decatur. I was navigating from the rear seat, peering out through the open window for landmarks. There, off our left beam, was a rectilinear lunar landscape, pocked by neatly spaced craters.

"Hey, Kern, what the hell is that?"

Kern authoritatively called back that we were now in the heart of "Stearman Alley," and reminded me that we had passed a couple of large, abandoned World War II military training strips. Those craters up ahead, he said, were the remnants of an old Army Air Corps bombing range.

I didn't think so. Nobody could drop bombs in neat rows like that. I had my own theory.

"No way Kern," I called forward. "That's an oil field up ahead."

"An oil field?"

"Oh yeah Kern. We're in Texas! Those are test bores for a big old oil field."

We flew over for a look.

As we came in low hundreds of furry, Mad-Hatter creatures scurried in every direction, tumbling head-over-ass for their holes. We scratched our heads. Minks, maybe? Or chinchillas—yeah, wild, Texas chinchillas. Nah. We were in Texas. Out here, chinchillas and minks would be immense, as big as German shepherds back home. Probably they were some kind of western woodchuck. Whatever. These critters were apparently quite private, and smart as hell about passing aircraft. In the few seconds it took us to cross their cratered community, the place was instantly deserted, empty as a ghost town, as everybody dove for their holes. Except for a few stragglers racing in pellmell from the prairie, and some tumbleweed blowing across the edges, nothing moved.

There were dozens of those colonies across Texas, out as far as Midland, where the desert begins. We learned to play them just right. If we approached downwind with the sun in front of us, so the gophers weren't spooked by our engine noise or shadow, we could gradually sneak in with gentle turns and observe their habits. They were lovable little devils, scampering about and bumping into each other in furry collisions, coming out of their holes on the fly, standing upright and inquisitively peering up at us with their babylike paws wedged against their cheeks.

Wildlife observation gets quite boring, however, and it was a lot more fun to terrorize the bastards. Kern developed our prairie-dog aerial assault tactics, but after a couple of colonies I took over the controls myself and perfected the technique.

Coming in with the sun behind us, we'd shut down the throttle and quietly glide in over the middle of a colony. The trick was to get about fifty prairie dogs all in one place, and then inch over with the rudders so that the Cub's shadow made a direct hit on the crowd. The plane's shadow was generally about three seconds ahead of us. As soon as it hit a big concentration of prairie dogs, they all dove at once for the nearest holes. At that instant we firewalled the throttle to give the fur-balls an extra shot of adrenaline from the noise. It was better than yelling "Fire!" in a movie theater. As we passed over and looked straight down, a dozen or more of the gophers were stuck headfirst in each hole, garroted at the neck, with a frantic circle of hind legs desperately kicking up a ring of dust. It worked every time, as good as a stun-grenade. Scare the bejesus out of fifty dense-packed prairie dogs, and they'll all dive at once for the same hole.

At the third or fourth colony, I remembered the Lance Moon Pies that we had purchased back in Oklahoma. As Easterners, we were not familiar with the Moon Pie, but apparently it was a popular food staple out west. Moon Pies consisted of two giant saucers of chocolate cake, held together like an Oreo with a caloric wad of sweet white cream in the middle. They looked filling, and we had a long flight ahead, so I bought a few and stuffed them in the baggage compartment. Now I wondered how a prairie dog colony would react to a Moon Pie dropped in its midst.

When the next colony came up, I took out the first Moon Pie, unwrapped it and resisted the temptation to try a bite, and opened up the side door. I shook the stick and took the plane from Kern.

I set up a nice, gentle glide toward the colony, with the sun on the tail. I figured that, with the forward momentum of the plane behind it, the Moon Pie would hit just about where our shadow was. So, I would release just as the prairie dogs all dove for cover. After we passed over, the prairie dogs would all extricate themselves from the holes, shake the kinks out of their necks, and discover that Moon Pie.

Bombs away, and it looked like a good drop. I powered up, but not too much, so I could turn sharper in a slower plane, and came back over the colony.

The Texas prairie dog, I can report, definitely goes for Moon Pies. It was like a single bucket of slop thrown to fifty starving hogs.

In one madass tangle of fur, tumbleweed bits, and trampled-over youngins, the whole damn colony declared war on itself. With all those craters around, theoretically it should have been difficult to see which one of them had been my Moon Pie drop zone. But in practice, it was easy. There was this writhing, slithering, gyrating pyramid of mammals down there, sixty or seventy furious little beasts scrambling over each other, clawing each other's eyes out and snapping shiny teeth to get to the prize, the Moon Pie at the bottom of the seismic heap.

The prairie dog must be related to the lemming. As the scrummage piled higher, more gophers ran in from the suburbs and jumped on, just because everybody else was doing it. How many prairie dogs can fit on top of a Moon Pie? At least a hundred. And it was all just a Hobbesian farce by now, because some big ole dominant male, burrowed in at the bottom, had probably snapped up that Moon Pie in six furious bites. But it was only a partial victory for him. With the weight of the whole colony upon him, that sucker had to be hurting, with complications from asphyxiation and sucrose shock.

I circled the colony a few times to see what happened next. After a while, the prairie dogs just got tired of being on top of each other, and they gradually slid off the pile and staggered home to their craters. I felt sorry for the ones on the bottom. It was obvious that they had been squished. After the others left, the critters from the bottom just lay there for a while, shellshocked and listless under the hot sun, and then they started scratching off on their bellies. I prayed for their survival. There were a lot of heavy-duty vultures and hawks circling those colonies all the time, and if one of those flattened critters dawdled getting back to his hole, he would be somebody's dinner before long.

I kept the plane well stocked on pastries after that, and this was one of the great pleasures of our coast to coast flight, feeding the prairie dogs. If an airport didn't have a vending machine with Moon Pies, I bought doughnuts or peanut-butter crackers. We could even throw out a bag of potato chips, unopened, and the prairie dogs would tear through the wrapping paper and greedily consume the potato chips in a matter of seconds. Those bastards were really starving down there. The big scrummage over the Moon Pie wasn't fair to the animals on the bottom, so I started altering my technique, to protect lives. Instead of releasing one, solitary Moon Pie or cracker, I threw out a bunch at high speed, so the baked goods were dispersed over a wide area by our slipstream. It

was a lot better that way because then only ten or twelve
critters jumped onto a single pile, and nobody got hurt.

In the afternoon, the headwinds had picked up, and circling
to feed the prairie dogs had consumed extra gas, and we were
forced to refuel before we reached Abilene. As we passed
Breckenridge in the central prairie, I calculated our time aloft
and fuel burn, concluding that we should land as quickly as
possible. Our only choice was the airport at Albany, a ranch
hamlet thirty miles ahead. The airport lay right on the north
edge of town, so that the runway looked like a continuation
of the street grid, and we whistled in just over the roofs as
we made our landing.

From the air, Albany looked quaint and ideally western, a
no-frills cowtown. As we descended to land we saw a dusty,
wide main street, wooden sidewalks, porches, and false-front
roofs. There were even hitching posts and a watering trough
for horses. It was the end of the Independence Day weekend
and the annual barrel races at the municipal arena were just
breaking up. Several groups of riders on horses were loping
through town, four and five abreast, manes and tails curved
up in the breeze.

I never forgot the view I had of one of them. A cowgirl on
a big Appaloosa was galloping up the street from the arena
to catch the other riders. As we turned for the airport, right
over her head, she neck-reined the horse around and I looked
straight down. The horse was prancing and whipping around
in circles, and the girl's blond hair and the fringes on her shirt
sleeves whirled like a dervish, and she waved up at us and
smiled, a pretty picture from the air.

The other riders raised their hats and waved too.

"Kern! Get a load of this, wil'ya? These people are just
riding their horses right into town."

"Darn it all Rink. I've been trying to tell you this all day.
Everybody rides their horse into town out here. This is
Texas!"

Still, I couldn't get over it. It never occurred to me that

Texas would be this old-fashioned, so close to its frontier roots.

It was only four in the afternoon and we could have done some more flying. But we liked the look and feel of Albany so much we decided to skip Abilene and stay here for the night. The airport owner gave us a ride into town in his pickup.

The hotel in Albany was a grand old-fashioned affair with a white adobe front, Mexican tile floors, and a big front desk made of ornately carved wood. Our room upstairs was large and tall, with a ceiling fan and immense, whorehouse-style beds. A set of tall vertical windows opened onto a railed balcony. The view was north, out over the board sidewalks and false-front roofs. The prairie beyond, dappled with sagebrush, glowed pink in the late afternoon sun.

We were hungry when we got in, and the hotel coffee shop had a special going—two "Texas-size" hamburgers and a large RC Cola, for ninety-nine cents. We brought the burgers up to our room, but they were inedible. It's an abomination, what Texans do to a piece of meat. Slopped on to both sides of the burger was a sauce, thick as swamp mud, that appeared to consist of mustard, pickle relish, jalapeño peppers, chopped onions, Tabasco sauce, and some other material that I can only guess at, but it looked awfully close to week-old, refried beans. We flushed the burgers down the toilet and decided to take a stroll through town.

The air smelled sweetly of sagebrush in bloom and manure piled at the hitching posts. All the horses were gone now, but there were still cowboys running up and down Main Street in their pickups, lots of pretty girls with sugary Texas accents, and, in the barbershop, men getting haircuts and a shave at six o'clock at night. In the window of the drug store, there was a stack of shiny straw cowboy hats, with thin, black string bands and metal grommets for air-holes, real, western-style headgear. Kern began to salivate. He didn't want one of these big heavy Stetsons anyway—it would be too hot inside the plane. But these straw jobs looked perfect, and we went in.

Kern bought himself one of these immense, ten-gallon

jobs, which made him look perfectly ridiculous, but he was happier than shit with that big cowboy hat on so I made an agreement with myself not to be embarrassed standing next to him. I settled on a black ball-cap emblazoned with a state map and a logo in yellow lettering, DEEP IN THE HEART OF TEXAS, which I thought looked just right with my Ray-Bans. Thus attired for the wide open west, we swaggered out to the street.

Next door, there was an old western cafe, and we sat down for some chicken-fried steak.

Nobody was fooled by our hats. Because of our penny loafers and paisley shirts, which were difficult for people not to stare at, everybody could see that we were from out of town, way out of town. But these Texans were very sweet-natured and kind, not at all like those yahoos cropdusters back in Arkansas. They all wore broad Stetsons, pointed boots, and ornate belt buckles, and they kept stepping over to our table and introducing themselves. Nu Jursa! I could have listened to that nasal twang all night. Everything was a "thang," everybody was an "ole boy" or a "gal," and if the folks in Albany, Texas, liked something a lot, it was a "humdinger" or an "all-day horse." They couldn't get over the fact that we had flown all the way from the East Coast, just to land in little ole Albany.

"Piper Cub, hunh? Ain't that kinder like a Model T or sumthang? Hot-diggety-damn. You boys is all bidness."

We felt like a pair of real cowpokes, back in the room, dialing home for the first Texas gam. We carried the phone and two chairs out to the balcony and Kern kept his cowboy hat on while he spoke with my father. The moon rose over the prairie as they talked. Kern told him all about our day, and described our routes. My father was worried that we were flying too hard, and thought we should take a rest once we got over the Rockies. He wanted us to plan a one-day layover in El Paso, which Kern was resisting by being non-committal.

When I got on, my father launched into a long reverie about Texas, making me sit through this ridiculously extended chat about all the great Stearman men he once knew out here, the ranches he had seen from the air, the whole nine yards of Lone Star blarney. I wasn't in the mood.

"Hey Dad," I snapped. "Thanks for telling me all about Texas. But I'm *in* Texas right now. I don't have to hear about Texas from you."

My father sounded hurt, and I immediately regretted what I had said. I couldn't understand myself. In the morning, crossing the Little River country, I missed him. Now that I had a moment or two to share with him, I was acting up. It was almost as if I could tolerate him theoretically but not in person. Kern was a lot more patient that way and could put up with the bullshit, a major difference between us, but I didn't have very long to dwell on this because my father had already changed the subject.

"Listen here," my father said, "How's the waterbag doing?"

Shit. Now I had to revert to that mode.

"Dad, the waterbag's just great. That old Stearman guy in Arkansas showed us how to rig the bag flat on the landing gear, so there's less drag. The cap faces backwards."

"Good. Good. Any problems?"

"Well, just one thing Dad. The bag loses water in flight. Every time I check it, it's down a gallon or two."

"Yup. It figures. Same thing use to happen to me. Now, to fix a problem, son, you have to understand it. Tell me, what's happening here?"

"Ah, let's see. Engine vibrations. The engine vibrations are forcing water out through the cap."

"Nope. Think son, think."

"All right. The seams are bad. Water's leaking out through the seams at the bottom."

"Nope. Try again."

"Dad, c'mon. I've been flying all day. I'm tired. Couldn't you just tell me?"

"All right. Look, it's evaporation. That waterbag is sitting out there in the sun all day, and you've got engine exhaust blowing over it too. All that heat evaporates the water right through the canvas. In the old days, I used to lose a quart an hour out of one of those bags."

Evaporation. Of course. How could I overlook a development that basic? I was lying so fast I couldn't keep track of all the scientific ramifications.

"Right Dad. Evaporation. So, what do I do?"

"Well c'mon son, that's simple. Every time you land to top off the gas?"

"Yeah?"

"Well, fill the waterbag too."

CHAPTER 14

FOR FIVE HUNDRED MILES EAST OF THE CONTINENTAL DIVIDE, the high plains of Texas and New Mexico sweep up as a long, imperceptible incline, rising steeply at the end as the stately massif of the Rockies comes into view. From our dawn take-off at Albany to our afternoon arrival at Carlsbad, New Mexico, where we launched for the Guadalupe Pass, we climbed more than 2,000 feet in land elevation, to almost 4,000 feet above sea level. We flew west through Sweetwater, Lamesa, and Seminole, the fabled "southern route" of the early air-mail flyers, but a pilot must fly that stretch at least once to understand what the land is doing to him. Usually we were looking only five or ten miles ahead, not enough to sense the corrections for height we should have been making. All morning, the ground seemed to be stealthily rising up and trying to swallow the plane. Every hour or so we realized our land error and climbed to avoid obstructions and terrain.

The country, too, changed. After Midland, Texas, the beige and red prairie, with its occasional clumps of green draws, rapidly gave way to sandy desert littered with boulders and rocks, the earth all dirty yellow and black, with spectac-ular mesas and ravines forming the serrated foothills of the Rockies. There were bizarre, disc-shaped cirrus clouds that day, screening the sunlight into weak shadows. The feature-less terrain obliterated into featureless sky, erasing the horizon. Deprived of clear ground reference, Kern occasionally experienced problems with vertigo, or spatial disorientation, and was forced to fly by peering constantly at his turn-and-bank indicator and altimeter. I had my hands full navigating by the compass and my time-elapsed calculations. We were flying through an extra-planetary abyss. Even the towns we passed along the way, many of which we never actually saw, had a far-off ring. Big Spring, Odessa, Pecos.

Farther along the clouds broke up and the sun scalded down. Oil fields, the first that we saw, popped out of the empty landscape. Dozens of black and orange derricks methodically pumped away, and the dirt tracks leading up to them radiated off into the desert like the spokes of a sundial. But the oil installations must have been unattended most of the time because there was virtually no sign of human activity below.

Adding to our feelings of flying into a lunar cosmos, it was to be a day of mishaps and freak events. The big mountain pass ahead, which we knew we would brave by midafternoon, seemed to be pushing us back, warning us off by a series of aberrant mechanical and natural frights.

As we turned in for our first refueling stop of the morning, at Avenger Field in Sweetwater, the tail suddenly rattled and shook as violently as a truck hitting a pothole. The airframe resounded with a bang! The sticks sagged, heavy and hard, the nose dropped, and I had to grab the controls myself to help my brother pull the plane away from the ground. He lunged with both hands for his stick and yelled back.

"I've got the stick! You work the throttle and rudders! Just get me down Rink, work me down."

It was a pretty decent spot of flying we did that morning, but we couldn't appreciate it right away. We didn't know what had happened to the plane. All the possibilities ran through my mind. Had we collided with another plane? Maybe we'd lost our elevator struts and the tail was about to vibrate off. Or a bird-strike—we'd seen low-flying vultures all morning. They were awfully big birds, and if one of them was hung up on our rudder, the plane might act like this.

It only took us a half-minute or so to reach the ground, but that's a long time when your heart is pounding like a pile driver. Kern was holding up the plane all right, but with little jerks and bumps, because two hands cannot be as coordinated as one. All the way down he kept yelling for me to work the throttle and rudders better for him, which wasn't an easy thing. A single mind flying alone gracefully choreographs the body—stick hand, throttle hand, the feet on the rudders—into a coordinated landing approach. Two minds doing it together, especially two frightened minds, are an uncoordinated jumble.

"Power, Rink!"

"Not that much! C'mon!"

"Trim. Give me some nose up."

"Wind drift! Jesus, could you watch that? Left rudder, Rink."

But gradually I got into my brother's head and got the hang of that strange descent. We mushed into a soft cushion of air over the runway. To help stall the plane, I furiously cranked in all the nose-up trim I could get, scraping some skin off my knuckles against the metal flange on the carburetor-heat knob as I flew the handle around. I didn't notice the blood on my pants until we stepped out of the plane.

At the gas pumps, which were deserted at seven in the morning, we couldn't find anything wrong with the plane. There were no dents or breaks in the fabric, everything was in place, and when we took off the inspection plates on the tail and peered inside, everything seemed to be in order. But the stick was completely dead on us and we could never fly the plane as it was. It was a mystery. My brother sat on the wheel of the Cub with his chin in his hands, miserable with himself. Our plans for reaching the mountains that day seemed dashed.

The airport mechanic arrived in his pickup a few minutes later. He was a tanned, gentle fellow in a greasy ball-cap, and he smiled knowingly when we explained what happened. He reached into his pocket for a key and unlocked the fuel pumps.

"You may as well gas up now," he said. "Let me get a couple of thangs from the hangar. You'll be outta here in ten minutes."

When the mechanic returned he was carrying a flashlight, needle-nose pliers, and a shiny galvanized-steel spring, slightly larger than the ones used on screen doors, fresh out of its box. He reached inside the tail inspection plate up to his elbow, grappled and winced, and came back out with two broken pieces of a rusty spring.

"It's what I figured," he said. "Busted elevator spring."

"Goddamn it," Kern said, angry at himself. "It's the one part I didn't fix."

"Ah, go easy on yourself young fella," the mechanic said. "Nobody replaces an elevator spring. You fix 'em when they break. You're just lucky that I got a new one that fits."

"What would break a spring in flight like that?" my brother asked.

"Well, where you flyin' from?" the mechanic said.

"New Jersey."

"Nu Jursa! Whoa here. Are you them boys on the radio?"

"We don't have a radio in this Cub."

"No! The AM band boys. You're all over it. Evrabaddy's lookin' for you boys. They're saying you're the youngest aviators ever to fly coast to coast."

We were astonished. It was the first indication we had that there was press interest in our flight, and it had never occurred to us that we might be the youngest aviators to fly the continent. It seemed bizarre to us, too. Here we were out in this lonely, remote stretch of Texas, which felt like the end of the world, and we were enjoying the isolation and the complete freedom from everything we knew. Meanwhile, newscasters were talking about our flight on the radio. Both of us instinctively suspected that my father was behind it. He was probably trying to build as much interest as he could, so there'd be a big splash once we got to California. Neither of us minded very much. We just hadn't expected my father to pull a fast one like that on us in the middle of the country,

and we hadn't expected newscasters to be interested either.
What did everybody see in this trip?

"Anyways, that's what did it to you," the mechanic said.
"You been flying in a lot of turbulence?"

"Yeah, lots," my brother said. "Straight, almost, for three
days."

"Well, it's too much for an old spring like that," the mechanic said. "She just gave out in the stress, that's all."

The new spring that the mechanic had wasn't designed for
a Piper Cub. It was for a Piper Pawnee cropduster. But by
crimping back the ends of the spring and making adjustments
on the armature of the elevator, the mechanic adapted it for
the Cub. As he set the new spring in place, the mechanic
explained that the controls would be lighter now.

"The thang'll be kinda loosey-goosey on you now, know
what I mean?" the mechanic said. "But it'll be better. Real
responsive-like."

The airport owner and his wife arrived and opened up the
pilots' shack. We went in and bought some crackers and soda.
The mechanic came in for his morning coffee, and we all sat
outside on the porch and talked.

The air was pungent with the dry, woody smell of the high
plains early in the morning. There was a thick coating of dew
on the macadam ramp and the gas pumps, and glistening on
the sagebrush beyond—surprising, I thought, for this dry terrain. The biggest jackrabbits I had ever seen were bounding
across the ramp, running circles around each other.

The woman walked out to the pumps to empty the waste
barrels. Returning, she called to her husband.

"Dear," she said. "Look at that pretty little Cub on the
ramp. It's perfect. Perfect! I've never seen a plane so beau-
tifully restored."

Kern beamed, took off his cowboy hat, and ran his hand
through his sweaty, flaxen hair. I was laughing my ass off for
him that morning. Kern saw me doing it, looked over and
smiled, and started laughing at himself too. He looked ridiculous in that big ten-gallon hat he'd bought for himself. But
he was happy and self-confident out here in the far reaches
of Texas. I could see him changing and growing, it seemed,

with every leg we completed, and he was a lot more fun to be with when he was relaxed on the ground like this. I couldn't get over how much I enjoyed being with him now.

"Ah, lookey here," the airport owner said. "Are you them boys from Nu Jursa? It's on the radio. Everybody's trying to find you two."

"Yeah. That's us," Kern said, but he felt a little sheepish about it. "Look. I'm just doing this to build time for my commercial license. We didn't do this for publicity."

"Oh it's okay!" the fellow said. "This'll be good for aviation, you know? They'll be a pack of people waiting for you once you get over the mountains this afternoon."

The airport owner was a licensed pilot who flew the Rockies all the time, mostly in big Cessnas and twin-engine planes. He went over the maps with Kern and me and showed us how to fly the Guadalupe Pass. From west Texas, it was better to cross northwest into New Mexico and launch for Guadalupe Peak from the north. Then we could head almost due south for the twin Guadalupe Peaks, flying a parallel course with the mountain range until we reached the pass. That way, the Guadalupe Range would protect us from the prevailing wind from the west until we were up above 9,000 feet. Facing the pass straight on for fifty miles would just expose us to heavy winds and leeward turbulence.

The owner at Sweetwater didn't discourage us from taking on the pass, but he didn't make it sound easy either. There were a couple of planes on the strip with 85-horse engines, a Luscombe and a Cessna 140, that had been through the pass, so it could be done. The big thing to watch, he said, was altitude loss. We should turn and face the pass about three or four miles out. If, during the first mile toward the pass, we could hold our altitude and course against the wind and the turbulence, we'd probably be okay. But if we started losing height and couldn't regain it, we should turn back right away.

He said one other thing that cheered us.

"It'll actually get better for you *inside* the pass. It's like the eye of a storm in there, a lot calmer. So, the last mile going in, when it's hell, just know it'll actually be better inside."

As we turned to go, Kern pulled out his wallet. We owed

them for a new elevator spring, labor, a tank of gas, crackers and soda. The three of them just stared at us and smiled. They wouldn't take our money.

Kern tried to insist, but it was no use.

The owner removed his tattered ball-cap and ran his hand through his hair.

"Boys," he said, "Just go. Evrabaddy's real excited for you two. Fly hard, and you'll make the mountains by noon."

We refueled again at Wink, Texas, a tiny desert hamlet just south of the New Mexico border. The gas jockey there was a gaunt, unshaven ranchhand type with holes in his boots, filthy jeans, and a hideously sweat-stained straw hat. While I supervised the fueling, Kern walked across the ramp to stretch his legs.

"Ah, listen here fella," the gas jockey called out. "Check out the hangar."

Kern doubled back for the hangar, figuring that there must be some kind of nice airplane in there, a restored biplane or something, that the gas jockey wanted him to see.

As he filled the wing tank, the gas jockey kept looking over his shoulder toward my brother and the hangar, and he spilled gas on the fabric.

"Hey," I said. "You're spilling gas. Watch that wing."

"Frig the wing. Watch your brother."

"I said, watch that wing! You're spilling gas."

"And *I* said, watch your brother."

A sound like a hundred snare drums and cymbals going off all at once resounded from the hangar, echoing off the corrugated tin walls.

Kern came running out of that hangar almost airborne. His cowboy hat blew off, and his big brown eyes were as wide open with terror as the Gettysburg dead.

Crashing into the Cub's wing strut, Kern leaned on it for support. He was panting and heaving, trying to catch his breath. Meanwhile, the hangar in front of us was rattling and heaving with a deafening roar, like it was about to come loose from its foundation.

"Jesus Christ, Rinker. Jesus. Lord."

The gas jockey fell off the wing, laughing hard, a mad dervish of gas hose, 80-octane fuel and clattering ladder. Haw, haw, haw, haw! He hadn't laughed this hard in months, since he sent the last jackass in penny loafers into the same hangar.

"Snakes," my brother expelled. "Snakes. Hundreds of them, thousands. *Rattler snakes.*"

It was true. Still bending over with laughter, the gas jockey led us over to the hangar and we crept up to the shadowy interior by the door. He threw the door wide, and the roar of rattlers went off again, so loud I held my ears. There were thousands of rattlers in there, in wire cages stacked all along the walls, with a large, open pit near the far end crawling with a hundred or more snakes all twisted around and slithering over each other. Smaller, wooden cages, stacked in the middle of the floor, held a huge colony of breeding rats— rattler food. A few of the snakes from the open pit began slithering over for the door as soon as they saw the light poking in, and Kern and I jumped back.

My father had told us a story once from his Texas days, about a young air cadet returning late at night from a drunk in town. Against all standing orders he took a shortcut through the prairie and walked across a runway. From the barracks they heard his screams, and everyone scrambled into Jeeps and drove out there. The airman was already dead, scarred by more than a dozen rattler bites. To me, it was just more barnstorming blarney, typical of my father's need to concoct stranger, more macabre tales as his standard fare of tailspins and midair collisions wore thin over the years. Turns out, though, the one about the rattlers was true.

"Oh yeah, haven't you heard about this?" the gas jockey asked. "Don't you ever, ever cross a runway at night in Texas. Them rat'lers will get you before you ever see them."

Rattlers are heat-seeking reptiles. From the frequent deaths of their mates, most of them knew to keep off heavily trafficked roads at night. But small airport runways are generally deserted, and after sunset, when the desert cools quickly, the rattlers crawl by the hundreds onto the warm macadam strips. At Wink, and a number of other airports around, the owners had developed a lucrative second income, harvesting the snakes at night with ten-foot snake poles and selling them live by the pound to meat-packing plants in Dallas and San Antonio. In some parts of Texas, fresh snake meat was still considered a delicacy. But most of it was packed like tuna into cans and shipped to Asia. Once a month, a big semi rolled into Wink and hauled off the rattlers.

The chucklehead gas jockey had a fine time describing to everyone in the pilots' shack how he had scared the balls off another out-of-town pilot. But he had a fraction of decency left. One of the people inside told him that he'd heard about us on the radio, so he too wouldn't let us pay for our fuel either. We were on the freebie roll again, and everyone seemed to be behind our flight now, cheering us toward the mountains. As a makeup gift, the gas jockey gave us several tins of rattler meat.

"Coast to coast, huh?" the gas jockey said. "Well, good luck. Evrabaddy's rootin' for ya."

The heat was up, our height above sea level was now almost 3,000 feet, and it took us forever to get off the runway at Wink. The Cub dismally wallowed in the climb. We were just one hop away from launching for the pass, and we didn't want any extra weight. As soon as we were out of sight, mushing up over the gray-beige desert, we threw the tins of rattler meat out the window.

Now that we had reached the hard desert, we knew that we were supposed to follow one cardinal rule: remain over highways in case the engine acted up. But from Wink we would have to fly all the way back to Pecos to pick up a road. We looked at the map and decided to take a shortcut, flying northwest until we picked up the Pecos River, which we could follow up toward Loving and then into Carlsbad, New Mexico. The midday heat had churned up some low cumulus clouds, which clung to the foothills of the Rockies in the distance, so we would have a decent horizon. We struck out over open desert for Carlsbad.

Kern let me fly, and I was enjoying it, skimming the bottom of the clouds in a Texas sky and ruddering over now and then to look for the Pecos River.

Whabang, Whabang, Whabang, bang, bang, bang, bang, bang, bang! Shit.

What was happening? Violent, irregular vibrations were shaking the plane.

The stick and rudder pedals trembled. The engine cowling up front leapt so violently on its mounts I was afraid that it was going to cut loose and cartwheel into the windshield. The airframe and fabric shook. We were finished, done for, fifty miles from the nearest airport over uninhabited desert, without so much as a dirt road underneath us. It was exactly the situation we had vowed to avoid. Instinctively I throttled back and slowed the plane.

Kern took the controls right away.

"Don't panic Rinker! We've still got an airplane here. Navigate. I want to know our exact position."

He inched the throttle forward and set up a slow flight at about sixty-five miles per hour, and we limped across the desert like that, saving every inch of height for as long as we could, with the front of the Cub banging violently and the floorboards trembling and vibrating underneath us.

We couldn't figure out what was wrong. The rpm on the tachometer was smooth and consistent, the oil pressure and temperature normal. The engine was responding well to the throttle. It was a partial engine failure of some kind, we guessed. Four-cylinder Continentals were famous for their endurance, even with a cylinder out. We knew of pilots who had kept damaged engines running for half an hour or more. But it didn't seem likely that we could make Carlsbad. The plane was shaking even more violently than before, and everything from the altimeter to the windows was rattling. And now the turbulence had picked up too, and it was very difficult to fly it properly in the slowed, vibrating plane. As the nose porpoised up and down, we were very uncomfortable, so drenched with sweat that our shirts were wet, and our hearts pounded along with the plane. While I looked for spots below where we might land, Kern struggled to keep the Cub straight and level and to maintain our altitude. He was ex-

tremely disciplined and levelheaded about that—he didn't
want to lose an inch of altitude until we had decided what to
do.

But it was a nauseating sensation, wallowing along in a
wounded plane like that, and it was hard to resist the urge
to just ditch the plane. It would be a relief, going down in
the desert, and I began to sweat and tremble from that hor-
rible claustrophobia known to pilots and their passengers in
a panic. At any cost, I wanted out of that plane.

"Kern! We can put her down. If we ditch sideways and
wipe out the wheels, we'll be fine."

"No! No Rink. I'm not ditching 71-Hotel. I've got an airplane here. I think we can make Carlsbad."

It was a hellish hour, getting to Carlsbad. But after about
twenty minutes, by making minute adjustments to the throttle and trim, Kern found a kind of queasy, nose-up attitude
that reduced the vibrations and the trembling of the controls.
We were still being kited all over the place by turbulence
but we could stand being in the plane.

But our trip was doomed. I knew that my brother was
thinking the same thing. Every second that we ran the engine
was only damaging it more. Even if we made it to an airport,
we probably couldn't afford the repairs or, more likely, the
new engine we'd need. We'd have to leave the plane in New
Mexico and take a Greyhound bus home. The indignity of
that seemed pathetic. Everybody knew about our trip by
now, and it was going to end just east of the Rockies with
engine failure. And what fools we'd been. Without a radio,
we couldn't call in our position as we went down.

And the waterbag. The fucking waterbag. I looked down
to the hardtack desert below us. I wasn't the least bit worried
about walking out—we both could make the fifty or sixty
miles to Loving, even in our penny loafers. But we probably
wouldn't last until evening without water. Suddenly it
seemed incredibly imbecilic for us *not* to have a waterbag,
and incredibly wise for my father to have suggested one. We
had boxed ourselves into exactly the situation he warned
against. Barnstorming blarney had provided for this contin-
gency, but we hadn't listened.

Whabang, Whabang, Whabang! Sticks and floorboard and baggage compartment thundering, we struggled over the desert.

Making agonizingly slow progress over the scorched and rocky wasteland below, we finally picked up the Pecos River and followed it north into Loving. But it was work, nasty, hot work, all the way. When the big strip at Carlsbad came into view, my brother pushed back his cowboy hat, rested his throttle hand on the instrument panel, and handed me back his Ray-Bans to wipe free of sweat.

"Rink! We're going to make it. We're fucked, but we've made it to an airport."

Waffling onto the runway at Carlsbad, we shut down the engine and coasted into a pile of tumbleweed on the side of the runway. I threw open the door and jumped out to inspect the engine.

As soon as I could see the plane from the outside I started to laugh.

"Kern! It's fine!"

"What?"

"It's just the cowling gasket! It blew off in flight. It's nothing! Just some ripped fabric."

The rubber and asbestos gasket that ran along the underside of the engine cowling and two of its three metal fittings were hanging down to the ground. Those fittings were another casualty of all the turbulence we'd flown the Cub through. In flight, one of the fittings had sprung loose, fell out into the slipstream and sucked the rest of the gasket out. Only one fitting held, and the rest of the assembly dangled out underneath the plane like a kite tail. The banging and vibrations were caused by the heavy metal fittings striking the landing gear and the underside of the plane as we flew along at over sixty miles per hour. The cowling was jumping up and down from the kite-tail effect of the heavy gasket and fittings billowing in the slipstream. This in turn set up secondary vibrations along the rest of the airframe that shook the plane.

The damage was relatively minor—a badly scraped landing gear, and a long, neat tear in the fabric underneath the plane—which we could probably fix ourselves. I was over-joyed that the plane wasn't damaged any more than that. But our assault on the mountains was delayed by at least a day.

But the airport breed, a crop-dusting man, in fact, saved us again. There was a large fleet of Piper Pawnee cropdusters from Seminole, Texas, working out of Carlsbad that week. They were spraying irrigated farms up around Artesia and Roswell. Every night the duster crew staged their planes back at Carlsbad for maintenance and repairs. A four-passenger Cessna-180, stuffed up past the windows with oil, parts, and tools, served as the operation's traveling shop.

When we pulled onto the Carlsbad ramp, dragging the bro-ken gasket along the taxiway underneath us, the crew chief for the crop-dusting operation, a licensed mechanic, was lounging under the wing of the Cessna. He got up and strolled over for a look.

"Lost your gasket, huh?"

"Yeah," my brother said, trying to hide his disappointment.

"Hey," the duster chief said, "Are you them boys flying to California?"

"Well, we're supposed to be," Kern said.

"Jeez, it's a big deal now," the man said. "You're all over the radio. There's a bunch of reporters waitin' for you in El Paso. They called here lookin' for ya."

"I guess they'll have to wait until tomorrow," Kern said. "We've got to get this plane fixed."

"Tomorra? Whad'ya mean, tomorra?" the duster chief said. "It's just a gasket—window dressing, noise abatement, extra weight. On my Pawnees here, I rip 'em off as soon as they come from the factory."

This cheered us some, because a Pawnee was just a recon-figured and enlarged Cub, with a big engine thrown on front and the wings mounted on the bottom instead of the top. Probably this fellow knew what he was talking about.

To prove the point, the duster-chief squatted beneath the cowling, pried off the remaining fitting with a screwdriver, and ceremoniously threw the dismembered gasket across the ramp.

"There," he said. "Now you've got a real airplane."

He looked underneath the Cub, walked over to his shop-plane, and came back with linen fabric tape, coffee cans of dope, and a blowtorch.

"Lookey-here," the duster chief said. "My planes are all up and I don't have a thang to do until tonight. If you boys are still game, I can have this Cub airborne in an hour."

"Really?" Kern exclaimed. "That would be great."

"It's nothing. Go get yourselves some pop."

The duster chief gave the underside of 71-Hotel what he called a "hot patch." His Pawnees were hitting sage brush and hopper trucks all the time, ripping tears in the fabric, and the operation lost too much money if they kept a plane out of the air all day just to patch some fabric and let the dope dry. So he "hot-patched" fabric all the time.

Slapping a length of linen tape over the tear in the fabric and painting on some dope, he gingerly flamed it dry and hard with the blowtorch. Two coats of nitrate, torch it, two coats of butyrate, torch it. He even produced a spray can of official Piper white paint and touched up the patch and the scrapes on the landing gear. When he was done, we couldn't even tell that the plane had been damaged.

"Okeydokey," the duster chief said. "That patch ain't never comin' off. My Pawnees? The hot patches are the strongest part."

That duster chief liked Kern. I could tell from the way the corners of his mouth trembled when he smiled that he got a big charge out of my brother. He couldn't resist a boy this earnest, all sunburn and freckles, the penny loafers and the man's cowboy hat on a boy's head, sticking out like a burro's ears.

"Son," the duster chief said, "Anything else bothering you?"

Kern took off his cowboy hat.

"Well, the engine, sir. We've just really pushed it hard across the desert—all those vibrations and everything. We're going to fly the mountains this afternoon. What do you think?"

"Stand by," the duster chief said. "I'm giving this Cub an annual inspection, right now. Go inside in the shade and relax. I said an hour and I meant it."

Kern was fiddling with the cowboy hat in his hands.

"Ah, well see. I don't think we have enough money for an annual."

"Ah, frig your money son. This is nothing for me. I can do an annual faster than a skunk can piss scent."

We knew a good mechanic when we saw one. If there was anything wrong with the Continental, we were confident that the duster chief would find it.

The duster chief brought his toolbox over from the Cessna and threw open our engine cowling. He pulled all the rocker arm covers, the plugs, and the filters, checking carefully for metal filings and other telltale signs of trouble. He ran compression checks on the cylinders, and went over the magneto ignitions, the wiring, the manifolds, and the carburetor. He didn't like the way the Continental was idling up at these high altitudes, so he propped the engine himself and adjusted the mixture and timing.

We used that time to plan our flight across the pass. It was a Tuesday afternoon, and there weren't any local pilots or geezers around Carlsbad that afternoon. They would have told us that there was one major fault in our plans. We were planning on launching toward a 9,000-foot mountain at the height of density altitude conditions. It was two in the afternoon, when the heat, turbulence, and headwinds were at their worst. We should have waited until evening, or better, the next morning, when a lower sun and cooling temperatures might have given us another 500 or 600 feet of service ceiling. But we didn't think of this ourselves and we were determined to fly as soon as the mechanic was done. It was the worst time of day to do it, a foolhardy moment to attempt our ascent.

Our route of flight was obvious. We could see that we'd pick up the bottom of the Rockies as soon as we took off from Carlsbad. A southwest-running spine of peaks lay just a few miles from the field, and it climbed steeply up toward Guadalupe Peak. As the airport owner back in Sweetwater had told us, the ridge line of the peaks would protect us from the worst winds during our long climb. On the map, the terrain-colorings changed as dramatically as we would have to fly, from the soft beiges and grays of the 4,000-foot desert floor to the ugly smudge of orange and black peaks that rapidly swept up to 9,000 feet. But we would need more than that to safely cross the Pass—10,000, 11,000, even 12,000 feet, whatever we could coax out of 71-Hotel. We knew that we faced a difficult hour of flying, but we weren't raising any objections against ourselves. We'd flown too hard all day to turn away from the mountains now.

The duster chief called us out to the Cub. Everything was fine, he said. The compression on the cylinders was strong and he'd only found one plug that was fouled with oil, ordinary enough on an old Continental engine, and he'd cleaned that and regapped the spark. As we took off and climbed, he said, we'd be surprised by the extra noise. Without the cowl gasket, the engine would roar. But it was only noise and we'd get used to it after fifteen or twenty minutes. In fact, the engine would run a little cooler and better without the cowl-gasket, because more air could get through now.

Kern went for his wallet.

"Look, maybe I should just try and pay you what I can afford. I want to be fair about this."

"Put that away son," the duster chief said. "What you owe me is that mountain. Get across. This trip of yours is gettin' kinda famous. There's people waitin' in El Paso."

It was a wonderful feeling I had for people, the afternoon we launched for the pass. All day, all week in fact, strangers were buying us meals, giving us free tanks of gas, fixing up our plane, and cheering us on west. I was afraid of that peak ahead, and I admit it. But I wanted that mountain now—not for myself, not even for Kern and me together. Everybody had been good to us and expected us to get across, so now we had to pay them back and do this thing.

There's one last memory I have of Carlsbad, New Mexico.

Under the baking sun, with the desert wind pasting my hair
to my perspiring forehead, I stood underneath the tail of 71-
Hotel and held it level to the ground on my shoulders. Kern
was up in front of the wing on a ladder, fueling the tank
himself. He wanted the plane level so that he could squeeze
in every last ounce of fuel. It was only sixty miles to the pass.
But we'd be climbing at full throttle all the way.

Guadalupe.

Looking south from the Carlsbad ramp, I could see the
purple-black rim of mountains towering up toward the peak.
I wasn't going to like it up there one bit, I knew, but then
Kern yelled from the cockpit and it was time to go.

"Contact!"

Kern. Somehow he always got us through. My only choice
now was to grit my teeth and fly, so I threw the prop, ran
around to the back, and strapped myself in.

CHAPTER 15

THE RUNWAY ELEVATION AT CARLSBAD WAS 3,293 FEET ABOVE SEA level. We could see right away what the high altitude conditions and the scorching heat did to 71-Hotel's performance. Wallowing down the sticky macadam, we ate up nearly a third of the runway before we labored into the air. This was not a good omen for our assault on Guadalupe.

The sun at its zenith burned through our glareshield and the engine roared louder than ever through the opening created by the missing gasket. Kern gingerly climbed us up to a safe height above the desert plateau. At 1,000 feet, once he could see that the engine was running smoothly, he hauled back on the stick and hung the plane on its prop. We would need a very high "angle of attack" to climb in this thin, hot air. Uncomfortably nose-high, throbbing with the vibrations of the straining Continental, we would not see over the nose again for more than an hour.

The black wall of the Rockies rose on our right, climbing higher and higher as the range slewed southwest. It presented a tantalizing, maddening barrier. Each time the altimeter bobbled up another few hundred feet, up past 4,000, 6,000, then 8,000 feet, we looked directly out the side and found ourselves nearly level with a conical summit, or a jagged, naked pinnacle of rock. Over the mountain, there was a slice of clear air and we could see to the west. But the sensation of space opening up and the joy of seeing over to the other side was always short-lived. There was always more wall rising ahead of us to the right, black-gray and sandy, with spectacular rock-slides and grotesque outcrops and false ridges that made my mind race. The Rockies were a quandary, both beautiful and cruel. How could mountains be so endlessly enticing to the eye, yet so impassable?

As we climbed we were rifled by the westerlies, which lifted up the right wing and resounded over the fabric like a drum roll. The wind slammed against the far side of the mountain, rocketed straight up and over the peaks and then roiled up thousands of feet more in a magnificent, invisible volcano, depositing down on us its leeward turbulence. We were ascending into a furious eddy of air that stretched all the way down the range. The pounding from the west was so continuous that my brother flew with the right aileron pushed up to keep the wing down, keeping the plane straight with the opposite rudder, so that we climbed in a queasy-feeling slip. The high angle of climb we were forced to main-tain against the steadily thinning air was disorienting. Now I was attacked by the worst kind of vertigo, one of my own mental creation. From his position up front, my brother could still see the peaks out of a portion of his windshield. But my view was almost completely blocked by the pitched-up nose and the downed wing, and I hated the agonizing feeling of a mountain that I couldn't see rising to my side. I was sitting at the bottom of an obtuse triangle that had been turned awkwardly on its side. At the apex, up over my brother's head, there was only clear sky, burned white by the sun. Over my right knee, I looked straight down to the rocks.

But once in a while the wind pounded us hard enough to lift the wing again, and then I could steal a quick glance left into the tepid slipstream. We were inching along the little blacktop highway that paralleled the east face of the moun-tains, down through Carlsbad Caverns, Whites City, and Pine Springs. With the steep climb, the engine developing only two-thirds of its power in the thin air, and the wind pushing us back from the range, our progress was excruciating. At best we made only fifty miles per hour over the ground. And we were alone, completely alone. Everything below us was life- less—hardbed desert on one side, colorless rock on the other. There wasn't even a passing car that I could judge our pro- gress by. We were punishing ourselves and our plane fruit- lessly, it seemed. Our fuel would be exhausted by the climb, leaving nothing for the pass.

Kern didn't seem to notice. As we clawed up in that queer climb, I looked forward to him, perched high above me, al- most over my head. His cowboy hat, nonchalantly pushed back on his head, bumped up against the cockpit struts when- ever we hit turbulence. With his left hand he held the throttle all the way forward in a lock-grip, and with his right hand he kept up the nose with the stick firmly in his lap. I begged him with my racing heart and trembling limbs to feel my agony and discomfort. Then he might level the wings and lower the nose. We could turn back now, before we were inside the mountains and it was too late. My brother did look back several times, quickly, so that he didn't lose control of the plane, flashing that determined half-smile of his. But I didn't want to show him how I felt so I smiled gamely and gave him two thumbs up.

It wasn't simply bravado, or reluctance to betray my cow- ardice to my brother. The sun and the throbbing plane, the mountains rising unseen over my right shoulder, surrounded me in a kind of hallucinogenic chamber, carrying me beyond myself. This was fear becoming spiritual. I wanted that mountain badly, and the pulsating cockpit and the sun were lulling me into a senseless, anesthetized state that blurred out fright.

During that climb, I thought a lot about Saint-Ex and Er- nest Gann again. Nothing in particular in their writings came back to me, and in any case I was too dulled by the throbbing engine and airframe to recall their books clearly. I just thought of Saint-Ex and Gann, the men. They were always scaring the hell out of themselves in airplanes, then coming back down and transforming the experience into meta- physical poetry. They were very candid about their fears in the air. Saint-Ex was even candid about his own death, which he expected at any time. In his last book, *Flight to Arras*, written while he was a fighter pilot during World War II, Saint-Ex analyzed his chances of surviving the war and concluded that they were nil. He prepared himself and his reading public for his inevitable demise by creating the impression that he was indifferent to his fate—no one should even search for him once he was downed. The only purpose in his life had been the existential search for meaning in the air. Dead, there was no point to Saint-Ex anymore. This was prescient enough. Returning from a mission over North Africa in 1943, Saint Ex was jumped from behind by German fighters, who filled his P-38 full of holes before he could lose them. He fell to a watery, unknown grave somewhere in the Mediterranean, and no trace of him or his plane was ever found. Saint-Ex appeared to have willed the ultimate existential act. He had vanished, and the only part of him that was left was his writings. Would he know fear during his last moments? He didn't know. He only knew that he felt resigned to death, thinking about it on the ground.

These were the kind of dreamy, melancholy thoughts I had, inching up to the peak. The effects of the heat, the throbbing of the plane, and the lack of oxygen brought a lot of this on, I suppose, but the worst part was not being able to see out the side. Once we cleared 9,500 feet though, and I could see a clear patch of air for a while, I felt better. The important thing, I told myself, was keeping my head and making myself available if Kern needed any help.

It was chilly, up at 10,000 feet. Neither of us had ever flown a plane that high. Judging the distance from an intersection on the road below, I guessed that we were now approaching Pine Springs and the cut through the mountains. Without asking my brother I reached forward on both sides and pulled shut the windows. It was a shock, closing off that slipstream. The absence of wind blowing over my face only made my vertigo worse, and my arms and legs trembled involuntarily.

At 10,500 feet my brother leveled the wings and the Guadalupe Pass came into view. The pass was an immense **V**, opening up between the twin Guadalupe peaks, more than a mile across at the top. At the summits, black, vertically crenellated sides guarded the opening, but lower down the slopes rounded out and softened to a soothing beige. Rockslides and windblown sand collected in the crevices and overflowed to the valley floor. The ferocious headwinds ripping through the cut blew up a hazy inferno of vapor and dust. We could already feel the first ripples from the wind tunnel ahead—sharp, choppy buffets and powerful, elongated downdrafts.

We were still three miles from the pass, flying a parallel course with the mountains, so that the peaks themselves appeared to us at right angles. Even though our altimeter read above 10,000 feet, which should have put us well above the summits, they still looked higher than we were. At the time I thought that our sideways angle distorted the view, but we later realized that the density altitude conditions contributed to a large altimeter error, by as much as 1,000 feet. In fact, we were still below the peaks. In any case it was an academic question. Though we remained in a climb and we were penetrating an ascending column of air, the Cub was nearly maxed out before we reached the mountains. We would gain only another 900 feet.

When we were directly opposite the big space of hazy air in the middle of the V, my brother hove over 90 degrees, to directly face the pass and the headwind. The wings immediately answered to the force of wind and pushed the nose up even higher. Momentarily leaving the throttle unattended, my brother yanked hard on his seat belt.

"Rink! Pull your harness tight!"

"It's tight!"

"Well pull it harder. Here we go!"

Perhaps we waited three seconds for the first belt of turbulence to hit us. Perhaps it was thirty seconds. But time soon meant nothing. Once it hit, all time ceased.

Whong!

It happened very quickly and violently. One second we were level and facing the pass, squinting down out the sides to see the clear patch of V ahead of us, the next second we were down so hard on the left wing that the tip was pointed straight onto the desert, 90 degrees over. Sky, desert, and mountain wall gyrated around as in a centrifuge. From the force of the blast, our shoulders banged up against the throttle casement and our feet momentarily went weightless off the rudder pedals.

It was a physically arduous thing, getting out of it. My brother lunged forward with the stick to arrest a stall, pushed hard over on the ailerons and rudder, and waited for something to happen. There was no determined half-smile now. He was scrambling up there, fighting G-forces with his arms and legs, to get the plane upright again. But we were now so high, over 11,000 feet on the altimeter, and the force of the blast was so strong, that the controls simply wouldn't answer. In that high, thin air, there literally weren't enough molecules passing over the controls to receive our commands. Our Cub just wasn't meant to be that high. Unbelievably, the wing tucked under even farther, and we hung there motionless and weightless for a few seconds more, suspended on one side and almost inverted, before the plane slowly righted itself.

Damn. We'd lost 300 feet. Kern felt the stick for flying speed and hauled back again on the nose to regain the lost altitude. We had just enough time to catch our breath before the next blast hit.

We were just a fisherman's cork bobber, severed from the line, careening over white water and rocks. The next two miles to the pass were like that, our wings rocking violently over, against which our flimsy controls seemed almost powerless. But by skittering and jockeying the stick sideways in a kind of mad wiggle and dance, my brother kept us tracking straight toward the middle of the pass.

This area just outside the pass was the notorious back quadrant, where the wind racing through the cut had already boiled over itself many times, churning up a wake turbulence on itself. The wind and the air disturbances here are generally worse than within the pass itself. As we got closer to the mountain wall, about a mile off, we began to probe a calmer patch of air. Now the wings were slamming over only 20 or 30 degrees.

I still didn't see how we'd make it. The peaks looming on

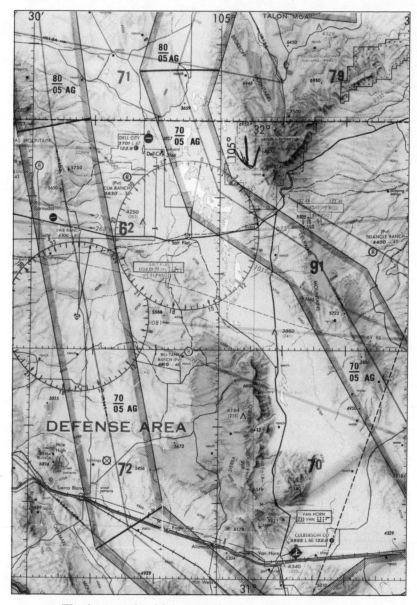

*The deserts, a hard beige and black, stretched monotonously
to the horizons until the walled massif of the Rockies
came into view.*

either side, just ahead, were still above us. The winds and
the downdrafts kept beating us back. Passing 11,500 feet,
Kern dipped the nose a bit to penetrate the headwind and
make some forward progress. Then he hauled back again to

regain the altitude. But as soon as he lifted the nose we got beaten back once more. We were just crawling to the pass, motionless in the headwind, like crabs scrambling up a beach in the intervals of waves, then spinning backward again in the receding surf.

Now the steep sides of the V were clearly visible just ahead of us, a fractured and veined massif of rock sloping up to meet us. In the turbulence, we were often pitched sideways, nose down. The aperture of the pass was quite narrow down below and didn't fill the windshield, so that it didn't seem possible that we could fit through. From these strange, uncontrolled attitudes, immense boulders and broken-toothed pillars of rock came into view, as if they were spinning up sideways to meet us. Individual rocks boldly stood out from the mass—I felt that I could see every pit mark and sandy abrasion. From a distance the pass had a harsh beauty. Closer in, it was ugly and gritty.

Hypoxia, or aeroembolism as the old pilots called it, is oxygen starvation. We had now been flying at 10,000 feet or above for over half an hour, the period of time it normally takes for pilots to feel the effects of oxygen denial. We had been concerned enough about hypoxia while crossing the mountains to discuss it several times before the trip, but it is typical of hypoxia that pilots forget all that they have learned once they are suffering from it. Hypoxia can work oppositely on different pilots. Some pilots become euphoric, swell with a sense of well-being and want to climb their plane even higher. Others turn morose and lethargic and are flooded with panic. As a flying team we were suffering both effects. I was definitely of the darker persuasion. Frightened and claustrophobic in the glassed-in interior of the plane, desperate to see again over the nose, I was boiling and shivering all over at once. Kern up front seemed content, and his smile had returned. He was happy to finally be in the mountains and a calmer patch of air.

Kern never seemed to lose his flying sense either. Fishtailing with the rudders, dipping the nose a bit and then goosing back with the stick, he worked to squeeze out of the plane and the wind every last foot of air.

Now it didn't matter how either of us felt. We were inside
the pass, and the edge of the mountain range on either side
of us had disappeared. Ahead we could only see burned white
sky, ugly walls of sand, and black veined rock. North and
south had ceased to exist; there was just an east-west hole in
the rock. We couldn't turn back now, because the walls looming up on either side of us were too close, denying us a turning radius. And if we'd given up the wind on our nose, we
would immediately have plunged to the rocks.

That final entry into the pass was a hallucinogenic blur for
me. There was so much heat and noise in the cockpit, the
glareshield above my head looked too hot to touch, and now
the walls on either side of the pass tumbled up, quite close.
There were moments when I looked out and the twin peaks
were more or less level with us, and other moments when we
were in a downdraft and they disappeared above the top of
the wing. I felt exhausted, wanting to cry, but not wanting
to, overwhelmed by a desire to escape into sleep.

I'd read about this, too, in war books, and Robert L. Scott
in *God Is My Co-pilot* had written about it. In the middle of
the worst combat mission he'd ever flown, or struggling to
hoist an overloaded DC-3 over the Himalayas, suddenly he
would be overwhelmed by the urge just to give up and fall
off to sleep.

Yet with panic arrived a great inner calm and resignation.
My father and my brother had been too cavalier about this.
It wasn't safe taking on the Rocky Mountains in an 85-horse
Cub. So what? Cratering into the walls would be immensely
pleasurable right now. I wouldn't fight it, and the experience
would be interesting, extrasensory, even. In a hurry, it would
end this misery of light-headed, claustrophobic flight.

I was startled awake from this torpid fatalism by my brother
calling back.

"Rinker! Take the controls."

"What?"

"Take the stick! It's your airplane! My arms have given
out. I can't hold it up anymore."

My heart must have doubled its output just then, because
I was instantly awake. Kern needed me to fly, and I was

overjoyed to be able to do so, as if I been thrown a life-rope. Gaining control of the plane, I knew, would revive me.

I grabbed the stick in my lap, wiggling it and the rudders a bit to show him that I had the plane. He immediately stretched out his arms and cracked his knuckles, then began massaging his muscles. Clutching the struts over his head, he leaned forward over the instrument panel and peered out to the walls of the pass.

"I'm going to keep a real careful eye on these peaks," Kern yelled back. "You fly."

I was shocked by what I found. I caressed the controls forward and back to feel the play of air over the wings. There was almost nothing there. In that high air, we were flying just a few miles an hour above the stall. The great wind on our nose was the only thing holding us up.

We flew that way through the rest of the pass. It could have been six minutes, or twelve, or twenty. It doesn't matter. Time had disappeared. I fought the turbulence and the downdrafts and kept the wings level, and didn't give up an inch of height. I was fixated on altitude, an antidote for my hypoxia, or maybe a symptom of it. When my brother handed me the plane, the altimeter read 11,600 feet, and I was determined not to lose a foot.

"Eleven-six."

That was my mantra. Eleven-six. I wasn't going to give an inch back to this mountain.

"Eleven-Six," I kept repeating to myself, drunk on those numbers.

I constantly peered forward to the altimeter on the instrument panel up front, whacking my brother on his shoulder when he let it get in the way. The little hand on the dial couldn't move off that *6*, and when it did, I wiggled and fishtailed and nudged the stick to move the nose into better wind, to get us back up.

"Eleven-Six. Eleven-Six. Eleven-Six."

My other fixation was my throttle hand. There was only one place for the throttle to be—all the way forward. I braced my arm in a lock-grip against it and never once relaxed the pressure.

It was an odd, wondrous experience, flying like that. Kern had handed the plane over to me, so matter of factly. Now we were so nose-high that he was perched almost directly on top of me, as if I were following him up a ladder. I didn't worry at all about our position against the peaks because I could see him peering attentively from side to side. He was alert, in control, and I was gratified every time he showed the slightest movement, because it showed that he wasn't keeling over from hypoxia, which would have left me all alone with the plane. He gave me hand signals from the instrument panel, or reached back and squeezed my legs, steering me left or right as we crawled past the outcrops inside the pass. He was the eyes, and I was the flying arms and legs. With him riding above me like that, and the throbbing, pulsating plane and the winds, I was an Atlas holding the whole works up, hoisting us over the pass.

I was very confident too, and all dangerous, indolent thoughts of cratering into the sides left me. We could easily make the rest of the pass, flying this way. There was still a lot of flying to do, and turbulence to fight, but I was euphoric about our progress so far and the rest of the challenge, now that there was some adrenaline flowing from me to the plane.

I was still deprived of vision and couldn't see much. All I was doing, really, was staring straight up over Kern's head to polarized sky, and fixating on the altimeter and Eleven-Six. I coordinated the stick entirely by seat-of-the-pants feel and the altimeter and airspeed indicator. I couldn't see the sides of the pass anymore because the angle of the wings was too high, blocking my view out the side. But I trusted Kern up front to correctly judge our distance from the walls. With tran-scendent happiness and belief, I just hung on and flew Eleven-and-Six.

Eleven-and-six. Eleven-and-six. I held it for as long as I thought I could stand it, but still we weren't through the pass yet and I held it some more. My arms were starting to hurt but I didn't want to give up the plane until I absolutely had to. The far-side turbulence was supposed to be awfully bad too, and I wanted Kern fresh and rested for that. That cheered me some too, because I realized I was suffering the effects of hypoxia but I still had enough left to think.

Buffet-jolt, buffet-jolt, wham-wham-wham. This was very different turbulence now, unique, very choppy and quick, with violent sideways movement that shook the stick. Good. I never welcomed a spot of bad air so much, because this meant that we were beginning to hit the rotor turbulence on the far side.

I could do this for another minute, I thought. Summoning that last ounce of strength beyond all strength, I flexed my muscles against the throttle and the stick and counted to sixty.

"Kern! Are we through?"

"Just about! Just about."

"All right! Listen, take back the plane."

"It's my airplane!"

My body cracked with relief. My throttle arm was as hard as cast iron and there were spasms and coils in my shoulders and hips, from the mental and physical tension of holding up the plane. But there wasn't any room in that tiny cockpit to stretch myself out, so I just sat there like a scarecrow in the wind, bobbing and jerking on a stick.

We had enough presence of mind to remain high for another ten minutes. If we tried to descend through the hellgate of air on the windward side, the violent downdrafts would suction us back into the mountain. So we just hung up there as long as we could stand it, bong, bong, bong, bong in that awful air, Eleven-Six, Eleven-Six, hating with every bone in our bodies the God who made mountains. But I was mentally at rest, now that I knew we were past the peaks and that my brother had the plane. I closed my eyes and leaned my head on the window railing, exhausted and physically drained but satisfied with myself. I waited for the calm air to return and the sound of the engine idling as my brother let us down.

Finally, gulping in air as we fell, we dove for oxygen and the desert floor on the far side. It was a visual relief to finally be able to see out through the windshield and the side windows, and I realized that I must have dozed off for a few minutes as Kern held us up through the rotors. We were clear of the mountains now.

In the desert just beyond the pass there were shallow salt flats filled with water, a blue meringue shining under the sun, stretching north and south. Tiny white caps and gently swirling pools lapped up against sand, an exotic, bizarre marine display after so much time staring at desert and hard rock. The air above the liquid flats was cool, and it cleared our heads. Over desolate mesquite country, we steered due west for El Paso, seventy miles away.

We were immensely contented now, enjoying the kind of deep, peaceful sense of well-being that is nourished by delivery from danger and fatigue. The big barrier, the only real obstacle that stood between us and the Pacific, had been crossed. Since November, and more intensely since May, I had worried about the Rockies. I didn't see how we could possibly cross them in a Piper Cub. Now we'd finally done it, even if I couldn't account for the aerodynamics of it. We were done and through, and there was no further need to figure it carefully and subject our crossing to logical analysis. It wasn't logical at all, in fact it was downright irrational, what we'd just accomplished. I would never know how close we came to killing ourselves getting through that pass, because my side vision wasn't adequate enough to judge that. Maybe we flew the mountains perfectly, maybe not so well. But none of that really mattered now because we were whole, on the far side. The gateway to California had been breached. I was overjoyed that it was behind us.

The country was changing again. The blacks and hard yellows of the high desert were giving way to the tessellated ochers and painted sands of the low desert on the western side of the Rockies. The country was falling toward the ocean again. The flying was easy and Kern shook the stick when we came up on a ranch, and I took the plane and dropped down to buzz the cows.

El Paso rose out of the desert like an emerald. Glittering roofs, green lawns and yucca trees were framed by the graceful, sweeping oxbow of the purple Rio Grande. It was the first habitation of any size we'd seen since Pittsburgh.

Our fuel cork was riding on EMPTY again, but we felt inured to worry now. We had the windows open and all the way across the mesquite I kept glancing back over the tail to the fading wall of the Rockies and the two peaks guarding the pass, until they disappeared into the blue meringue of water on the salt flats.

Guadalupe. Before that day I always thought of Exupéry and Ernest Gann, and the early airmail pilots who flew the pass, as distant, heroic figures, brave men who conquered peaks. They seemed very aloof to me and I could never emulate them. Now I felt closer to them all, and I had learned something else. It wasn't bravery. Bravery isn't what it's cracked up to be. They were just stubborn, that's all, and afterward they were very tired.

CHAPTER 16

As we taxied in at the busy general aviation airport at El Paso, an anxious knot of reporters and cameramen jostled near the pumps. All across Texas, the geezers and the gas jockeys had said, "You're on the radio." But we didn't expect a reception as big as this. As we shut down the engine, microphones on booms came orbiting in through our open windows and photographers were fighting for position up by the prop. There were a few newspaper reporters there, but these were mostly TV people, scrappy and full of elbows. They all shouted into the cockpit at once.

"How do you feel?"

"Boys! Yo! Can you tell us how you feel?"

That was the thing about broadcasters that we would learn. Facts? They were incidental. First, everyone wanted to know how we *felt*.

In fact, we felt terrible. Our faces and arms were burnt brick-red, our heads ached from hypoxia hangover, and our seatbelt welts chafed. I wasn't happy to see this swarm of reporters, crowding around the plane and banging their cameras on the fabric. But Kern didn't seem to mind. The trip so far had been a jumble of new landscapes and events. Swale to river, prairie to desert, rattlers to mountain pass, and all of

```
22

2423
     PLANE 7/7 BA
   EL PASO, TEX. (UPI)--TWO TEEN-AGED BROTHERS FROM NEW JERSEY,
WHO COULD BE CALLED AIR PIONEERS IN REVERSE, LANDED AT INTERNATIONAL
AIRPORT AT NOON THURSDAY IN A TINY PRE-WORLD WAR II PIPER CUB.
   THEY REBUILT THE 23-YEAR-OLD PLANE AND ARE FLYING IT TO LOS
ANGELES.
   KERN BUCK, 17, AND RINKER BUCK, 15, SEEMED AS UNCONCERNED
ABOUT THE TRANSCONTINENTAL FLIGHT IN THE TINY 90-HORSEPOWER CUB
AS IF THEY WERE ON A HOP ABOUT THEIR LOCAL AIRPORT.
   "WE HAVE LOST A FEW BOLTS AND NUTS AND HAD A LITTLE DIFFICULTY
LANDING AT ABILENE, TEX., WHEN AN ELEVATOR SPRING BROKE," KERN
SAID.
   "WE GOT DOWN OKAY THOUGH, AND FIXED IT OURSELVES."
   KERN HAS A PRIVATE PILOT'S LICENSE WITH 140 HOURS FLYING TIME
AND IS WORKING TOWARD A COMMERCIAL LICENSE.
   "THE CUB IS A 1943 MODEL WITH A SLIGHTLY LARGER ENGINE THAN THE
ORIGINAL," HE SAID. "WE SPENT ALL WINTER REBUILDING AND RECOVERING
IT AND PUT 17 COATS OF DOPE ON THE FABRIC AND ONLY FINISHED THE JOB
JUST BEFORE WE LEFT."
   THE YOUNG AVIATORS LEFT NEW YORK LAST SATURDAY AND EXPECT TO
LAND AT LOS ANGELES JULY 9. KERN SAID HEADWINDS ON THE TRIP HAD
KEPT THEIR AVERAGE SPEED TO 90 MILES PER HOUR.
   THEIR ROUT WAS FROM NEW YORK TO HARRISBURG AND PITTSBURGH,
PA., THEN TO COLUMBUS, OHIO; INDIANAPOLIS, ST. LOUIS, MEMPHIS,
LITTLE ROCK, DALLAS, AND ABILENE BEFORE EL PASO. THEY LEAVE
E
 L PASO O

   THEIR ROUTE WAS FROM NEW YORK TO HARRISBURG AND PITTSBURGH,
PA., THEN TO COLUMBUS, OHIO; INDIANAPOLIS, ST. LOUIS, MEMPHIS,
LITTLE ROCK, DALLAS, AND ABILENE BEFORE EL PASO. THEY LEAVE
EL PASO ON FRIDAY.
   THEIR SINGLE-ENGINE PLANE HAS ONLY TWO SEATS. THEIR FATHER IS
ALSO A PILOT.
      E-JT842PCS..
```

it had worked a magic on his character. He was ready to meet the press.

Without really trying, Kern was a dreamboat for those reporters. Earnest as a novitiate, blushing all over when he flashed that broad smile of his, he was a natural for the cameras. (Later, my mother complained that I was always "scowling" in the news photos, while Kern, she thought, had "the nicest smile.") Neither of us understood what the fuss was all about. As far as we were concerned, we were just two kids from New Jersey, pursuing our own private dream. But these reporters seemed determined to turn our flight into a national hullabaloo. We were genuinely surprised and caught off guard by all this attention, and that contributed a lot to the naïve, aw-shucks attitude we projected. The reporters loved it. America was a different place then and all the heroes had crew cuts, platinum-blond wives and drove Corvettes. The media was devoted to this cult of innocence and that is what they hoped to find in us.

"Rink, look at these guys out here," Kern muttered under his breath as we climbed out of the plane. "They're going nuts for us."

"Yeah. What are we supposed to be, the astronauts?"

"Are you Kernahan Buck?" one of the reporters yelled.

"That's me."

"Mr. Buck! How do you feel?"

"We're fine fellas," Kern said, pulling on his cowboy hat and shaking hands all around. "Real fine. Hi, I'm Kern Buck. I'm glad to meet you."

The three network affiliates in El Paso, the ABC, CBS, and NBC local stations, had each sent a crew. They clutched wire service bulletins on our flight and an article from the *El Paso Times* announcing our expected arrival. One of the stations had brought along their anchorman, a tall, blond Adonis in a tan polyester suit, primping himself in a little mirror before he stepped up with his mike. The other stations had elected to narrate over their footage back at the studio. Even before we landed, the TV crews were fighting over us. The station that had brought its anchor thought that they were entitled to interview us first, which the other two stations didn't think was fair.

Kern dove right in. Something had happened to him over that mountain back there. I was amazed by his easy familiarity with the press.

"Hey, guys, whoa, relax," Kern said. "We just flew this little Cub over the mountains, and we're tired. You can't fight over us, okay? Everybody will get their interview, I promise. Right now, I have to go inside."

"Wait!" several reporters yelled at once. "You can't go inside yet. We have to do the interview!"

"Guys," Kern said, "I gotta go inside. I need a toilet, bad."

Haw! Everybody roared with laughter and started taking furious notes. No detail, apparently, was beyond their interest.

As we stepped inside the small airport terminal, one of

the reporters handed us his pile of wire copy and clips. We locked ourselves in the men's room, sat on the toilets in adjoining stalls, and read our press. When Kern was done with each clip, he handed it to me through the bottom of the toilet stall.

It was astonishing, confronting ourselves in print for the first time, reading all the palaver that had been published already, most of it lifted out of the original *Indianapolis Star* story and quotes from my father. Wire-service writers who had never even interviewed us perpetuated the Jack-and-Bobby motif, calling us a pair of "Kennedy knockoffs." In another story, we were "air pioneers," and "diffident about our exploits." In the age of the Kennedys and the astronauts, diffidence was greatly prized and it was an angle to play up, even if it was total horseshit. According to United Press International, "The Buck boys seem as unconcerned about their transcontinental flight in a tiny 85-horsepower Cub as if they were on a hop around the local airport."

The silliest malarkey, of course, originated with my father. It was obvious from the articles that he was carefully managing the coverage from home, the way he ran one of his political campaigns, sitting up all night in his library with both phones busy. He was the one keeping the Kennedy fantasy alive. One of the reporters had asked my father what "inspired" our trip. " 'The boys never forgot John Kennedy's inaugural address,' said their proud father, Tom Buck. 'Ask not what your country can do for you, but rather what you can do for your country.' "

The virtuous appeal of two boys from a large Irish-Catholic family was another reliable theme. It was the original "family values" pitch and my father knew just how to milk it.

"We think it's far better to have the kids attracted to wholesome adventures like flying," he sermonized in one article, "than have them running off to discotheques in Greenwich Village."

"Ah Jesus Kern," I said, talking through the bottom of the toilet stall. "I think I'm going to puke. Better than a discotheque? What *is* a discotheque?"

"Yeah!" Kern said. "I never told Daddy I was inspired by John Kennedy's inaugural address. I completely forgot that Kennedy ever said that stuff."

"Yeah. Probably even Kennedy forgot about it. Some speechwriter like Daddy makes up all that crap."

The strange thing was, I was supposed to be the cutup and ham in the family, outgoing with strangers. But I didn't want to deal with the reporters. Kern was very comfortable with the press coverage, however, and immediately understood what it meant.

"Rink, look," he said. "Daddy's going to eat this stuff up back at home. This is great for him. Let's just spoon-feed these guys whatever they want to hear."

"Yeah. No problem Kern. Just shovel the Kennedy shit."

Now that we were over the mountains, nothing bothered us, and we were determined to enjoy ourselves. We agreed that Kern would handle all the reporters while I found a motel. We were both exhausted and ached all over from the ride through the pass, and we couldn't bear the thought of sleeping outside with the plane.

"And none of this Motel Cheap stuff either Rinker," Kern said. "Splurge! Luxury accommodations."

Kern was in a joyful, buoyant mood. As we walked back through the airport lounge, several pilots came up to us, clapped us on the back and shook our hands. Kern cocked his cowboy hat back on his head, laughed, and shook hands all around.

"Rink, I just can't get over this," he said. "Everybody thinks this is such a big deal."

He pushed through the glass doors and went out to face the reporters. His gait was stiff from flying the deserts all day, and his arms and the back of his neck were so burned it was painful just to look at him. But he was glowing all over, cocksure and game, elated to be over the mountains. I never forgot that image of him from behind, through the glass doors. The sun was glinting off his cowboy hat and throwing bright splashes of yellow and purple off his paisley belt. Here in El Paso, he was a completely different person.

Along the wall of the pilots' lounge there was a bank of

phones beneath plastic-embossed color posters depicting several local motels. Apparently El Paso was a popular tourist destination, with everything ordered for convenience. When I found a motel that I liked, all I had to do was pick up the phone, and a clerk on the other end of the line answered right away and took the reservation. I chose a motel that featured pictures of beautiful women in bikinis lounging by the pool, lavish meals served by chefs in white hats, and a loving, affectionate couple propped up by pillows in a king-sized bed, smoking cigarettes and watching color TV. Color TV was a must, I decided. We still didn't have color TV at home. When I picked up the phone and made the reservation, the clerk promised to send out a motel van right away.

When I got back out to the plane, Kern was jauntily leaning on the propeller with his cowboy hat perched high, posing for pictures and answering all the reporters' questions. The reporters weren't interested in the technical aspects of the flight, factors like the weather, the turbulence, or getting over the Rockies. Mostly all they wanted was a bunch of hooey—how my father had taught us to fly, how we decided to "relive" his youth, what my mother had to say about all this. We caught up with a lot of those stories written after the El Paso press conference a couple of days later, in local papers in Arizona. It was all baloney, some of it very rancid baloney. If Kern and I failed to say what the reporters wanted to hear, they just dialed up my father and got him to say it.

"Kern and Rinker have always been affectionate and close," my father lied in one of those articles. "In a family of eleven children, you learn to care."

Jesus, Mary, and Joseph. Almost anything could get into a newspaper. But I didn't understand the point yet, and I wouldn't for years. Jack Kennedy was dead, and we still hadn't gotten over that. The tragedy of Vietnam was unfolding. The country was rocked to its foundations by the civil rights struggle and student protests. America just wanted a good dose of innocence that summer and we perfectly fit the bill. The Jack-and-Bobby look-alikes bouncing out to California in their homemade Piper Cub was a heartwarming tale for the masses.

Besides, Kern gave very entertaining interviews, in his dumbass, silly old way. He was a total greenhorn but didn't seem to know it.

After the interviews, the TV reporters wanted to do a voice-over shot of Kern and me looking at our map laid flat over the tail of the Cub. While the cameras were rolling, one of the reporters yelled out.

"Boys! Where are you headed next?"

We looked on the map, which happened to be the Phoenix sectional. It was obvious that we'd have to make a fuel stop at a place called Tucson, Arizona. Neither of us had ever heard of Tucson before. Kern stabbed Tucson on the map with his finger, and stared straight into the cameras.

"Tucks-on," he said. "That's where we're headed next. Tucks-on, Arizona."

Haw! The reporters couldn't believe it, and everybody started to howl with laughter and furiously scribble on their notepads. Here were these two kids from Nu Jursa, peddlin' across America in their penny loafers, in a Piper Cub without a radio, and the dumb little shits didn't even know how to pronounce Tucson.

But Kern was on a roll and he wasn't stopping. Another reporter yelled out.

"And what's after that—what's your route of flight?"

We checked the map again, and it looked like this small city right along the border with Mexico, Yuma, was another logical stop. From there, it was just a hop, skip, and jump across the Salton Sea into southern California. Kern smiled again into the camera.

"Yumma," he said. "After Tucks-on, we'll land at Yumma."

Haw! The reporters laughed their asses off, and they had their angle now. *The Beverly Hillbillies* fly coast to coast. They all howled again when we did the Brakes, Throttle, Contact! routine and taxied the plane over to the tie-downs. I could see them shaking their heads as we taxied off. Jesus. These tykes actually made it over the Rockies in that crate.

Our van arrived. As we were piling in with our pillowcases and our bag of maps, the television crews were loading their gear into their own vans. Watch at 5:30, they said. You'll be on the local news.

We dawdled, getting back to the motel. The van driver was a nice fellow and he insisted on giving us the VIP tour of El Paso. We liked that low-slung, antiquated city out on the far edge of Texas. The driver showed us the big cattle yards and auction hall, the railhead, the iron bridges crossing the river into Mexico, and the adobe Old Town. Everybody drove around in dented pickups and wore Stetsons or sombreros. El Paso was very slow-paced and twangy, and we were starting to relax.

"Here, just take the key," the man behind the desk at the motel said. "We'll check you in later. Room 19. And run! They just said on TV that you're coming up next, right after the commercial."

Clutching our pillowcases, we ran down the flagstone walk and past the blue swimming pool. Halfway down to Number 19, a room door was wide open and the color television set blared. Filling up the screen—cowboy hat, blue button-down shirt, white Levi's, Ray-Ban case on the paisley belt—was Kernahan Buck. We pulled up short and watched from the open door.

"Well, the only tough part was crossing the Rocky Mountains," Kern was saying on the screen. "But, obviously, we made it."

Kern looked great on color television. I'd only seen one or two color TVs so far, mostly on display at the Sears Roebuck store. I couldn't get over how realistic the picture was.

Inside the room, on one bed, was a man with a big smoky cigar, a flattop haircut, and heavy, lace-up logger's boots. On the other bed, propped up with pillows, were two attractive women, a blond and a brunette, a lot younger than the man.

"Hey, girls, get a load of this!" the man said. "These two boys from New Jersey are flying a Cub, coast to coast."

The people in the room looked very friendly and we didn't want to miss any more of Kern on color television, so we just edged through the door to watch.

"Ah, excuse me," Kern said. "Do you mind if we see this?"

"Sure, be my guest," the man said, waving his cigar in the air. "These two goddam little kids, see, they're flying a Piper Cub coast to coast."

"Yeah," Kern said. "We are those kids."

"Well Jesus H. shit!" the man bellowed, blowing out a huge cloud of cigar smoke.

The fellow looked to the TV. Cowboy hat, blue shirt and white pants, Ray-Bans on the paisley belt. Then he looked to Kern in the doorway. Cowboy hat, blue shirt, white pants, Ray-Bans on the belt.

"Well I'll be damned," he said.

The women on the bed clapped their hands and squealed.

"Everybody quiet!" the man barked. "We'll watch this, and then we'll talk."

So we stood there in somebody else's smoky room, with the women on the bed giggling behind us, watching ourselves on TV. The segment on us only lasted a minute or so. They showed the interview with Kern, the Brakes, Throttle, Contact! routine and, of course, the "Tucks-on" and "Yumma" gaffe. Kern looked great on the air, but when the cameras panned to me, I hated myself. My nose was too big and my voice, when I yelled "Contact!" broke into an embarrassing falsetto.

When it was all over everybody exploded off the beds and made a fuss over us. The man, barrel-chested and a fast, hearty talker, stepped over and pumped our hands. He waved his cigar as he talked.

"Girls, get a goddam load of this, wil'ya? These are the boys! Jesus H. Christ. Congratulations fellas! Coast to coast in a frigging Piper Cub. You got a radio in that thing son?"

"No radio," Kern said.

"Shit! That's even better!"

That is how we met Robert Warren Pate, a glorious headcase of a man, and the find of the trip.

He was a flyer himself, he said, a former Stearman man and a B-52 jockey for the Air Force. He'd flown out from his home near Sacramento, California, just this week in the fam-

Robert Warren Pate, a glorious headcase of a man, and the find of the trip.

ily Cessna. Today, they'd all been flying around the Guadalupe Mountains themselves, taking pictures.

Pate's story was as improbable as his appearance, which, when he pulled on his rumpled Stetson and stood tall in his

247

logger's boots, gave him a *Treasure of Sierra Madre* look. He was a poet and a songwriter and a self-educated archaeologist, a retired Air Force pilot and rocket scientist whose exploits, according to him, had been reenacted in several movies and books. John Wayne, he said, had played him in one movie; Steve McQueen was looking at the next one. Now, at forty-three, he was retired from all that and making a living hunting buried treasure. His exploits sounded stunning. Had we ever heard of Drake's Cave along the coast of northern California? Well, he was the one who found it. Montezuma's Lost Treasure in the Guadalupe Mountains? He knew where that was too. Did we know there was billions of dollars worth of silver and gold buried up on Guadalupe? We'd flown right over it, practically. He'd tell us about it over dinner.

The women were beautiful and petite, the perfect foil for Pate's gruff front. Ellen, Pate's wife, was compact and athletic, with a pageboy bob of brown hair, freckles, and a broad, pert smile. She bounded right across the room and gave Kern a bear hug. Elsa, Ellen's younger sister, belonged on a Beach Boys album cover. She was tall and very blond and bouncy, with a bashful, seductive smile, and piercing blue eyes. After Ellen was done with him, Elsa crashed into Kern and gave him a long sexy embrace.

"Congratulations!" she said to Kern. "You look great on TV!"

"Gee, thanks!" Kern said. "Ah, excuse me, what's your name?"

"Elsa."

"Well hi Elsa. I'm Kern. Kern Buck."

Ellen and Elsa began hugging Kern and planting kisses on his cheek, stepping back with their hands on their hips to size him up. Kern stood there with his arms spread wide, smiling and laughing, enjoying the attention he was receiving from these women.

I was pissed about it. This always happened to me around Kern. Women always fell head-over-heels for the shy, vulnerable type, Kern, and treated me like a doormat. Besides, we'd just been on TV, and these great-looking California girls were interested in the pilot, not the navigator. I was being ignored, over in the corner.

Hey, Elsa, I thought, come on over here and give me one of those hugs.

Elsa finally did come over, stood about three yards off, and politely shook my hand.

Pate lit another cigar and cleared the room.

"Jesus, women. Stop slobbering over these goddam boys. Let 'em get cleaned up and take a shower. We're all going to dinner."

When we got into the motel room, Kern stripped down and changed into his swimming trunks.

"Rink," he said, "You know what I want to say to you about this trip?"

"No, what?"

"Well, on the phone, you've really handled Daddy like an ace. I admire that. I don't want him to get into the habit of always talking to me first. While I take a swim, you call home."

What the hell. He was the pilot-in-command.

So, I dialed home, collect, for the El Paso gam. When my father picked up he already knew where we were. More reporters had called. He was relieved that we had made it safely over the mountains and exultant when I told him that Kern had given me the controls halfway through the pass. That was such a "good" thing for Kern to do, my father said, typical of his generosity toward me. This annoyed me, because it had nothing to do with Kern's generosity. His freaking arms gave out.

"Hey, how's the waterbag?" my father asked.

"Ah shit Dad."

"Rinker. Did you just say shit?"

"No. I didn't say shit."

"No. I heard it. You said shit."

"Dad. I didn't say shit. It's probably a bad connection or something."

"Goddamit Rinker. Stop saying shit."

"Dad. I did not say shit. I said, 'It's it.' "

"It's it?"

"Yeah. It's it. The waterbag. It's right here in the room."

"The waterbag? In the motel room? What's the waterbag doing in the motel room? And don't bullshit me. You just said shit. To your father."

"I didn't say shit."

"Bullshit. You said shit. And you just said shit."

"Shit."

"Ah Jesus Rinker, stop saying shit. What if your mother was listening in?"

"If Mother was listening in, she'd hear me say shit."

"Ah Jesus. Stop saying shit, wil'ya? Mother could be listening in."

"Good. Then she'll blame you, for teaching me to say shit."

"You see? You just said shit. Again. You said shit."

"Shit."

"Ah shit. Rinker, you're saying shit."

"Shit."

"Stop saying shit!"

"Shit."

"Rinker, you are not to say shit to your father. Do you understand?"

"Shit."

"Ah shit."

"Hey, Dad, shit. Okay? Shit. Shit, shit, shit, shit. I mean, I am fifteen years old. We have just flown eight hundred miles across Texas and made it over the Guadalupe Pass and you are yelling at me because I said shit. Well, shit. I mean, you know, shit. Shit, shit, shit, shit. If I want to say shit I am going to say shit. Got it? From now on, I say shit whenever I want to. It's better than this 'Ask not what your country can do for you' shit."

"Ah shit Rinker. Don't talk to me this way. You're spoiling everything, and saying shit."

"Shit. Shit, shit, shit, shit, shit. Okay? Don't tell me not to say shit."

"Ah shit."

"Yeah . . . shit."

"Why are we fighting like this?"

"I don't know. Shit."

"Where's Kern?"

"Swimming."

"Well, go get him. I want to talk to someone responsible."

"Ah shit Dad. Let's just let him swim."

Robert Pate saved me from this infinite regress of shit. In the middle of my twenty-fourth shit, he came sailing through the door without knocking, carrying a large thermos of lemonade, glasses, and ice. He poured a glass for both of us.

From the looks of him, Pate was no Pillsbury Doughboy. I'd already heard him say shit several times, so I knew that he wasn't going to mind that. He knew a phone call gone south when he walked in on one. He yanked the phone from my hand and cupped his palm over the mouthpiece.

"Name?"

"Tom. Tom Buck."

"Tom?" Pate began. "Tom Buck? Well listen here, this is Robert Warren Pate. My wife and I are just having the time of our lives out here with your wonderful boys."

Pate had the touch. He told my father that he was an old Stearman man, that he'd flown B-52s and practically every other plane the Air Force ever had, and designed half the rocket systems too. This kind of information about a man tended to relax my father. They were perfect together on the phone, two old Stearman men and grand bullshitters, comparing notes on World War II military flying.

Pate told my father that he'd keep an eye on us and show us the southern route into California which, he assured my father, he knew better than his "wife's ass." The waterbag came up, Pate picked up on that instantly, and he hurled my father a monstrous bag of dung on that subject, making it sound as if we had the goddam thing. My father was worried about another thing. He wanted us to lay over and rest for a day in El Paso. Pate said that he would take care of that too. By the time they hung up I could hear my father laughing on the other end of the phone, happy that we were now in the hands of a great old Stearman man.

Pate leaned back in the chair and blew a few smoke rings. I liked the man, right away. He reminded me a lot of this crazyass priest we had back at school, Father Lucien.

"Shit, hunh?" Pate said.

"Yeah, shit, Mr. Pate."

"Robert. Call me Robert, son."

"Shit, Robert."

"Yeah, well, shit, I know what you mean son. I got out of Missouri when I was sixteen years old. We were dirt farmers, poor. It was the middle of the Depression. You know what one of the last things I ever said to my father was?"

"No, what?"

"Shit. That's all there was left to say. Shit."

"Yeah," I sighed. "Shit. I try and get along with my father, you know, but sometimes . . ."

"Hey, stop worrying about your dad, all right?" Pate said. "I cheered him up good. He's happier than shit right now. This kind of thing happens on a big trip and you can't let it get to you. Right now, we should concentrate on having some fun."

"All right Robert."

I told Pate not to bring up the one-day layover, because Kern was dead-set against it. Probably, we'd just fly into Arizona tomorrow, and then call home and tell my father that we were still in El Paso.

"Don't say a word," Pate said. "I'll handle it."

The Pates were tired from flying all day too, so we ate in the motel dining room. In the booth, I got wedged in between Pate and Ellen, and Kern and Elsa sat together on the other side. All through dinner, while Pate regaled us with some great barnstorming blarney, Elsa was mooning over Kern and paying him compliments, telling him what a great pilot he was. Kern smiled bashfully and blushed right through his sunburn. It was an awful waste of a woman, I thought, stashing Elsa over there with Kern, but there wasn't anything I could do about that now so I just sat there and enjoyed my chicken-fried steak, listening to Pate's incomparable tales.

During dessert, Elsa put her arm around Kern's shoulder. "Kern," she said. "We had a fight with Robert today, up in the plane. He doesn't like the way we take pictures for him."

"Gee, that's too bad," Kern said.

"Well, not really," Elsa said. "Ellen and I are on strike now. We're not flying with Robert tomorrow. We're just going to hang out by the pool. Stay with us, just one day. You need a rest. You're going to make it to California, easy, by the end of the week."

Elsa had her nails dug lightly into Kern's shoulder and she was dangling a spoon over the rim of a glass, making tingling sounds on the ice.

"Oh sure Elsa," Kern said. "I mean, yeah. We're laying over a day in El Paso. All along, that's been the plan."

CHAPTER 17

IN THE MORNING, PATE LEFT THE MOTEL AT DAWN TO GO FLYING.
Throughout the 1960s, he spent most of the summer in El
Paso, taking off every day for photo-recon missions out over
the Guadalupe Range. Over the winter, back in Sacramento,
he analyzed the pictures. He was convinced that he could
locate the site where the fabulous treasure of the Montezuma,
the last Aztec emperor, had been buried in the mountains in
the sixteenth century. As a matter of fact, he had already
stumbled across the site, once, but then lost it, which we
would learn more about that night. Before he left that morning, Pate told Ellen and Elsa to open up a restaurant tab for
us and make sure that we enjoyed a relaxing day.

It was balmy, out by the blue motel pool, definitely my
idea of luxury accommodations. Elsa was stunning in her red
tank suit, and there were several teenage girls vacationing
with their families at the motel, sunning themselves in bikinis
and listening to transistor radios, slipping like seals in and out
of the warm water. Ellen Pate, appalled at our sunburns, laid
us down on chaise longues and administered a welcome and
relaxing massage of suntan oil. Elsa and Kern had a great time
out on the diving board, practicing their flips. Ellen was a
school teacher and liked talking about books, and she seemed

impressed by the amount of reading I had done. Actually, half of those books I had read in Cliffs Notes, but I could always throw a good line to a classy older lady and make her feel like I was going to be the next Ernest Hemingway, so I enjoyed myself. We ordered an early lunch from the restaurant and ate it at a table by the pool, and it was Ellen Pate who introduced me to the margarita.

Meanwhile, back at press headquarters in New York—my father's paneled office at *Look*—the phones were busy. He was beginning to sense, as he put it, that we were going national. One of the big television networks had called and requested an interview with us that afternoon in El Paso. They were flying a producer and camera crew up from Dallas on an afternoon flight. But because the crew wanted to jump right on the next flight back to Dallas, they wouldn't have time to drive across town to the general aviation strip. Instead, my father agreed to have us meet them at the big international airport.

Without a radio, technically we were not allowed to land at El Paso International, a controlled field with an FAA traffic-control tower. But there were ways around the rules and my father was good at that. He phoned the FAA tower supervisor at El Paso, explained the situation and obtained a special clearance for us to land by light-gun signals. We learned about all of this when a motel clerk ran out and told us that we had an urgent phone call from my father in New York.

Kern took the call, and wasn't very happy about it, but my father had him boxed in. Everything was all set up. They were using Runway 22 at El Paso International, and all we had to do was report on a right base, wiggle our wings, and wait for a green light-gun signal from the tower. We didn't have much time. The network camera crew was already in the air out of Dallas.

So we did that dumbass thing, annoyed at my father for intruding again. First, we had to put up with the waterbag jive, now this. In the middle of our day of rest, we'd be flying with the big jets into El Paso International, without a radio, no less. Changing quickly out of our bathing suits, we dashed off to the general aviation strip in the motel van.

Landing without a radio at a controlled airport wasn't that unusual, as long as certain FAA procedures were followed. We vaguely remembered the light signals from *The Private Pilot's Handbook*. A red light from the tower meant discontinue approach. Flashing green meant stand by. A steady green was clearance to land. What we couldn't have known was that the FAA tower supervisor that my father had spoken with at noon was nearing the end of his shift. He never alerted the incoming crew that a red and white Piper Cub would be appearing in their airspace. As we entered the pattern at the international field and began waving our wings, Kern was busy staying clear of other planes. I watched the tower for the light gun. First, we got a long, ominous red. Then I saw green.

"Green light Kern!"

"Steady green, or flashing green?"

"Ah shit, I don't know Kern. Green. There it goes again."

So, we landed. As we rolled out a big cargo plane roared over our heads and pulled up its wheels.

"Rinker, you better be right about that green light," Kern said. "That plane just did a go-around."

But I was wrong, dead wrong. We had never been cleared to land. The gas jockey at the general aviation terminal was waiting for us, and he pointed over to the FAA control tower.

"They just called," he said. "And they don't sound too happy. They want you over there, pronto."

Kern exploded with rage. He decided that it was better to confront the FAA without his cowboy hat and angrily tossed it in the baggage compartment.

"Godammit Rinker. Your ass is grass right now. They can pull my license for this! It could screw up our whole trip."

It was a long walk across the tarmac to the tower, then up several flights of echoing, steel-grate stairs to the top.

We knew a tight-ass when we saw one, and the FAA tower supervisor was unmistakably the type. He was expressionless and curt and wore a shiny white shirt with epaulets and a plastic pocket protector full of pens. He knew all right that we were those kids flying to California—his wife had seen us last night on TV. But the rules were the rules. We had "busted his airspace" and landed without clearance on a flashing green light. He'd been forced to divert another plane. He didn't care about my father allegedly calling ahead to alert the tower. No one had called *him*.

Kern was professional and calm, and elected for the kiss-ass approach.

"Okay, sir, we respect the rules," Kern said. "The rules say phone ahead for permission, wave your wings, look for the green light. That's what we did. That's our position."

"Position?" the supervisor snapped. "That's your *position*? So, you're taking a position already, hunh? Well, you don't have a position. You have a violation. I'm legally entitled to pull your license right here. That's a *position* too."

I detested authority so much, especially plastic pocket-protector authority, that I could hardly see straight. And I was furious at my father for setting up this senseless interview at the international strip, even more than I was angry with myself for mixing up the flashing and steady green lights. We should have ignored my father's latest intrusion and stood up the television crew. Right now, I could have been safely back at the motel pool, drinking margaritas with Ellen.

From the doorway of the tower, I heard the scrape of heavy boots on the metal steps.

"Say, what's going on here?"

It was Pate. He had been right behind us in the airport traffic pattern, returning from his flight over the mountains. He was surprised to see our Cub over the international airport and had heard the radio chatter about the "intruder" over the field. He rushed right over to the tower after he landed.

There was none of this "yes sir" "no sir" obsequiousness to Robert Pate. Twenty years of government service had hardened him to pocket-protector types. Lighting up a fresh cigar, waving his Stetson in the air, he lit into the tower supervisor.

"Say, do you know who these boys are?" Pate growled. "They're flying a Piper Cub, without a radio, coast to coast. You should be begging them for their autographs. Green light or no green light, nobody's going to bust them."

Pate intimated that he had a lot of powerful friends, senators and Air Force generals and the like, and he was just enough of a kick-ass guy, standing there with this silver belt-buckle on that looked as though it cost $500, to intimidate a pocket-protector turd. "Somebody's butt is going to be sausage for this one," Pate said, "And I'm the kind of guy who will make sure that happens." Besides, he said, he was behind us in the pattern and had seen everything. If the tower wrote us up for a violation, he would submit his own report and vouch for us. The FAA regional office, he said, would file this one under "Chicken Shit."

I didn't think that Pate's approach was going to work, and neither did Kern. Every time Pate stopped to catch his breath, Kern jumped in and pleaded with him to stop.

"Robert, please, relax," Kern said. "I can handle this. This fellow here, he's just trying to do his job. I've got a position, and he's got a position."

Mr. Pocket Protector really liked that. Pate's appearance in the tower annoyed him, and now this sunburnt kid was interrupting to say that the FAA was just full of swell guys, trying to do their jobs. Even when he'd just busted your airspace, Kern was too earnest and lovable to resist. When Pate finally shut up, the tower supervisor explained that the rules required him to file an incident report, but he would be recommending that no action be taken. Once we returned home, Kern would probably have to file a routine reply to the report.

We thanked him, and quickly got the hell out of there. Down on the ramp, Pate clapped Kern on the back.

"Perfect buddy, just perfect," Pate said. "We aced it."

"We did?" Kern said.

"Oh, shit yes," Pate said. "The FAA's always trying to violate me too. Fuck 'em. All you gotta do is give 'em the good-cop bad-cop routine. And Jeez, you're a natural at the good cop. Say, where's your cowboy hat? There's a film crew over there, waiting."

We ended up enjoying our interview with the television crew. On a one-on-one basis, away from the melee of a press conference, broadcasters could behave quite politely when they wanted to. The crew was relieved to learn that the other networks hadn't found us yet. The producer and the cameraman obviously enjoyed us a lot and they were very interested in our personal backgrounds and the details of our flight.

We learned a lot about television and its filming methods from that crew. They filmed Kern and me taxiing the Cub around the ramp a couple of times, and we did the Brakes, Throttle, Contact! routine with the cameras rolling, then we walked out to the plane from the pilots' shack with our maps spread out in front of us, discussing our routes. Without the cameras rolling, the producer had us talk into the microphone for five minutes about our flight. I didn't get that at all. Now they weren't going to have pictures that went with their sound.

I was intensely curious about that. Kern wasn't much interested in the actual mechanics of news-gathering, what was happening behind the scenes. But I was fascinated by it.

"Hey, I don't understand this," I said to the producer. "If you want to interview us about our flight, why don't you just take pictures of us talking about it?"

The producer explained that he didn't want to file our story as a standard news piece. Once we arrived in California, he said, our flight would be big news, "even bigger than it is now," and the network would have exclusive background material. The story would be prepared as a weekend feature. They would use the shots of us landing in L.A., which they could pick up from their local affiliate, and then splice in some of the shots they were taking now in El Paso. But these would be used as background visuals. The core of the story would be our voiceover narration about the flight. This made sense to me, but I still didn't understand why the network was going to so much trouble.

"You really don't have any idea how big a story this is, do you?" the producer asked me.

"Well, sort of," I said. "I do now. Reporters are calling my father at home every night. But my brother and I just thought of this as a summer lark. We never thought anybody else would care."

The producer smiled. This happened to him a lot in the news business, he said. Participants in the middle of events had no idea what they meant to a larger audience. In our case, he said, people were captivated by what we had done. "Millions of kids" would kill for a chance to see the country from a Piper Cub. It was an adventure story, the American dream. Everybody was rooting for us to make it to California and television just couldn't ignore a drama like that.

I was beginning to understand all this, but it wasn't as if my head was swelled by what the producer said. We still had a long stretch of desert to fly before we reached California, and then maybe we could worry about fame. But I wasn't ready for it. It wasn't why we made the trip. I could see that our flight was already beyond just Kern and me. People took an adventure like this, and breathed into it their own dreams and thoughts, imagining all kinds of things that weren't there and ignoring things that were, and then a force takes over and it's not your trip anymore. I wasn't sure I wanted that. The fuss and bother of media coverage, the jumble of events since we landed in El Paso, were beginning to unnerve me. I missed the desert, the isolated country we had just crossed. I just wanted to be up in the throbbing cockpit again with Kern, anonymously banging along in turbulence, out in lonely airspace where nobody could find us.

After the interview, we helped the camera crew break down their equipment and shuttled them back to the commercial air terminal in Pate's rental car. We decided to leave the Cub at the international airport. In the morning, Pate could radio the tower from his own plane and get us clearance to take off.

On the way back to the motel, Pate bought a six-pack of cold beer and offered us one. Kern declined, because he had to fly in the morning, but all I had to do was navigate, so I took one. It was my first can of beer, and I liked the taste of that cold, foamy brew going down. It was like an injection of spring water, sending invigorating pins and needles into my burned face and arms. The can dripped a cool ring of perspiration onto my lap. What was the big deal about alcohol, anyway? This beer, not to mention the margarita I had wolfed down at lunch, didn't affect me in the least.

In the car, Pate prattled on about Montezuma, who had

fought a brave but hopeless war against the Spanish conquistadors in the sixteenth century. Finally, after Spanish conqueror Hernando Cortés had chased most of the Aztec forces up to the Rio Grande, Montezuma dispatched a small band north of the river to bury the Aztecs' fortune of silver and gold in the mountains. The mystery of where Montezuma had buried his gold died with him, in 1520, and for centuries pre-Columbian scholars and archeologists had speculated on the site of his lost treasure, even whether it really existed. Among the small international coterie of treasure-hunters, it was known as Montezuma's Tomb. Pate was convinced that he could find the treasure, which was probably worth billions. In fact, he told us again, he'd already seen the site.

He would tell us all about it tonight, Pate said. Ellen and Elsa wanted to cross the river into Mexico and go for dinner in old Juarez, and they wanted us to come along. The change of scenery, Pate thought, would do us good.

"Hey Rink, Mexico!" Kern said back in the room. "This Pate guy wins the Bullshitter of the Year Award, but at least he's taking us to a foreign country."

Kern didn't like Pate as much as I did. I didn't think he was grateful enough for the way Pate had bailed us out of trouble with the FAA, and I was annoyed about it.

"Hey Kern. Ask not what your country can do for you, but rather what you can do for your country."

"Okay, Rinker, okay. Sorry. You're right. The Bullshitter of the Year Award goes to Daddy."

Toward sunset we crossed the bridge on the Rio Grande, stopping briefly at the Border Patrol checkpoint, and then Pate drove down through the narrow, twisting streets to Old Juarez. Kern and I were both excited to be traveling "south of the border." It didn't seem possible that a place so confusing and exotic could be right over the river from Texas. Teenage girls in skimpy, skin-tight tank tops propositioned us from the street corners, and vendors hawking T-shirts and bags of fruit leaned over from the filthy gutters. The Pates seemed to know their way around. Robert kept honking the horn and shooing away the people shoving jewelry and cheap leather belts up against the windows of the car.

We went to a place called Taxico. In the front, there was a crowded bar with flamenco dancers and a loud Mexican band up on a stage, where we stayed for an hour and watched the show. I was quite impressed with my ability to consume margaritas, on top of the second beer that I drank in the shower back at the motel room, without feeling any negative effects. I wasn't getting drunk, I told myself. The only thing that seemed to happen to me under the influence of alcohol was that Elsa, dressed in culottes and a sleeveless blouse, was even more seductive and beautiful than she had been in a bathing suit earlier in the day. There were other positive developments, I thought, once a boy became a drinker. I discovered for the first time, for example, that my powers of conversation were wickedly brilliant. Even Elsa seemed to appreciate this. The more margaritas I drank, the more obvious it became that she was coming down with a ferocious crush on me. Of course, she was sitting with Kern right now, but that was just for show. Back at the motel, she was going to ditch him and then secret me off to one of the chaise longues on the dark edges of the pool. By my third margarita, I was absolutely convinced of this. Elsa was in love, with me. Drinking just wasn't the evil that my father and all of his friends in Alcoholics Anonymous cracked it up to be.

Off to the side, connected by a hallway lined with pictures of celebrities, was a quaint old Spanish-style restaurant, one of the best in Mexico, Ellen said, where they gave us a nice booth. I wobbled over there behind the rest, unsteady on my feet, and proud of it. A certain loss of balance was inevitable the first time you drank. As a dinner host, Pate was generous and grand.

"Boys," he said, waving the menu in the air, "Order whatever you want. Tonight, we're celebrating your big flight."

Elsa sat across the table with Kern again, and I was wedged in between Robert and Ellen, but I wasn't upset. Elsa would make her big move for me back at the motel.

Besides, I liked Ellen a lot. She was very nurturing and considerate, and put her arm around me and stroked my shoulders while we talked, which no grown, married woman back on the east coast would ever do. I'd heard about this. Ellen, I decided, was very "California." Aunt Joan, Uncle Jim's wife, was the same kind of person, very affectionate and warm and not afraid to touch people while she talked. And feelings. Feelings! Jesus, California people were really big on that. When we sat down, Ellen told me straight off that Kern and I were doing "wonders" for Robert. In fact, we'd even helped Robert and Ellen's "relationship." Last night, they had stayed up late, talking about us. For Ellen, the conversation had filled in a lot of gaps about Robert. Our trip, she said, reminded him of his own youthful barnstorms across the country, and she'd heard a lot of details he'd never mentioned before.

We ordered dinner and had a good time. Pate kept trying to limit me to "just one more" margarita, and Ellen and Elsa kept slipping me refills from their glasses. Finally Pate got annoyed, banished all alcohol from the table, and ordered me a cup of coffee.

All the while, Pate entertained us with barnstorming blarney as grand as any I'd ever heard. He was a marvellous yarner, with good pace and rhythm and excellent arm and legwork on the imaginary controls.

In a booze-induced flash, I suddenly realized something important. If Pate was my father, I would resent his ceaseless string of tall tales. But Pate *wasn't* my father and I was enjoying every minute of him. Maybe I was being too ornery about this. I should be able to appreciate what others saw in my father. Everybody else loved being around him, listening to his grand talk, the same way I loved listening to Pate. Pangs of loneliness for my father, as bad as back in Arkansas, hit me again. But then the coffee came and I drank a cup and felt better.

Pate said one other thing that night that helped me understand and resolve a huge misgiving I had about my father. I never would have realized it without him.

Like my father, Pate has escaped the Depression by learning to fly. Initially, the Air Corps would take him only as a radar operator, and he didn't qualify for flight training until the end of World War II. He trained in Stearmans about the same time my father was instructing in Texas, and didn't see combat until the 1950s, in Korea.

"I bet your father's still bitter about not seeing combat in the war," Pate said.

It was true. My father never had seen combat, and he was self-conscious about it. It was something of a dark secret in our family, a subject we weren't supposed to bring up. When we were younger, and my uncles visited every summer for the big family reunions that were held at our farm, they all sat under the large shade oak on our back lawn and entertained us with their war stories. My father sat off to the side, uncharacteristically quiet, steering the conversation back to the Depression, or the barnstorming era of the 1930s, as soon as he could. He was horrified about his lack of war experience, and even lied about it to cover up. Indeed, that was happening right as we sat in the restaurant in Old Juarez. In one article about our flight that we caught up with in Arizona, my father identified himself as a former pilot with the famous Eighth Bomber Command in Europe. He told another reporter that he flew torpedo-bombers in the Pacific.

Kern was fascinated by it too. His face lit up with wonder when Pate said that.

"Robert, why?" Kern asked, leaning across the table. "I mean, my father's a great pilot. You should see him do aerobatics in his Texan. With a wooden leg! So what if he didn't fight in the war? He helped in the war, and he's a great flyer."

"Well," Pate said, "There are thousands of guys like that. I had the same problem myself after World War II, and I didn't get over it until I finally got a Mig in my sights in Korea. The Pentagon way overestimated the number of pilots it needed for World War II. Most of them ended up doing thankless work—training, ferrying, test-flying. That kind of flying was every bit as hazardous as combat. Shit. Training in Stearmans? We lost pilots every day. But nobody ever made *God Is My Co-pilot* for a frigging flight instructor. You felt excluded, a failure. Everybody else was getting their asses blown off on Iwo, being heroes, and you were back at the Officer's Club in Florida, drunk as a skunk. Some guys

couldn't get over it. That's why we all call ourselves 'Stearman men.' The Boeing Stearman was the most glorious aircraft ever made, boys, and we flew the bejesus out of that
wonderful whore. It's all we've got from those years."

Jesus. I couldn't believe this was happening to me, in a
restaurant down in Old Juarez. I was actually beginning to
feel normal about myself. And if nobody would ever accuse
my father of being quite normal, at least his personality was
beginning to make some sense to me. Barnstorming blarney.
The great Stearman men of the west. Why was that any different than Mr. Feakins across the street, the ex-Marine with
great war tales, or for that matter the Black-Irish Prince, Jack,
and his PT-109? Everybody had a past that they couldn't
escape, a past to embellish for the young, and they could only
talk about what they knew.

"But look, enough of this," Pate said. "I want to tell you
my big one. Would you like to hear my big one?"

I'd had a second coffee by now and I was feeling a lot
better.

"Sure Robert."

Pate ordered a double-brandy from the bar, belted it back,
and then he lit a fresh cigar and launched into his tale.

Every good old Stearman man has a "big one." Pate's started
according to form, with a routine flight during World War II.

In 1944 Airman Robert Pate was assigned to ferry a Stearman from Lakeland, Florida, to Fresno, California, as part of
a formation wing of 25 planes. It was September, the height
of the squall season, and he didn't have a radio. It was supposed to be a routine game of follow the leader. For navigation, the only thing the Air Corps gave him was a
large-scale chart of the continental United States.

I could tell right away that Pate's big one came right out
of the Stearman man's bible. My father told a variant of the
same tale, and so did all the old Stearman men. During World
War II the Air Corps didn't have enough hangars to house all
of its trainers. When the fall hurricanes swept up through
Stearman Alley, every pilot and cadet on the field was dra-

gooned into service, to fly huge formation-wings of Stearmans north, to get the planes out of harm's way. Those flights, invariably, were disasters. The storms frequently overtook the stragglers and forced them down. Twenty years later rice farmers and loggers were still discovering crashed Stearmans in remote Louisiana bayous and Cumberland ravines, the skeletons of the pilots still strapped into their cockpit harnesses. The most famous of these flights, a kind of Exodus of Stearman lore, was the "Lost Flyers of Biloxi." In September 1943, more than one hundred Stearmans took off from Biloxi, Mississippi, in the face of a raging hurricane, and fewer than eighty of them safely reached a field up north. Many of the downed planes still haven't been found. As boys, Kern and I had a macabre fascination for those lost Biloxi pilots. They had disappeared into something as mysterious and suspenseful as the Bermuda Triangle. *Reader's Digest* published articles about the "Lost Flyers of Biloxi," and so did many of the aviation magazines.

God, we had trouble all along, [Pate began] the weather all the way out was crap, even past the desert dryline in Texas, and the wing commander they gave us couldn't fly his ass out of a chute sack. He was always getting lost. But I had to follow him and stay with the formation. Those were the orders.

It was a wild trip, and all kinds of weirdass stuff happened. In Arkansas, the first night, the base commander wasn't expecting us and all they had to feed us in the mess was pickled pig's feet—awful stuff, which most of us heaved over the side the next day. We buzzed a lot of trains and had dog-fights up above the clouds. Even that idiot leader joined in that. But planes kept dropping out. Some had engine trouble, others lost the formation in the clouds. One guy, who was a friend of mine, had a whore that he liked to fuck in Wichita Falls. He wiggled his wings when we got out over the Red River, see, like he was having engine trouble, and that was the last we ever saw of him. By the time we got to west Texas there were only ten or twelve Stearmans left.

That leader was just a jackass. When we got to the New Mexico line, where I knew the mountains began, he couldn't see anything under the clouds so he headed south. He was supposed to be climbing and flying us west, or steering us through the Guadalupe Pass. But he was taking the flight into Mexico. Frig the orders, I said to myself. I am getting this plane to Fresno. I let some clouds get between me and the formation and wandered off, pointing the Stearman west.

Away from the pack, I firewalled and punched through the clouds. I broke out on top at 8,000 feet. God, it was a mess up there. I could see some of the peaks of the Guadalupe Range ahead of me, but others were obscured in the clouds. I was flying in and out of clouds all the time. The map wasn't any use to me now, and I tossed it under the seat. All I could do was keep going for air—10,000, 11,000, 12,000 feet—and in the turbulence keep the compass locked on a due course of 270 degrees. Once the mountains disappeared underneath me, I figured I'd wait twenty minutes and let down, praying that El Paso was still in front of me.

When I got right over the mountains, with a big, motherless peak just ahead of me, the engine started to run rough. All that moisture in the clouds was ganging up on me, and I was picking up carburetor ice. Oh it was just a pitiful feeling. Over the mountains. On top of clouds. I couldn't turn back because the clouds behind me were just as bad as in front. And now my frigging manifold gauge is showing twenty-two inches of mercury, then eighteen. I tried everything to keep that engine going. When the gauge got down past fifteen, that old Continental just quit and I had myself a dead airplane. But I still had 800 feet or so on the peak ahead of me and I held the stick up as long as I could, coasting over the top. There was a hole in the clouds just past the summit, and I could see a system of ravines down below it. Just before I stalled, I made it to the hole and dove.

As I went through that hole in the clouds I just said to myself, "Well Robert. You're done for. It's been a

good, short life. You were poor and a nobody back in
Missouri, but you got out, learned to fly, and made it
into Stearmans." Good. I was proud of myself, but now
my time was up. Everybody else was getting killed in
the war over there, so why not me?

I mean, you can't let down into the middle of the
goddamn Rocky Mountains and survive. But it was
strange, a strange feeling. I didn't give a shit. I was so
tired from being in the Air Corps for two years, so sick
of flying hard all week, I didn't mind dying right then.
Lots of my friends had died already. From the altitude,
I was oxygen-starved too, and cold, very cold. It just does
crazy things to you, aeroembolism. I accepted death at
that moment—wanted to go, even. Lord, just give me a
wall to crater into, and hurry up about it. I was ready to
die.

And, you know, I was just this young, hardass airman
then. I was meant to die in these peaks, I said to myself.
Shit, how many airmail pilots have crashed in the Guad-
alupes? Dozens. I'd just crater in with them and call it
a life. In a minute or two, I promised myself, when there
was nothing ahead of me but rocks, I would just push it
into a wall as fast as the Stearman could go and get it
over in a hurry.

But there were these ravines under me now, twisting,
winding ravines, a whole city of them, falling down the
range and generally dropping in altitude. I just followed
them, dead stick, where they took me. It wasn't a
straight downhill ride, the way they show mountains in
movie pictures or anything. The mountains slope down,
then back up, sideways even, but I just kept following
clear space where I could. Sometimes the wheels were
clearing the rocks by ten feet and sometimes four hundred.

That's when I saw Montezuma's Tomb. I want to say
it was thirty seconds after I came through the cloud
hole—God, if I only knew *exactly* where it was today—
but there's just no reckoning time in a situation like that,

dead stick in the Rocky Mountains. It could've been three fucking seconds.

Whatever, see. I came to this huge, deep intersection of ravines, way down in the belly of Guadalupe, with these tall, massive walls of rock rising on three sides of me. The only way I could turn was right, and hard right. I just had those wings right over, almost snap-rolled, holding top rudder, you know, to keep the nose pointed through the hole in the rocks.

My God, what's that? My Motherless Lord. What in the name of God is that? Craning my neck out, looking straight down over my banked wings, I'm looking at the most beautiful, magical sight of my life.

Ah Jesus boys, I wish I could describe it just right for you, I wish there were words. I only saw it for five or six seconds, while my wings were over. There, in a deep, deep hole hidden by these kind of needlelike pinnacles, just below that big intersection of rocks, was the most beautiful castle man has ever built. Two perfectly carved pillars rose straight into the air. They were symmetrical, perfectly matched, maybe a hundred feet tall apiece. They were connected by a long, curving wall, with windows cut out and flat platforms behind, as if armaments were planned. The sun was catching it just right, backlighting it from the hole I'd just come through—in fact, that's the only guidance I've got now. It was about ten-thirty in the morning, see, I know that from my logbook, and I'm still trying to figure that angle of light from the sun that day. Anyway, I knew as soon as I saw that castle that it wasn't something that occurred in nature. Deep, deep in a hole in the Rocky Mountains, somewhere near the Guadalupe Peaks, somebody had built this beautiful structure. They had carved those pillars perfectly in stone. And it wasn't accidental. It was there for a reason.

Okay, I am crazy now, see? I have got a dead airplane in the Rocky Mountains. I am aeroembolism nuts. But I'm desperate, wild with curiosity and desire. I have just seen the Eighth Wonder of the World or something. I want to fly the plane back up there and see that castle again, mark the spot, so I can come back and explore. Get the airplane back around Robert, get it back around. You've got to be able to find that thing again. But I'm falling, falling, see, I've got to keep falling with the ravine and let that castle disappear behind me, or I'm dead.

I wasn't paying any attention to the airplane, looking at the instruments or anything. All I could do was fly with my head out in the slipstream, see, this side and that, slithering with the rudder pedals around the rocks, diving down through the ravines. It all happened so fast. Bang, the big intersection comes along, wonk, over hard with the wings, Jesus Motherless Christ, what's that castle down there, gotta find it, gotta find it again, quick, try and mark it on the map, no, that's crazy, gotta try and save myself, and then the next thing I know I'm falling through the ravine and looking for clear space and up front the engine is rumbling and the airframe is shaking hard all over, whamp, whamp, whamp, whamp, smoke's belching from the stacks, the prop's windmilling hard, and every goddamn orifice on that Continental is spitting steam and ice and screaming a furious shockheat. My stick was shaking real hard, the instrument panel was vibrating, and the flying wires were jumping up and down, like a guy being electrocuted, and I'm red-lined now on the speed, I had that gorgeous whore red-lined and more, but the wings are staying on. God, that's the thing about Stearmans, that magnificent airplane, there isn't a bastard yet who's pulled one apart in the air. It just held, that Stearman just held. Rumbling and rattling and banging the bejesus out of herself, that mother Stearman held. The whole frigging thing over the mountains had just happened so fast, and I was oxygen-starved mad. I had never shut off the magnetos. I hadn't closed the mixture or fuel—why do that anyway, when you're planning on cratering into a wall?

Now, what the hell's going on here? Steam and smoke are exploding off that engine, whamp, whamp, whamp my stacks roar. And you know, my damn stick and rudders are coming back on me now too. They've got some wash going over them now. I looked quickly to the manifold gauge and the bitch is showing me eighteen inches. Well Jesus Christ. I had my airplane back. Coming out of the clouds, down now below 8,000 feet, the carburetor had cleared. In a few seconds I was showing twenty inches and maybe 2,100 rpm. Hell, I could almost fly those ravines normal now. There was no reason to climb, and I couldn't have anyway. But I was level now, when I wanted to be, with lots of air coming over the controls. I was almost over to the other side and I could see it was clear to the west. All the clouds had been bunched up on the east side of the mountains.

God, the feeling of coming off those mountains, with my engine running again. I was planning on dying, see. But shit, Robert Warren Pate has fucked that one up too, he can't even kill himself, and damn I'm coming off the far side of Guadalupe with an airplane that still flies and my pants all full of piss, so I figured I was still alive.

But I couldn't believe what I had just seen. That was driving me wild. I came out about two miles north of the Salt Flats. I figure that I crossed about six miles north of the Pass. It was just this spiritual experience for me. I was gulping for air and diving for the desert to get more, and was sort of laughing and crying at once. I was just twenty-one and didn't know how to handle all that emotion, a brush with death like that. And I was in awe of what had just happened to me. I had violated orders and broken off from the pack, going for air over the Rockies, alone, the whore Continental dies on me, and then I had come right through the most dangerous part of the mountains in this spectacular way.

Something was protecting me, guiding me to that spot, this hidden castle, see, right near Guadalupe. I was di-

rected there by a spiritual force. It took me years of re-
search to figure out what it was. The literature out of
Mexico says: "The Emperor's delegation placed the
treasure deep inside the mountains, marking the spot
with battlements and two stone pillars reaching for the
sky." I know what I saw was Montezuma's Tomb. Now,
every year, I come back. I am going to find it too, the
spot where I came through the mountains. It's my mission, my religion. If I can just recreate that flight, my
path through the mountains in the Stearman, I will find
Montezuma's Tomb.

Well, you don't say a whole lot after listening to a big one
like that. For sure, it was one of the best Stearman tales I'd
ever heard. We all just sat there at the table staring at our
coffee cups, brooding in the heavy, pregnant silence, and
maybe Ellen and Elsa had already heard that one a dozen
times, but even they were moved.

Somewhere in the middle of Pate's soliloquy, I just followed him right over the mountain and over the top of my
father. It was my second trip through the pass. It was just a
moment, a flash, but when I was past it I was past it forever.
I didn't care any longer about what happened between my
father and me. He was a talker, a bullshitter, an exhibitionist.
He couldn't sit in a plane without looping or rolling it and
he couldn't enter a room without dominating everyone in it.
So what? Here was Pate, rich and successful, retired at forty-
three, spending the summer in El Paso with these beautiful
women half his age. He was a bullshitter too, a grand, grand
bullshitter, perhaps beyond even my father's powers. There
were just talkers in this world, that's all. There was Pate, and
there was Tom Buck. Suddenly I saw myself more clearly.
Nobody blamed my father for who he was, and nobody
blamed me for being his son either. He was, that's all. And I
was, too. And I could exist in a separate space from him and
be whatever I wanted.

I was exhausted by dinner and drink, and by Pate's yarning.
We left the restaurant and walked for a while around Old
Juarez. On the ride back to El Paso, Kern rode up front with

Pate, listening to him yap more blarney all the way up over the border.

I fell asleep between Ellen and Elsa in the backseat. I can't remember who it was, Ellen or Elsa, but one of them put their arm around my shoulder and nuzzled me off to sleep. I was satisfied with myself and the night. We were over the mountains now and safe, in El Paso. A woman's body comforted me. I can't say that I knew it right away, that night, but eventually I did understand what had happened. Pate's wild Stearman ride over Guadalupe liberated me. I wasn't quite past being angry and embarrassed about my father. But I could see my way through to it now.

In the morning, Pate woke us an hour before dawn, and we found coffee and doughnuts at an all-night diner on the way to the airport. I was still hungover and woozy, and would battle sleep all day. But the coffee and the prospect of an easy day of flying across the southwest revived me. In the pilots' lounge, Pate went over the maps with us. The southern route was easy—a straight shot. All we had to do was pick up Highway 10 north of El Paso and follow it up through Deming, Lordsburg, Cochise County, and Tucson. After that, Highway 8 took us right into Yuma.

Pate got us off the international field by calling the tower on the radio in his Cessna and telling them we were departing in formation, as a "party of two." All we had to do, he said, was follow him down the taxiway, then firewall right behind him on the runway. On the ramp, he gave us a thumbs up and wiggled his wing ailerons to signal that the tower approved.

It was a beautiful sunrise, the most beautiful of the trip. High, wispy cirrus clouds, deep purple and black, collided with pink and orange fringes from the sun poking over the horizon. When Pate advanced his throttle, Kern stayed with him, and we climbed out briskly in the smooth air, wing-to-wing. Pate lingered with us a bit, flying us west to the Rio Grande. Then, cigar clamped between his fingers, he saluted us and banked east, disappearing off toward Guadalupe.

I was moody about it, watching Pate and his plane fade toward the mountains off our wing. I never laid eyes on him again, but I never forgot him either. He was a great old Stearman man and I don't see how we could have done El Paso without him.

CHAPTER 18

WE DIDN'T REALLY MEAN TO RUN THE BUS OFF THE ROAD IN Arizona. It was just one of those things that happened along the way, like Elsa in El Paso or the rattler snakes at Wink.

We were running along Highway 8 between Gila Bend and Yuma, having made great time across the deserts of New Mexico and Arizona all day. The highways ran straight as an arrow, torpid and flat, and the navigation was easy. Between Deming, New Mexico, and Cochise County, Arizona, Kern let me sleep off my hangover for a couple of hours. I awoke to the breathtaking mesa country of southern Arizona. Immense outcrops of black and gray, some of them pinnacled and some of them flat, mounded up from the painted deserts, and the corridors in between them were softened by the shadows of passing clouds. The beauty of Arizona was almost too extensive to take in, and the steady throbbing of the Continental made us drowsy. I guess that's why we did in the Greyhound. We'd been flying hard for five days and now we were bored as snails.

It was one of those long shiny land yachts, running east on the highway. From twelve or fifteen miles out all we could make out was a large incoming object. Closer in, we could see that it was a Greyhound bus, with the red and gray dog

Teen Fliers Face Arizona Deserts

Hope to Reach Yuma Today

By RICHARD BIGELOW

Two teen-age New Jersey brothers took off from El Paso Airport, El Paso, Tex., today in a 28-year-old single engine plane they are flying in a 8,000-mile double crossing of the United States.

Kernhan Buck, 17, and his brother, Rinker, 15, of Sand Spring Road, New Vernon, spent yesterday preparing for the "worst day of all"—today's flight across the deserts of Arizona.

The final destination for the two youths is Capistrano, Calif., which they plan to reach tomorrow by 1 p.m.

Plane Cost $300

"Tomorrow's the worst day of all," Kernhan said yesterday. He is piloting the plane, a Piper Cub, his father, Thomas Buck, bought for $300 and he and his brother completely rebuilt.

"Today's flight at 12,000 feet across the desert will take us pretty far from civilization," Kernhan said.

"Basically," he reported, "we're going to fly a straight route to Yuma, Ariz., staying within gliding distance of a

(Continued Page 3, Column 1)

UPI Photo

DARING LADS—Kernhan Buck, 17, at right, and brother Rinker, 15, of New Vernon prepare to leave El Paso, Tex., in transcontinental flight to Los Angeles in 23-year-old plane they rebuilt. The boys, flying without radio, hope to be there tomorrow.

Kern insisted on buying a cowboy hat in Texas, and he was jaunty and self-confident after we crossed the Rockies.

leaping through the logo painted on the side and a large green sundeck on the roof glaring under the sun.

We went down for a look. Kern had been flying the yellow centerline of a highway all day, so it was just a matter of thinking the stick forward a bit. When we passed through 500 feet and kept going down, I looked forward to Kern. He had this beguiled smile, and was staring at the yellow line. When we were boys, Kern and I used to hypnotize the roosters down in our barn, flipping them over on their backs and drawing a chalk line on the floor out from their eyes. The rooster stared inverted at the line, mesmerized and perfectly still. We'd go in for dinner and return in an hour. The rooster was still there, inverted, staring at the line. That's what my brother looked like right now. He was fixated on the bus and the yellow line.

I suppose Kern would have leveled off at some point, but the bus driver was a buffoon. About a mile off, he started flashing his lights at us, as if we were some overloaded family station wagon wobbling into the passing lane, too slow to get back in time onto our side. I disliked bus drivers on principle and now this jackass was flashing his lights.

"Yo, Kern!" I yelled over the noise of the engine.

"Yeah Rink."

"Chicken?"

"Chicken, coming up!"

While the bus lights ahead frantically blinked "Give Way," Kern firewalled and put the Cub five feet above the yellow line on the blacktop. Jesus, I thought, these closing speeds really pick up at the last minute. Downshifting now, and starting to brake, the bus was still doing 45 or 50 miles per hour. Full throttle, in a headwind, maybe we were doing 65 or 70 over the ground. From there everything happened very fast.

A half mile out, the bus driver swerved lane-to-lane a few times, as if the sight of a Greyhound on two wheels was going to make us pull up. Then, briefly, he tried the frontal approach, burrowing straight for us with his lights on high beam. But he could see that this wasn't going to work either. One-hundred yards out the driver yanked over his steering wheel, which threw out his front tires at angles, and the bus rotated and slid sideways. The painted hound on the side appeared to be skittering ass-first onto the dusty shoulder, like a burro going over the Grand Canyon. Tire smoke, black exhaust, and sand sprayed up over the sundeck.

As we hauled up over the bus, sand blasted the prop and the cockpit smelled of diesel and burnt rubber. Down through the mushroom cloud I got a pretty good view of the terrified occupants of the bus. The driver wore a tan uniform with gray epaulets and a Greyhound cap, and was violently shaking up at us with his fist. The tourists in the sundeck were staring up through the tinted glass with their hands clutched to the seat railings—several rows of cheap cowboy hats attached to gaping mouths.

We flew out over the desert and kept our tail to the rear

of the bus, so they couldn't get our registration numbers. Looking back over the rudder, we watched the driver destroy his transmission getting back onto the road. Wha-bump, wha-bump, wha-bump, he rocked that heavy ten-wheeler back and forth on the shoulder, digging furrows with the rear wheels and throwing up magnificent geysers of sand. The scene reminded me of the annual spectacle at school back home, during the first big snow, when everybody stood around the parking lot and cheered as that crazyass Father Lucien, our science teacher, smoked his Buick Wildcat out of the drifts.

"C'mon buddy!" Kern yelled. "Rock that mother! Rock 'er."

Jesus, I thought. When that Greyhound pulls into the terminal in Tucson, the mechanics are going to be shitting bricks.

Finally the Greyhound found some traction on a lower level of sand. Rear end jumping, the exhaust pipe digging into the desert so deep it threw back jets of ignited sand, the heavy galleon bucked and kicked onto the highway. Puffs of white smoke shot up when the rubber hit the road, and the bus sped off.

We cheered and flew on toward Yuma. Momentarily, however, the Beaver Cleaver in him got the better of Kern. He was worried that the bus driver, once he got to Tucson or Phoenix, would report us. It was the kind of thing that would occur to Kern and not to me, and he was still rattled by that brush with the FAA back in El Paso. I thought about that for a moment. Then I leaned forward and yelled over the roar of the engine.

"Hey Kern," I said. "You're the driver of a one-hundred-passenger bus, right?"

"Right."

"And you pull into that terminal in Phoenix and tell the boss: 'Hey, I just got run off Highway 8 by a Piper Cub!' "

"Got it Rink. We're in the clear."

Yuma was the west, the old, far west, and we spent the rest of the afternoon strolling the town. The older section had several prewar cafes, Indian craft shops, and hardware stores featuring items like saddle blankets and canteens. Cowboys and Navaho ranchers pulled up in pickups loaded down with bales of hay and sheep. We bought new wallets at a leather shop and dawdled in an art gallery featuring color photographs from *Arizona Highways* magazine, trying to identify some of the mesas and painted deserts we had just crossed.

Next door, there was a Mexican restaurant fragrant with cooked spices, and we decided to eat there because we liked the way the tables were arrayed around an open-air court with live cactus and wild flowers growing in the sand. We couldn't read the menu, which was handwritten in Spanish. A large, smiling woman came out of the kitchen and told us to just sit there and relax. For $5 apiece, she said, she was going to feed us. For more than an hour the dishes kept coming out— a cold fish cerviche, enchiladas, a salad with warm dressing, side plates of rice and beans, and a liqueur-flavored custard for dessert. Except for chicken-fried steak in Arkansas, it was the best meal of the trip.

When we got back to the motel, Kern changed into swimming trunks and disappeared for the pool. I called my father again. Despite the disastrous shit-shit-shit El Paso gam, Kern and I didn't even discuss this division of labor any longer. We accepted this as routine. The calls home were stressful, with my father quizzing us about our routes, asking about the waterbag, and now directing the press. The fiasco at El Paso International had left a residue of anger in both of us. Kern wasn't making a big show of avoiding my father, but he'd get away with it if he could. Whenever we landed at an airport, it was my job to squeak all the bugs off the windshield and make sure that all of our maps for the next flight leg were in order. When we got to a motel for the night, I called my father.

This sixth and last call home, the Yuma gam, could have been another disaster, but I seemed to be learning how to handle my father better. When I reached him collect, he was annoyed because we had failed to watch television for the past two nights, and thus missed ourselves on the news. He couldn't understand why we weren't more interested in that. And every time I called, it seemed, Kern was conveniently taking a shower or swimming in the motel pool.

"Rinker, where's Kern?" my father asked. "I want to talk with Kern."

"Dad. He's swimming. He asked me to call because he wants to take a swim."

"Swimming. He's always swimming. What are you guys up to anyway? Is Kern dodging me for some reason?"

"No Dad. He's swimming."

"Swimming, jeez. You're supposed to be flying an airplane coast to coast, but everytime you call, Kern's in a goddamn swimming pool. I know you guys. You're doing this for a reason. Why couldn't Kern call?"

"Dad, if you want, I'll go and get him."

"Nah, nah, nah. Let him swim. But have him call me when he gets back. I've talked to Uncle Jim and there's some details about your arrival in L.A. tomorrow. I need to talk to Kern about that. But do have him call me, you hear?"

"Sure thing Pop. He'll call."

That was easy, I thought, hanging up. The Yuma gam was the big one for me. Why couldn't I always be polite like that, and just take his shit? It didn't matter in the end. It took nearly two thousand miles of country, six hard days of flying and six phone gams, to reach this point, but I was there. When he wanted to be, my father was the world's biggest pain in the ass. But it didn't have anything to do with me, because I could always ignore it.

So, I went out to the pool for a swim myself, and told Kern to call my father.

Everything was arranged for our arrival in California the next day. Kern and I would follow the southern route from Yuma to San Diego, rest and refuel, then follow the coast up to the little paved strip at San Juan Capistrano in Orange County, the nearest airport to Uncle Jimmy's without a radio tower. My father expected lots of media—the three networks, Associated Press, United Press International, all the L.A. stations, with more still logging in at his New Jersey command post. He would call Uncle Jimmy himself and tell him to expect us at one p.m.

Before we went to sleep a reporter from the Yuma paper called. He wanted to interview us at the airport in the morning. Neither of us really wanted to do another interview, but we were planning on leaving early for the airport anyway. Kern was concerned because the new paint job on 71-Hotel looked dull after fifty hours of flying. He wanted it to look neat and clean for our arrival in California, so Aunt Joan would be impressed with our plane. The reporter could interview us while we were washing the Cub.

That night, at two or three a.m., we were awakened by the loudest thunderstorm I had ever heard. In the desert, there weren't any trees or lakes to absorb the rolling claps of thunder, and the walls of the motel and the mattresses on our beds shook. We were excited about flying into California the next day, and neither of us could sleep after that.

Ducking the rain outside, I ran down the motel alley to the Coke machine. Kern and I sat up on our beds, talking with our Cokes in our laps and the light on, listening to the rain pounding down on the tile roof.

"Rink, Daddy's real excited now. I think he's getting more out of this trip than we are."

"Yeah. He's real happy now Kern. He bugs the hell out of me, but he's happy."

"Rink, you know what you oughta do?"

"No, what?"

"Make an agreement with yourself. That's what I do. No matter what Daddy says, how much he riles you, blow it off. Never show your feelings to the guy."

"Kern, I know. I realized that tonight. But thanks. You always need to have your thinking double-checked."

"Okay, but there's one other thing. It's like Daddy and all those AA meetings."

"Yeah?"

"Whenever you make an agreement with yourself, you have to stick to it."

In the morning, at the Yuma airport, we were delighted to see that we didn't have to wash the plane. The thunderstorm had scrubbed 71-Hotel clean. We waited for the reporter out on the bench at the gas pumps, enjoying the open views out to the desert. It was a beautiful Friday morning and several pilots had showed up early to get a head start on their weekend flying. The airport manager and a couple of geezers came out and sat with us on the bench. Yuma was a friendly strip and everybody wanted to hear about our coast to coast flight.

One of the geezers had made tea. He was pouring out a cup for everyone from a large thermos when the detail from the United States Border Patrol showed up. Three green and white pickups with flashing cherry lights pulled in through the airport gates, drove across the ramp, and took positions around our Cub.

Kern and I ran over to the plane. I could see right away that this was a serious group of lawmen, or at least they considered themselves serious lawmen, but mentally they looked pretty far down the evolutionary chain. Their uniforms bristled with insignia and badges and their belts were heavy with guns, walkie-talkies, and mace. On top of sullen, porcine faces, the border patrolmen wore these ridiculous-looking shellacked straw hats, too small for their heads. Instead of the shellac, the officer in charge wore a gray felt Stetson.

"Mornin' boys," said the gray hat. "We're here to inspect this plane. There was an illegal crossing from Mexico last night by air, and we believe this to be the aircraft. Everything's gotta be stripped—floorboards, seats, engine covers, all the inspection plates."

My brother protested, explaining that we had landed yesterday afternoon, before three o'clock. We could prove it. There were plenty of witnesses who saw us land, and we even had a fuel receipt.

The gray hat snapped back.

"I don't give a rat's ass when you say you landed. This is a standard airport check. Routine."

"Routine?" Kern asked.

"Yeah. Routine. Where are you boys from?"

"New Jersey."

"Well, good. A long way from home, I guess. This is the way we do things out here."

I didn't like this dipshit gray hat one bit, which was a dangerous mood for me to get into. I was the kind of kid that cops took one look at and decided to pick on, because I displayed such a "rotten attitude." They were always nabbing me for blowing up mailboxes, or mooning old ladies, and once this local primate in uniform actually issued me a summons for passing a stopped school bus, on my bike. But I didn't mind, because I was used to it. They could pick on me all they wanted. But now my brother looked upset, which infuriated me.

This was one thing, actually, that I had swallowed right up to the pole from my father, his healthy loathing for cops. He had a good bickering manner to him around the law, denuding officers of authority by peppering them with a lot of difficult questions, taunting them with heavy verbal dosages of "My Ass."

And I was sick of the perils of this trip. There was always more peril. Thunderstorms, malevolent morons, rattler snakes, Pocket-protector FAA men—I'd had enough of that shit. I wasn't in the mood for this ersatz Wyatt Earp in the gray hat.

"Routine, my ass," I said to the gray hat. "We're not from Mexico. My brother just told you. We're from New Jersey."

The gray hat bristled and clutched both hands on his belt.

"Son, I don't know who the hell you think you are. I'm an officer of the law. A federal officer of the law. I have a right to inspect this plane and any other plane on this airport. Now, I've given you a lawful order to strip this aircraft. Are you going to obey?"

No, I wasn't. They weren't getting near 71-Hotel without a fight. My father's lawyer told me once that the best way around a cop was to throw out a lot of legal mumbo-jumbo, demands for warrants or probable cause. This stalled a lot of cops, because they could never remember whether the instructor back at the police academy told them they had to have a warrant for this situation or, shit, maybe the guy said we didn't.

What the hell. Give it a throw.

"My ass," I said to the gray hat. "Where's your warrant?"

"Now listen here son. Do you want me to call for help?"

"Help my ass! Where's your warrant?"

It bothered me a lot that my voice cracked every time I screamed "My ass!" I should have been able to deliver that in a calm, masculine tone, the way Clint Eastwood and Steve McQueen did it in the movies.

But it was working. The spectacle of the coast to coast kids getting busted by the Border Patrol was too much for the Yuma flyers. The whole airport exploded with rage.

While I screamed into one ear of the gray hat, the airport manager came over and screamed into the other. The geezer ambled over with his thermos of tea and called the gray hat a "flamin' jackass."

Apparently the Border Patrol was not well liked in Arizona. While the illegals streamed across the line down there, the Border Patrol was always up here, harassing the naturalized population. The border lawmen were especially detested at airports, where they were famous for pulling ramp checks on the wrong planes.

It got to be madness out there. Everybody was screaming at the gray hat, who by now could see that he had another Dodge City on his hands. Because it seemed to be working, and it felt so good, I kept yelling "My ass," even when nobody was listening.

"Listen here," the gray hat screamed, pointing his finger at my nose, "You stop saying 'my ass' to me, or I will *have* your ass."

"Oh my ass!" I said.

"Hey, officer, my ass too!" the geezer screamed at the gray hat. "Nobody's violatin' the law saying 'my ass.'"

"My ass! Golly, I like that," said the airport manager. "My ass! You boys from Nu Jursa are all right. Officer, what are you going to do? Call headquarters and tell 'em this boy's upsettin' you, saying 'my ass'?"

When the reporter from the paper arrived, he jumped in

too. He shoved a pile of clips about us in front of the gray hat. He was real shrewd about what he said too.

"Hey, fella, go ahead and bust these kids. The whole country is following their trip. Now the Border Patrol wants to strip their plane. It's a great story for me."

The Border Patrol crumbled. While the shellac hats stepped back into their pickups and lit cigarettes, the gray hat attempted to save face, asking to see Kern's license. Yup, T. Kernahan Buck, out of Nu Jursa. Tons of witnesses here, saying you landed yesterday afternoon at three. Guess we'll be leaving then. Have a safe trip.

Departing, the Border Patrol pickups flashed their lights and spun gravel and dust all over the airport with their wheels.

It was a victory, but Kern and I were upset. The Yuma flyers, however, clapped us on the back and laughed. They told us not to worry about it. This kind of thing happened a lot in Arizona, they said. The Border Patrol hated aviation, and aviation hated the Border Patrol.

After we were done with the newspaper interview, we shook a lot of hands and turned for the Cub. Just before we propped the engine, a bus load of Indian children arrived. They were all in a summer camp, and this was their annual excursion out to the airport. They were five- and six-year olds, round-faced and dark, with lovely black hair. As we taxied past them, they all started to cheer, really going wild for us for some reason, hooting so loud from behind the chain link fence we could hear them over the noise of the idling engine. Kern wheeled the plane around nearby and ran up the engine so they could watch.

The runway was right there. As he firewalled and raised the tail Kern called back.

"Rink, those are beautiful children. I'm giving them a flyby."

We turned at the windsock and banked back hard for the children, painting the sunbursts on our wings over their heads. From above, we could see them cheering and clapping, shiny black hair and brown faces jumping up and down in swells in the airport parking lot, beautiful Indian schoolchildren, dancing Arizona for us. Out over the desert we swept around low, dove for the strip and poured on the coals. As we went by the pumps, all the pilots, the geezers, and the children were waving, and the reporter was standing on top of the benches, both arms crossing over his head, and as Kern hammerheaded up there were hard blue horizons in the sky all around us, sparkling dew on the desert floor and a purple-black rim of foothills beckoning us west. I loved our trip, everyone we'd met and everything that had happened to us, the ceaseless unfolding of faces and terrain, swale to river to mountains, all of it joined and made intense by the thunderous Continental and the smell of burnt oil.

And so we flew west over the Colorado River and into California, past endless, undulating formations of sand dunes as fresh and as clean as beaches. Then the lush, irrigated lands of the Imperial Valley opened green for us, and El Centro and the Superstition Mountains went by. That leg was one of the longest of the trip, a little over three hours, and it was three hours of peaceful, carefree flying, when we owned the sky and everything in it.

Kern and I were silent in the cockpit, barely exchanging a word. It was a beautiful morning, with pristine desert scenery floating by under the wings, and we were almost there. We didn't want the trip to end, and it seemed too sacred a moment to spoil with talk.

Over the last range of mountains before San Diego, we got caught on top of the clouds. The Pacific Ocean had poured its morning surplus of fog onto the brown hills, and the moisture couldn't get past the high pressure on the eastern side. But there would be a break in the clouds for us, there always was. We held our compass course for ten minutes until it appeared, a hole just big enough for our wings. Spiraling down, we saw California all at once. We came out over suburban red tile roofs and water sprinklers making miniature rainbows over meticulously bordered green lawns. Every square foot of southern California seemed occupied by man, but it was a bright, ordered, and prosperous occupation. Just ahead of us lay Brown Field, and we flew over and entered the traffic pattern.

Screech-screech. Two tires down, in California.

Through heat mirages shimmering off the tarmac we could see another horde of reporters waiting for us by the operations building, jumping the gun on the Los Angeles media. But I couldn't have cared less about those reporters just then. It had been six days of hard flying and hell, and our waists and our stick hands were sore as roadkill. We were tired, we were burnt to a crisp, and our ears were ringing from the constant din of the Continental. But we were there. A sea breeze was blowing, and I could smell salt air from the Pacific ocean.

My brother was at rest. He was quiet and contemplative up front, a monk in his cell. He wiggled the rudders for me to taxi in. Resting his stick hand on the crash struts, he reached back with the other and squeezed my knee.

"Rink. We have done this thing. We made it, coast to coast."

CHAPTER 19

THE FIRST TELEVISION-NEWS HELICOPTER INTERCEPTED US OVER Oceanside. We were flying north up the Pacific coast in heavy smog, admiring the rat-packs of surfers on the waves below and southern California's vast acreage of swimming pools, when the chopper suddenly appeared out of the haze and hovered obnoxiously at our two o'clock. A long camera lens pushed out through the open window in the rear. Kern kept motioning them away, to get their rotor-wash off our wings. But every time Kern waved them off, this goofball television correspondent in the backseat unfastened his seatbelt and reached out his window, excitedly waving back. He was wearing a large rubber headset and talking into a microphone, as if he was broadcasting live. Of course I couldn't hear what he was saying, but it wasn't hard to imagine by watching his asinine jowls and happy, chattering teeth.

"Folks, they are now waving at us. The Buck boys are waving. Obviously, they're real happy to be in southern California."

What I would have been happy with, right then, was a wing-rack full of air-to-air missiles. Continuously raking us with its rotor turbulence, the copter wheeled and panned its camera at us from every angle, and then it dove at us from twelve o'clock high for the long head-on shot. Finally they tired of harassing us and settled into a safe position off our left wing.

Opposite Dana Point a large green exit sign hung over the San Diego Freeway. SAN JUAN CAPISTRANO. We followed the twisting two-lane road up to the top of the ridge. It took us a while to pick the airport out of the smog. We knew that the strip was tiny and difficult, because in San Diego a pilot had told us that San Juan Capistrano was legendary for its short-takeoff-and-landing flight school, where flyers about to ship off to Alaska as bush pilots were trained. But then the chopper clattered by and peeled off to the left, and we followed its rotor wash down to the airport.

It looked like a Hollywood movie set down there. The tiny airport and hangar were built into a bowl-shaped depression wedged in between two dusty canyons, surrounded by a serpentine irrigation canal. On the tarmac, a crowd of people waiting for us was ringed by the glinting rotors of more news helicopters and the blue waters of the canal. Everyone started to wave as we dropped into the traffic pattern and the whole airport looked excited and alert, the kind of place we were meant to fly hard for all week. I could even pick out Uncle Jim. Raven-haired and smiling, a foot taller than everybody else in the crowd, he was waving both arms over his head, like my father back home.

Turning downwind, Kern sized up the strip. The irrigation canal, with sloping cement walls, surrounded the airport like a moat. The runway was actually lower than the canal, paved into a basin. The strip was too short to glide down over the obstruction in the usual way. We would have to get low and slow over the canal and then side-slip briskly down over the wall. Our destination landing in California would be the most difficult one of all.

Kern always took a challenge like that and made it look easy. He got right down on top of the canal and kept us slow by holding the nose high and gradually adding power. Following the irrigation ditch around to the runway, he turned

90 degrees, slipped sideways down over the wall and leveled the wings just as we mushed into the stall. It was perfect, the first time. The runway was right there.

"Ah shit Rinker. Look at this."

All four helicopters on the ground had launched in a frenzy and darted over to the runway to photograph our arrival. They were completely blocking the runway and throwing up a dust storm that covered the whole airport. The only thing we could do was throttle back up and go around, praying that the choppers didn't climb underneath us and slice us up from below.

As we climbed and turned downwind, the helicopters rose in force and rat-tailed around in a crazyass formation behind us. They were real bronco-riders, those chopper pilots. When we descended again for the ditch, they all broke together and made a beeline for the runway to film our landing. But they were hovering so low on the runway, and throwing up so much dust, that it wasn't safe to land. Three times we flew San Juan Capistrano like that. Go around, fly the ditch, turn for the strip. Each time, down on the runway, it was Vietnam, snarling with Hueys.

After the third pass, Kern got mad. The blood vessels on his temples bulged and he cinched his seatbelt tight. He coiled up his body and moved his shoulders back and forth, the way my father and Eddie Mahler did, approaching an airshow field, transiting in muscle tone and mood from cross-country to acrobatic flight.

"Rink, I am going to lose these goddam choppers!" Kern yelled back. "Watch! Just watch me do this."

It was a very slick piece of flying Kern did right then. Ramming the throttle forward and going around, he faked right with the wings so the helicopters followed around downwind. Then he dove for speed and drew sharply back with the stick and we shot straight up through the hazy smog. Just before the stall he threw in all of his left aileron and plowed the rudder to bring the tail around. We snapped half-inverted 180 degrees into a wingover reverse, falling back onto our own propwash. Full stick down and we screamed for the far side of the ditch. All of this was done so briskly the helicopters above didn't even know they weren't on our tail anymore. This time Kern flew the inside of the irrigation wall, really smoking the plane around the turn. God, watch the accelerated stall, I thought. But Kern was aware of that too, and he kept pouring on more power and jabbing at the air with his outside rudder to make sure the Cub still had something left. All of this he did as one long and graceful sweep of the controls, so that each maneuver flowed smoothly into the next and I couldn't even discern that much was happening to the plane. There's no accounting for a young pilot as good as Kern was that morning in California. He was my father and Big Eddie Mahler, and all of the instructors and barnstormers back at our home strip, giving back all at once everything they had put into him over the years. Bonk he pulled out of the turn. Wham he crossed the controls, flying us sideways to bleed off speed. Slam he closed the throttle and then kicked in the last of his rudder and aileron to keep us in the sideways slip. All the while he was playing way over on the left side of the cockpit with the stick to hold us flat and nose-high in the slip, so the plane would be expended and have nothing left when we got over the runway. Mushing, we porpoised down over the canal. From the wingover up top to the slow-flight down here, a matter of thirty seconds or less, the plane had been stretched to every attitude and extremity of speed. Screech he planted the wheels on the first ten feet of the runway. But there was no stopping him now, because the helicopters had finally seen us and they were peeling back for the runway. Powering back up, Kern fast-taxied the length of the strip with the tail raised, took the corner at the taxiway on one wheel and made directly for the crowd with the Cub weather-cocked up on its main gear. When we were twenty yards out he reached for the magnetos and pulled the mixture control to shut down the engine and stood on the right brake, wheeling us around in front of everybody with the prop still clicking and dirt devils blowing off the wheels. Kern could really fly an airplane when he needed to and it was a very stylish arrival.

The crowd was cheering. There was a group of pilots from the San Juan Capistrano short field course standing up front, and they had enjoyed watching Kern work that tight little strip. The flight school director, who was also the airport manager, was the first to the plane, and he pumped our hands. Uncle Jimmy pushed through the crowd with his arm around Aunt Joan. Tall and tanned, with that gracious, broad smile that I remembered, he was dressed in one of those white, Mexican-style shirts that hung down over his waist, and these geeky, black hightop sneakers, very "California" I thought. Aunt Joan was dressed to the nines, in a white rayon skirt and blouse. My cousins, Kevin, Tom, and Kelly, came behind with a group of Jimmy and Joan's Orange County friends. It was obvious that Uncle Jimmy and Aunt Joan's friends didn't know anything about the small airport culture, because they were dressed for the country club instead, with lots of costume jewelry and pink golf pants. The print reporters started shouting questions and the photographers shot a lot of pictures. As soon as I got the door open Jimmy had his big arms around us and Aunt Joan kissed Kern, getting her bracelets and rings tangled in his hair.

"Oh Kern!" Aunt Joan said. "You look so handsome and tan! Just look at you!"

That was the thing about Aunt Joan that was great. She treated Kern as if he were Cary Grant.

"Real fine Kern. Real fine," Uncle Jimmy said. "Wow, what a landing you made. Wait'll I tell your dad."

"Uncle Jimmy, don't you dare tell my father about that landing."

"Real fine Kern, real fine. I am *not* telling your father about that landing."

The crowd surged forward. Everybody was poking the fabric and reaching inside to touch us and the throttle and stick, anything they could get their hands on really, and I liked all the excitement, the emotion and joy swelling off the crowd into us. It was the first moment that I felt that there was anything remarkable about our trip. But my feelings about that reception were curiously detached, as if all the excitement were directed at someone else. Everyone there was thrilled about our flight, their imagination of what a transcontinental crossing in a Piper Cub must have been like. But I was exhausted, tired of flying, and all I could remember was five days of nonstop turbulence and a blurry scramble through a mountain pass. I was stunned by the spectacle of it all, the queer logic of what excited people. Kern and I were oddballs, aviation nerds, sons of an eccentric, one-legged ex-barnstormer. One Saturday we took off and flew west for the mountains and the Saturday after that we hit the next ocean, and now we had this personal monkey off our backs. But nobody else saw it that way. This was America, where everything had to be exaggerated and hyped to the max. All of a sudden it was patriotic, what we had done. We were great American boys. I could practically hear the "Star-Spangled Banner" wailing away in the background. But that wasn't us. That's what everybody else was bringing to our flight. But I figured I could learn to milk this dog and enjoy our fifteen minutes of fame. Then the reporters started calling out questions all at once, elbowing each other, and snarling about who got to interview us first, and everything got back to normal. People kept pushing up through the crowd and asking for our autographs. Before I was even out of the plane, I had signed a dozen autographs on postcards and scraps of paper shoved into the cockpit. Some little brat even ran off with two of our maps.

The TV helicopters came clattering back down, and it was just a media brawl after that. My father had asked Jimmy to "supervise" the press coverage, but he was no good at it, not being the aggressive newshound and efficient greeter that his older brother was. The television producers kept getting angry at him for letting a competing newsman interview us first. One of the reporters got wind of the fact that Kern had dated the girl across the street from Jimmy's when he visited California in 1963. It wasn't exactly a hot romance. She and Kern played Ping-Pong in the cellar, and held hands at Disneyland. But somebody—Kern swears it was Aunt Joan, Aunt Joan says, nope, it was Kern—blurted out her name, Carol Brantley.

It was hot out on the tarmac and everybody got all bollixed up over that, dragging poor, sweet Carol, the proverbial girl next door, into the media shindig. As far as Jimmy was concerned, the story of our coast to coast adventure was now

YOUTHFUL PILOTS—Kern Buck, 17, ~~ther,~~ Rinker, 15, relax at Tustin ~~...~~

We were just the dose of innocence that the country needed before the tumult of the late 1960s began.

Adventure Ends Tomorrow

Two Morris Teen-Agers Flying

By PEGGY CARROLL

NEW VERNON — Today a small 28-year-old Piper Cub enters the last leg of its transcontinental journey from New Jersey to California.

At the controls is a 17-year-old New Vernon boy, Kern Buck, and navigating is his 15-year-old brother, Rinker.

Their sole navigational aid is a $9.95 alcohol compass.

The boys began their adventure Sunday when they took off from Basking Ridge in the plane they completely rebuilt themselves. The first part of their journey will end at 3 p.m. tomorrow when they are scheduled

to land in Capistrano.

Yesterday, they had reached El Paso, Texas, and ahead of them lay the roughest part of the trip — over the western desert and the Rocky Mountains.

Their father, Thomas F. Buck, of Sand Spring Road has confidence in their ability.

"They are probably safer than if they drove to Hoboken in a car," he said, "or got on a bicycle and rode to the swimming pool.

"We think it's better to have the kids attracted to wholesome adventure than running off to discotheques in Greenwich Village."

The boys have been around planes since they were little more than two years old. Their father, who has been flying since 1924, bought his first plane at 17; served with the Royal Canadian Air Force, and later with the U.S. Eighth Air Force during World War II.

As soon as each of his 11 children passed the toddler stage, he took them for their first flight. By the time they are 10 or 11, they have learned the rudiments of navigation and are competent "stick pilots," able to control the plane once it's off the ground.

Kern, a June graduate of Del-barton School, soloed on his 16th

birthday, got his pilot's license on his 17th birthday, and next month, on his 18th birthday, will receive his commercial instructor's certification. By the time he returns from his California jaunt, he will have logged almost 300 hours of flying time.

Rinker, a sophomore at Del-barton, is prevented only by age from taking his solo flight, his father said.

"He's navigator and ordnance officer on this flight," Bu~~ck~~ explained.

The boys have also had experience with gliders, ~~...~~ soloed on a glider ~~at ...~~ Airport last year ~~...~~ 14.

It was ~~...~~ boys be ~~...~~ the pl~~ane...~~ "A~~...~~ vise~~...~~ "I~~...~~

~~...~~, 15—made it ~~...~~mpleting a 7,500

28-day ~~...~~ng time, more ~~th...~~ ~~...~~ to fill out the 200 hou~~rs...~~ needed to qualify for a commercial pilot's license when he turns 18 next month.

The boys rebuilt the plane last winter, and obviously did a good job. Kern said they broke a spring once and had a "little trouble with the engine—nothing serious."

Otherwise, except for a little bad weather, everything went smoothly.

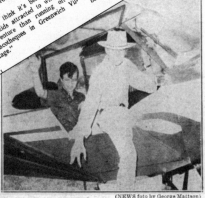

(NEWS foto by George Mattson)
Rinker (left) and Kern Buck have a happy landing in Piper Cub at Basking Ridge Airport.

Brothers, 17 ad 15, air their proficiency

By MARK N. FINSTON

"I would never let my boys drive to Atlantic City," said the strict father.

"But, of course, I would have no objection to letting them fly to Atlantic City in their plane," added ___ F. Buck.

Whether K___ Rinker, ___ child___

hours of work a we_ get the plane ship-shape_ July 5 the boys __ft Los Angeles ___ short da___ ___ them ___ by ___ion

in the Cub's cramped quarters. The boys would land every two hours to stretch legs and refuel. And they spent two weeks in L.A.

___iring tans at the home of ___ of their uncle.

___ is the best summer ___ spent," said Kern. ___ would have been ___ a radio." This ___ill enter Holy ___ he may major ___ might also ___someday

that. Flying might get boring."

Their father has been a flight fancier since 1935; his inspiration was Charles Lindbergh.

"Being in a plane is much safer than being on a highway," repeated Buck. He was questioned about the fact that he lost his left leg in an airplane accident in 1945.

"That was military flying," he explained. "Civilian flying is much safer than military flying."

"We only got really scared once," said Kern. "When we were over the desert, it sounded as if the engine were falling apart. When we landed we found it was just a heavy piece of tape hanging on the ___

themselves out of the cockpit, their mother took a look at the long, curly hair invading the eyeball province of Rink's face.

"Push that hair out of your eyes," said Mrs. Buck.

Rink, who was more interested in the applause and the photographers, gave a gentle push which removed not one hair.

"You're home, I see," sighed his mother.

For the rest of the summer, Kern will work on a farm, and try to get a commercial flying license. Rink will put up fences for his father and fly gliders on weekends.

Oh, yes, there's one more summer project. During those seven months of just plane ___ a week, the ___ir social life ___ced.

___do something ___ said Kern.

___ast To Coast

___ ___tary flight instructor in Texas.

"They are to follow the highways in the desert," Buck said. "The plane's wing are painted so they are easily visible in case of an emergency landing. The boys also carry with them a supply of water and six candy bars."

Each night at dusk, after traveling an average of 750 to 800 miles, the boys land in meadow-type airports in small towns and check in with their parents. Each day they file flight plans, away from main airways, with the FAA.

They are seeing a bit of off-beat America on the way.

"They landed Wednesday in a small town in Texas," Buck said. "They were amazed to see cowboys come riding into town at the end of the day. They even saw a 'lawman', complete with badge and horse."

In California they will visit an uncle for 10 days before making the return trip.

This September, Kern will head for Holy Cross College where he plans to prepare for a career in journalism.

"With his instructor's license," his father said, "he won't have to sell magazines to pay for his education. He'll fly his way through college!"

___ the ___uilding ___ight. ___ super- ___ a smile ___ my older

___ for the trip ___ — Kern at a ___ in a Bernards- ___er: Ricker ex- ___ting horses in New

___they left, their father during ___ out the plane ___. They got the instructions for ___ trip over the desert and ___untains from Alex Yankanis, ___ pilot for Ronson Indus- ___ries, who had served as a mili-

CROSS-COUNTRY TRIP—This Piper Cub took Rinker Buck, 15, in plane, and brother, Kern, 17, from their Morristown home to California. They arrived in San Diego Saturday. Kern is the pilot. Rinker isn't old enough for license yet. (AP Wirephoto)

contaminated by a love angle. We all knew that the papers would print Carol Brantley's name, which committed Kern to calling her up for a date. But seeing Carol again had never been a part of Kern's plans for the California trip, and he was surprised at the way her name had popped out of the blue.

And the waterbag, the freaking waterbag just wouldn't die. All week, my father had been regaling Jimmy over the phone about the waterbag, and Jimmy in turn had regaled Aunt Joan. On the way out to the airport that morning, in her Cadillac, Aunt Joan had told all her Orange County friends about the waterbag. So, there was sort of a waterbag coterie now— people in the know, people "close to the trip," a VIP list of insiders privy to information about the waterbag.

So, Aunt Joan and her friends decided to stroll over to the Cub to check out the waterbag. In the excitement of all this, however, Aunt Joan's internal gyros failed and she slipped backward into the Cub, right at the oiliest spot. Now she had the reverse image of a Piper Cub landing gear, in 40-weight oil, indelibly printed on her white rayon derriere. She forgot all about the waterbag.

"Jim! My skirt," Aunt Joan moaned across the tarmac. "It's ruined!"

"Ah Joan, relax," Uncle Jimmy said. "I'm trying to manage all these reporters here."

"But my skirt, Jimmy. It's ruined!"

"Dear, just buy yourself another one," Jimmy said. "You *own* a dress shop. You own *five* dress shops, for God's sake."

I felt terrible about it—not about the skirt, but about Jimmy and Joan. In our family, they were legendary for the warmth of their relationship. At our family reunions, all the aunts sat around talking about how rough it was being married to these Buck men. But Aunt Joan out in California, they all agreed, had it made. Jimmy was such a peach, and he and Joan never exchanged a harsh word. Now, just because we had landed, they were arguing for the first time in years.

"Ah Jeez Rink," Kern said. "Look at Aunt Joan's skirt. I knew we should have cleaned the gear off back in Yuma."

"Yeah. This is a zoo. Let's get out of here."

It was a relief when the last news-chopper finally lifted off.

We made arrangements for tying the Cub down at the airport for two weeks and piled into Jimmy and Joan's matching Cadillacs. I rode the lead Caddie with Uncle Jim and my cousins, and Kern and Aunt Joan followed behind as we twisted down the canyon road.

As soon as we hit the San Diego Freeway, Uncle Jimmy asked about the waterbag. He hadn't noticed it on the landing gear. I wasn't alarmed. Kern had always told me that Uncle Jim was somebody you could be honest with, like one of the "cool priests" up at school or one of our older cousins. He wouldn't sit on a boy for something, like my father would. Uncle Jimmy had already told me just to call him Jimmy.

"Jimmy," I said. "Can I tell you this?"

Jimmy has a way of talking. He explodes on words, one at a time.

"It's bullshit, right? The waterbag is *bull*. I just *knew* it. *Knew* it. *Oh*, that father of yours."

"Total bull, Jimmy," I said. "We never even looked for the thing."

Jimmy roared. He adored my father. As boys, they had shared the same room and Jimmy never stopped being grateful for the way my father had chipped in and helped support the family during the Depression. But he understood his older brother quite well and had a good sense of humor about him, and he loved it when my father's tall talk got him into trouble like this.

"Real fine," Jimmy said, still laughing. "The waterbag is bogus. But look, don't tell Aunt Joan about this. Her friends were really looking forward to seeing the waterbag and I don't want everybody to be disappointed."

Out on the freeway, the first thing I noticed was the traffic. Clearly, the automobile was a very serious preoccupation in southern California. Every vehicle on I-5, a dozen lanes across, glowed with wax and looked as though it was worn by its occupants as a piece of clothing or jewelry. Immaculately tanned and coifed men in long-nosed Jaguar XKEs glided by at eighty miles per hour, noiselessly darting across the lanes.

There were surfers and lots of pretty girls in yellow Jeeps. Even the bikers and the cops looked spotless and neat, as if they were impostors, headed for a costume ball.

The car just seemed to be everything in California. At Anaheim, we pulled off the freeway and headed in toward Jimmy's house in Tustin, gliding down sunny boulevards lined with palm trees, carpets of flowers and faux-Mediterranean façades. As we turned in for Jimmy's neighborhood, every garage door was thrown open and men and boys inside leaned over the hoods of cars, classic cars, a '51 Chevy pickup at the house on the corner, a T-Bird next door, lots of '57 Chevys and early-model Corvettes after that. While the men Simonized their Deuce Coupes in the shade, their wives and daughters were outside on the hot lawn, mowing the grass in bikinis.

We hardly had a chance to settle into the house, which was tastefully decorated by Aunt Joan in beige and earth tones, with lots of nubbly fabrics and African and Mexican masks, before Jimmy called us out to the garage. In California, as soon as a house guest arrived, the car relationship had to be established.

"Boys," Jimmy said, ushering us into his spotless two-bay garage, "First things first. Here's your vehicle."

There, in the bay next to Aunt Joan's Cadillac, was a Ford Falcon station wagon, their "spare car." It was several years old, but the red paint was like new and the grille and chrome trim gleamed like the brightwork on a yacht.

"Real fine," Uncle Jimmy said. "This is your car, boys. You can use it for as long as you're here. I don't care what you do with it, I don't care what time you get in at night. In fact, I don't care period. You're grown, mature boys—hell, you just flew an airplane all the way out here! Just don't get me in trouble with your father. Aunt Joan just loves you, and she wants you to have a good time."

Jesus. I always thought that this pie-eyed brother of mine was too extravagant in his praise of California. Aunt Joan and Uncle Jim couldn't be as great as he said they were. But Jimmy really seemed to mean this stuff. It was paradise out here.

Kern and I immediately settled into a routine, and most nights in Tustin we paired off with Uncle Jimmy and Aunt Joan. The California neighborhoods never seemed to shut down, and my cousins, who were younger than us, were always running off somewhere, driving go-carts with their friends or helping the man next door repaint one of his cars. Aunt Joan, who was a great cook and enjoyed company in the kitchen, sat at the table inside with Kern, slicing vegetables for a Mexican-style dinner and talking. She'd always told everyone that Tom's "darling Kern" was her favorite nephew. She was excited about him leaving home for college in the fall and wanted to know everything that had happened to him since he visited three years before, and all about his dates. Joan was very protective of Kern and determined to see him become a success, and she knew just how to make that happen. Dates. Kern, Aunt Joan thought, needed lots of dates with girls.

I sat outside in the garden with Uncle Jim. God, did I love California and Jimmy's garden. Back in New Jersey, at Easter, my father was always careful to buy my mother a couple of these bird-of-paradise flowers, and this special kind of pink orchid that she liked, and the damn things cost about $15 a petal. In the east, these plants were considered rare. But Jimmy had at least a dozen bird-of-paradise plants back there, as thick as overgrown lilac back home, and the orchids were a dime a dozen. Ringing the patio, in neatly manicured beds, were all kinds of mimosas and bonsai trees, flowering ginkgos and all the rest, with a carpet of grass so green and plush a baby could fall right off a swing and not get hurt. The fragrance of all these plants together was otherworldly, and there was always a gentle breeze blowing in from the Santa Ana mountains.

I had never spent much time with Jimmy, and it was a relief to dawdle away my evenings with somebody in the family who was so like me, but then again, so normal. We were both interested in the same things—politics and history—and read a lot, and Jimmy often felt intellectually lonely in Orange County, being the only registered Democrat for miles around. We gorged ourselves on talk. Jimmy's stories were expansive and grand and he reminded me a lot of my father, except that he seemed less insistent on proving a point, and more satisfied with himself.

Jimmy didn't mind if I had a beer once in a while. In fact, I had many beers in the garden with Jim. But we knew that Kern might be concerned about this so Jimmy would sneak the beers out of the refrigerator for me and pour them into a glass with a big 7-Up logo. From the kitchen, Kern and Aunt Joan would look out to the garden, and think I was drinking 7-Up.

Jimmy wanted to hear all about our trip, and he had already gotten wind of the shit-shit-shit El Paso gam and other problems I was having with my father, because my father had complained about it. Jimmy was seven years younger than my father, and after the Depression hit, my father helped raise him. He understood what was happening, and anyway, Jimmy was a just good egg, somebody I knew I could talk to. Even without the beers I would have opened up to him.

"Jimmy, I just don't know what to do sometimes. We flew all the way out here without getting lost, but every time I talk to my father I get the ninth degree. I'm bugged about it."

"Don't fight a problem, Rinker," Jimmy said. "Understand it. Look, your father is a total kick-ass man. God, you should have seen him scrap his way out of the Depression. He's got to dominate everything, because that's all he knows. That approach might have worked with Kern. But then you come along, thinking you have all the answers, and Tom Buck doesn't know what to do."

"Yeah. Great. So where does that leave me?"

"Rinker, you don't have to do a thing. Dodge the guy. Avoid him! Your father is so busy now with civil rights and politics, and God knows what else he's up to, he's not even going to notice if you just keep your head low."

Kern had said the same thing. This was the agreement with myself I was supposed to make back in Yuma. I was trying hard to listen. Kern and Jimmy couldn't both be wrong about the same thing.

California had its own light and smells. In the morning, fragrances of mimosa and birds-of-paradise wafted in through the bedroom curtains, and we woke refreshed. We ranged out in the red Falcon every day, spending long afternoons taking surfing lessons from the teenagers down the street, or visiting Disneyland and Knott's Berry Farm. Carol Brantley took us to Newport Beach a couple of times, and we got terrible sunburns. More reporters called for interviews, and Kern particularly liked a very thorough and accurate story on our coast to coast flight in *The Los Angeles Times*. When we flew the Cub up to the Orange County airport for a fifty-hour check, Frank Tallman, a famous Hollywood stunt pilot, strolled out of his hangar and made a big fuss over us. Kern took our cousins and the neighborhood kids for rides in 71-Hotel.

We were new boys out there, different boys. It wasn't simply Jimmy's creed of fun, or the absence of rules. He and Aunt Joan unconditionally loved us and couldn't have cared less about all the great ambitions my father had for us. Aunt Joan took Kern shopping in the malls, bought him new clothes, and told him how wonderful he looked in this outfit or that. Uncle Jimmy was excited when I came in from the beach one night and told him that I finally managed to "get up" on a surfboard. In California, you could just live day by day and nobody seemed to worry about tomorrow. Everything was fine, real fine as Jimmy said, and everybody liked Kern and I just the way we were.

A few days after we arrived in California, Uncle Jimmy returned from his job at Allstate Insurance one evening and told us that he had received an intriguing phone call during the day. A dignified-sounding gentleman by the name of Harold Buck had read about us in *The Los Angeles Times* and tracked Jimmy down to inquire whether or not we were related. We weren't, but Harold Buck was apparently a big wheel in southern California. He was a former close associate of the reclusive billionaire Howard Hughes and had retired many years ago as a director of Hughes's machine-tool company. He insisted on meeting his newly famous namesakes.

Jimmy felt sheepish about it. He didn't want to impose another visitor upon us, but he was too polite to give Harold Buck the bum's rush.

"Boys," Jimmy said, "Mr. Buck sounds very old. And lonely. Could you just meet the guy, for me?"

"Real fine," Kern said.

The next night Harold Buck appeared in the driveway and tooted the horn of his Cadillac. He wasn't feeling particularly ambulatory that night and preferred to meet with us in his car. He was a sallow, white-haired man with a hearing aid and impeccable, old-fashioned manners. We sat with him in his car for an hour and listened to Harold's long, lonely monologue.

He was so, so pleased to meet us. We reminded him of his own youth, striking out from the east for California. In the 1920s, he had risen quickly in the machine tool business, and then met Mr. Howard Hughes. Mr. Hughes was quite an aviator himself, did we know that? Mr. Buck wanted to show us the Hughes tool works. He could even get us in, he said in hushed tones, to the hangar in Long Beach where the biggest plane in the world, Howard Hughes's famed amphibious boondoggle, the Spruce Goose, was stored. Kern stalled for time, making up an excuse that we had to do some work on our plane. I was exhausted from surfing all day and fell asleep in the rear seat.

It was our most bizarre California experience. Harold Buck returned a few more times, usually unannounced. When he was feeling especially nonambulatory, a chauffeur drove him. We sat out there in the driveway in an air-conditioned Cadillac, drinking Cokes that Harold provided, listening to this rich old geezer chat away. He was always trying to interest us in the various properties he owned. For example, he ran an avocado farm up in the hills somewhere, and he wanted us to see it. Politely, Kern kept turning him down.

"Oh, Kernahan, please, don't apologize," Harold said. "Of course, you must be very busy now. But can't I at least bring you some avocados, as a gift? You can keep them in the plane and eat them on your return flight."

"Oh fine, Harold," Kern said. "Real fine. We'd like that a lot."

It was decided. For our return flight, Harold Buck would make us a present of avocados.

CHAPTER 20

AT THE END OF OUR FIRST, BLISSFUL WEEK IN CALIFORNIA, MY father impulsively decided to join us by hopping on an overnight airline flight to Los Angeles. This was another personality test for Kern and me. I was instantly depressed and furious about it and considered my father's decision thoughtlessly selfish, proof that he just couldn't let go of us and stay away. Kern was a lot more mature about it.

"Rink, guess what?" he said, bursting into our room at Uncle Jim's on Friday night, just after we had returned from Newport Beach. "Daddy's coming out! He's already on the plane. Uncle Jimmy just told me."

We both agreed that he had been furtive about it. This had never been part of the plan, and my father had simply called from the airport before he boarded a plane in New York. There was a "big mess" in his Los Angeles sales office, he told Uncle Jim, and his presence was suddenly needed to sort things out. It was the oldest ruse in the magazine business. My father had reached a nice point in his career. He was now associate publisher at *Look*, a classic holding pattern where talented executives waited for several years until the publisher finally stepped down. Because his politics had turned so radical, my father was beginning to sense that he would never be named publisher, but he wasn't worried about it. His sales record was strong and he was particularly gifted at solving the myriad crises that strike publishing every week, and the magazine didn't want to lose him. So he had a big corner office in New York, lots of secretaries, and an unlimited expense budget. There was always a "big mess" out in the L.A. office—my father had joked about it for years. Whenever he got bored with office routine, or just felt the need for racing along a balmy freeway in a rented Lincoln Continental, he had his secretaries book him a flight to "The Coast." As soon as he stepped off the plane he did everything he could to assure that the "big mess" remained a big mess. That way, he could return next month to see his brother Jim and goof off with his pals from the Hollywood film studios.

"What a coincidence!" he told Jimmy. "I can see the boys."

His plane would be landing first thing in the morning, and we were to take an early bus up to the Los Angeles airport and meet his flight.

I got over my annoyance as soon as I saw my father bound down the escalator at the terminal. He was a picture of fitness and sophistication. Tanned, with his Ray-Bans on, he was wearing a pink alligator shirt and one of those beautiful summer tweed jackets made for him by the best tailor in Dublin. Kern was elated to see him and ran over to the bottom of the escalator, and I always felt elated myself, seeing those two together. Kern and my father loved each other so much.

My father skipped off the bottom of the escalator in that funny gait of his and hugged us both.

"God boys, it's great to see you. You did this thing! Coast to coast in a Piper Cub. Everybody's going nuts for this deal back in New York. I'm just so damn proud of you I could scream."

"Yeah," Kern said, beaming. "But Dad, one thing bothers me about all this."

"What?"

"Well, Dad, it wasn't that hard. You know, we just got in the Cub every morning, flew all day, and now we're here. What's the big deal?"

My father looked like he was coming down with an awful case of indigestion.

"Jesus Kern, don't say that! If a reporter asks you, you tell him it was *rough*."

My father's briefcase overflowed with articles about us clipped from the New York papers, and Kern had a pile for him from L.A. We all stood around at the bottom of the escalator and looked them over, laughing about the way the newspapers in one town borrowed quotes from the papers in another, and all the Kennedy bull, which made it sound like Kern and I flown over the Rockies reciting John Fitzgerald Kennedy's inaugural address.

After we landed in California, the Associated Press had checked with the Airmen's Bureau of the FAA and concluded that we were "the youngest aviators on record ever to fly America coast to coast." It seemed a meaningless distinction to us. Somebody younger than us just might have flown coast to coast before, and in any case this wasn't a record we were even aware of trying to break before we took off. But the press seemed to need this, and embraced the concept of us breaking a record. It was a peg, an angle, a way to break the story down for readers and identify what the clamor was all about. (In fact, the "record" was bull. Years later, while studying for my instrument rating, I came across a book written by Robert N. Buck, no relation, a well-known TWA captain and writer on aviation subjects. In the 1930s, Robert Buck flew coast to coast at age sixteen, and even set a speed record doing it. What the hell, at least it was a *Buck* who really did it.) Kern and I were perplexed about it.

"Hey Dad," Kern said. " 'Youngest aviators ever to fly America coast to coast?' Don't you think maybe this is bull?"

"Ah c'mon Kern," my father said. "Learn to relax. When you get right down to it, everything's bull! Who cares? This is what the papers are saying so this is what's true. Milk it! Get used to it. Christ son, you're famous!"

Everything was going smoothly until we got out to the freeway, and my father turned his rented Lincoln north for L.A., instead of south for Uncle Jim's. All of the good men's shops, he explained to us, were in Beverly Hills, just off Wilshire

Boulevard. He was going to deck us out—new slacks and summer jackets, loafers, shirts, and ties. It was a ritual for him, something he enjoyed, buying us new riding chaps or leather bomber jackets for each new stage of our "careers" as boys. All of his clients and buddies in Los Angeles were insisting on meeting us, and he wanted us to look smart while he squired us around town.

Kern and I both rebelled, and my father was surprised by the intensity of our reaction. Something had come over us between New York and L.A. No, no, no, I said, I didn't want to waste a beautiful Saturday morning buying clothes. Kern backed me up. Aunt Joan had just bought him a new pair of white slacks. They were good enough. Besides, what were we going to do with all this loot? There wasn't any room in the baggage compartment to fly it back home in the Cub.

My father was angry about it, but he tried to make the best of a disappointing situation.

"All right then. Good. You don't need new clothes," my father said. "How about lunch? I'll take you to lunch at the Beverly Wilshire. Wait'll you see the Beverly Wilshire!"

"Dad," I said, "it's ten o'clock in the morning."

As it happened, I had a surfing appointment back in Orange County at noon. Kern was going to a beach party with Carol Brantley.

"Well fine boys, just fine," my father said. "Rinker's going surfing. Kern's got a beach party. I came all the way out here to see you two, and now I get to sit around the garden and twiddle my thumbs with Uncle Jimmy and Aunt Joan."

The rest of his visit was like that. It was a misunderstanding that lasted a week.

When we got back to the house in Tustin my father noticed a number of phone messages for my brother on the kitchen bulletin board. "Kern, call Hildegard Richter." Hildegard Richter, which truly was her name, was our biggest pain in the ass that week. She was the society columnist for the weekly newspaper back home and, what a coincidence, she was visiting friends in San Diego County when we landed after our coast to coast flight. She pestered us all week for an interview, even calling my father back in New Jersey, appealing for his help. With help from Uncle Jimmy and Aunt Joan, Kern invented a dozen excuses to put her off. Finally, when Hildegard just wouldn't give up, Kern agreed to drive down for an interview on Saturday, today. But then Carol Brantley called about the beach party and I accepted an invitation to go surfing. Then my father showed up on twelve hours notice. Clearly, Hildegard had to be eliminated from the program, but neither of us wanted to call that godawful woman and blow her off.

"Hey Kern," I said that morning, as we boarded the bus for L.A. "Fuck Hildegard. Let's just stand her up."

"Yeah. Okay Rink. It's definitely not the right thing to do, but let's just do it."

My father was furious about it. At Uncle Jim's he immediately picked up the phone and called Hildegard, apologized, and explained that we would be late. Then he stuffed us back into the Lincoln for the long drive to San Diego.

It was a hot, smoggy day, very dreary conditions for freeway driving, and the trip was a killer. The house where Hildegard was staying was way up in the hills somewhere and we got lost. At one point we were actually yelling to some neighbors from a lawn across the canyon, soliciting further directions. Hildegard was middle-aged and lumpy, and when we finally found her she greeted us at the door in this bright orange jumpsuit, "very California," she thought. To me, she looked like Winston Churchill in drag.

Hildegard led us out to chaise longues in the patio-garden and served us soda and some kind of apricot-flavored pastry that no human being would ever want to eat. My father sat there with us, throwing in his two cents every few minutes and palavering on to Hildegard about the waterbag. The garden was very California too, stuffed to the fences with flowers, fragrant and soporific. In the middle of answering one of Hildegard's totally dipshit questions I fell fast asleep.

My father was merciless on the ride home.

"Goddamit Rinker! Why can't you grow up and get with the program? I know Hildegard's a pain in the ass. But you gotta put up with people like this to get ahead. It's so typical of you, so obstinate, to nod off in the middle of a newspaper interview like that."

And I guess it was typical of me, too, to be miserable over the next three days while my father escorted us around L.A. We did the *Look* office, the movie studios, and had dinner up in the Hollywood hills in the palatial homes of his friends. Everywhere we went we were photographed and toasted, and we were also totally bored. I didn't fly to California for this. I just wanted to be back in 71-Hotel now, wandering the deserts with Kern. By the end of the third day my father could see that even Kern had had enough. Glumly, we all said goodbye as he put us onto a bus for Uncle Jim's. We would see him Saturday, at San Juan Capistrano, when we took back off for the east.

Saturday arrived, and it was time to fly back east. There was a small crowd waiting for us at San Juan Capistrano, a few pilots from the strip, some curious people from town, and Aunt Joan and Uncle Jim. Hildegard Richter showed up, blowing over to us in a cloud of perfume and another one of those hideous California jumpsuits. The Lincoln cruised in and my father bounded out, all smiles and colorful talk, as if nothing had happened between us in L.A.

"Hey boys," he said. "C'mon! Let's get going. Go down and preflight the plane. And where's the waterbag? Everybody wants to see it. Get the plane, and bring up the water-bag."

It was a long walk down the flight line to the Cub, and Kern was disconsolate. Two weeks ago, he was profuse in his praise for my handling of the waterbag situation. Now he couldn't see a way out and blamed me for lying too well. He sat on the wheel of the Cub with his chin in his hands.

"Shit," Kern said. "What are we going to do? Daddy is going to explode."

It pained me to see Kern like that, and I was angry. Partly, I was angry at myself for lying so well, but mostly I was angry at my father. He never told us he was coming out to L.A.

and would want to see the waterbag. If we'd known that, we either would have found one or told the truth. The whole farce was my fault, for taking such perverse pleasure in hoodwinking him as we crossed the country. So I would have to take responsibility and deal with my father.

"Kern, relax," I said. "I'll handle the waterbag with Dad."

Meanwhile, up on the ramp, my father saw no evidence of us readying the plane and the waterbag. Angered by the delay, he kangarooed down across the dusty strip toward the Cub. I stalked off to meet him halfway.

I can still recall that confrontation with photographic accuracy. My father was wearing a crisp white alligator shirt, blue twill pants, and a new pair of English-cut oxfords that he'd bought at a shoe store in Beverly Hills. We squared off midway down the flight line, near the tail of a brown Stinson.

Everything that was within me welled up. Instinctively I sensed that I would have to hit my father very hard and fast. I couldn't pull my punches and act contrite. I took a deep breath and opened up with both barrels.

"Dad, there is no waterbag. We never even looked for the stupid thing. There's no waterbag."

"Ah shit Rinky."

"Yeah, shit. You've been an absolute pain in the ass on this thing, and there's no waterbag."

"Shit."

"Shit is right."

"No waterbag?"

He didn't know whether to scream or laugh, and there was this falsetto amazement to his voice when he said, "*No waterbag?*"

"No waterbag."

"Jesus Rinker. Everybody up there is expecting to see this thing. They want to see the waterbag. You really mean it? No waterbag?"

"Dad, there is no waterbag. Do you copy that? No waterbag. It was a dumb idea when you brought it up. It was a dumb idea when you pestered us all across the country about it. It's a dumb idea now. We never even looked for that waterbag. You don't need a waterbag to cross America in a Piper Cub. We've proven that to you."

My father looked up from the dust, his face twisted in anger, but he did have these marvelous qualities, always. He could transition quickly to the next emotion and when he was wrong he wasn't afraid to say so.

"Ah shit Rinker. I'm feeling awful now. I blew it. I blew this thing."

He fished his pipe out of his pocket and took several long draws to calm himself down. He was really working at getting himself over the hill and into the next mood. Then his shoulders started to shake and he laughed so hard that he had to lean against the tail of the plane behind him.

"Well, I oughta be angry with you Rinker, but I'm not. I'm sorry. This whole thing is my fault. I can see that you're upset, and you have a right to be. You obviously didn't need a waterbag."

"Yeah, well, I'm sorry too. I shouldn't have lied about it."

"Nah, nah, nah. You didn't lie. You let me believe what I wanted to believe. And I was a horse's ass to want to believe it. But look, how's Kern on this? How's he taking it? Is he mad at me too?"

"Kern's fine Dad. Just leave Kern to me."

"All right. But I don't want him upset."

"Dad, he's always upset when you put pressure on him like this. Why can't you just back off sometimes, leave him alone?"

"Ahh God, Rinker. I'm just so upset with myself over this. It's my project now—leaving Kern alone. Jimmy's been kicking my ass about it all week. I've gotta let go and stop upsetting Kern."

"And me Dad. Me."

"You? What do you mean, you?"

"Me, Dad. Me. Everything's always Kern. Kern, Kern, Kern. What if I'm upset? You only care about Kern."

"Oh boy," my father sighed. "How was I supposed to know you felt that way?"

"You never asked."

"You never told me."

"You never listened. You only care about Kern."

"Rinker that's not true. Dammit-all, that's not true! Kern's the one I *worried* about, and there's a difference. Hell, I didn't have to worry about you. You're running track all the time, getting straight As, and all the priests up at school know damn well they should be kicking your ass for something, but they'll never do it because they like you too much. Shit, I happen to admire that. But Kern wasn't that way. He was shy. He didn't take to people like you did. Until I got him up into an airplane, I didn't know what the hell we'd do. Mother was worried about him. I was worried about him. I've always felt close to him and knew I had to do something. But I knew you'd be fine. Don't you get it? That's a compliment, son."

"Sure, I get it. Thanks for the compliment."

"Ah Jeez. What are you telling me? You feel slighted? Left out?"

"No, I don't feel slighted! I don't feel left out," I said. "I mean, you know, well, okay, yeah, maybe, so I do feel left out, sometimes. I guess. Whatever Dad. But if you're going to be upset because Kern's upset, then you have to be upset because I'm upset. Dad, I busted my ass on this trip. I delivered for Kern. But I'm not his gopher, running around being the second son all the time. I'm tired of that stuff. I'm just as important as him."

"Rinker, I know that. And if I've made you feel differently, then I'm sorry and I mean it. But there's reasons for all this. You don't know the half of it sometimes."

"Oh yeah? What's the half?"

"Ah c'mon Rinker. You're running late now. Everybody's waiting. We can get into that later, back home."

"No. I want to hear it now. What's the half?"

"All right! Okay, since you want to get into this and everything. Rinker, don't be afraid to take a look at yourself either. You're half the problem that I've had with Kern, always calling him a square for being who he is, making him jealous all the time because you make such a big splash with everybody up at school. It hasn't been easy for him having a younger brother like you. I was absolutely shocked when he said he wanted to take you on this flight. I mean, why didn't he just leave you home? Now, you're out here, and you didn't get the waterbag, and you're both making me feel like some kind of fifth wheel in this operation. Jimmy says Kern doesn't need me anymore and I should leave him alone, and he's probably right. Now you're saying the same thing. I'm practically out of this equation."

"Dad, you're not out of the equation. You just have to stop butting in, that's all. Whatever problems Kern and I had, we dealt with them. Just leave us alone. Stop bugging us."

"Yeah, I have to work on that," my father sighed. "God, this is as bad as an AA meeting. Look, just have some mercy on me, wil'ya? This is hard for me. Kern's leaving for college in a month and I'll hardly see him once we get home. That's the reason I came out here."

"Dad. You've got ten other kids. Why don't you worry about somebody else for a change?"

"I know that, Christ I know! I just had to make sure everything was straight with Kern, that's all."

"Yeah. Well look, don't do the same thing to me. I want some space Dad. I'm not going to solo sixteen airplanes on my birthday for you and all that other stuff. I need some breathing room."

"Well good. You want some space. I'm burned out on all this anyway. Maybe we both need some space."

It was time to go, and we were both talked out. Then Kern came around to the side of the Cub and stared up at us with his hands on his hips.

"Smile Rinker," my father said. "Laugh or something. Kern's looking over at us. See me? I'm smiling. Look at me smile! I'm laughing my ass off about this, right? That's what you tell Kern. Everything's fine and Daddy is laughing his ass off about the waterbag. Jesus Rinker, I need my head examined for this one."

Before he left, my father and I cooked up a cover story. He was desperate to have an excuse about the waterbag for everyone back on the ramp. So, we came up with this: Two weeks ago, I was refilling the waterbag in the men's room at the Yuma airport. Then I forgot it before we took off. But we were going to retrieve the waterbag at Yuma this very afternoon, on our way back east.

"All right then," my father said. "The men's room in Yuma. I'm going back up there to give Aunt Joan the biggest bullshit job of her life."

My father turned to go, then wheeled back to face me.

"Look, I'm glad we talked. Nobody ever does it at the right time. And I am proud of you two. You obviously don't need me back-seating you anymore, so don't even bother calling home every night, not for me. Just let Mother know where you are. And screw the waterbag. I'm sorry about it. The waterbag is history."

I watched my father hike up past the line of parked planes. It had been too long a walk for him, and now his bad leg was twisting out at the knee, scraping up dust. It was a moment of supreme conflict for me. I felt sorry for him, but satisfied for myself. Probably we understood each other a lot better now and he would try and leave me alone. But it was pathetic too. It had all happened over the waterbag.

I turned back to Kern and the Cub.

"What did he say, Rink?"

"It's fine, Kern. He's going to tell everybody we left the waterbag in the men's room at Yuma."

"Ah, Jeez. More bull. Look, I don't ever want to hear about that damn thing again."

Old Harold Buck arrived as we taxied up with the plane. His chauffeur had driven him down to San Juan Capistrano in a big stretch limousine. He sat on a folding chair out on the ramp, appearing very interested and asking a lot of questions while Kern and I showed him the plane. Then the chauffeur came around from the parking lot carrying an immense vegetable crate.

"Boys, these are your avocados," Harold beamed. "There's enough here to last you all the way back east."

It was the largest vegetable crate that I had ever seen,

larger, even, than the one Henry Fonda had to lug around in *Grapes of Wrath*. There was no way it was going to fit into the tiny baggage compartment of the Cub, but nobody wanted to disappoint old Harold so we just left it there by the wheels.

My father was chastened now and treading gingerly around Kern. But he did have a favor to ask—just one more favor, he said. After we took off, could we give everybody a flyby and then climb for altitude circling the field? We had to climb high before we flew east over the Santa Rosa Mountains anyway, and everyone here on the ramp would enjoy watching us go for air before we disappeared over the hills. Kern agreed.

We shook hands all around, kissed Aunt Joan, and squeezed into the Cub. My father came over and lifted the crate of avocados onto my lap. The crate was heavy, as heavy as having a grown person sitting on me, and when Kern tried moving the controls, my stick in the back seat butted up against the avocado crate. He would have only about half of the normal play on his elevator controls.

"Ah Jeez Dad," I said.

"Ah Rinker now just screw it and behave here for a minute," my father said softly. "Let's not upset old Harold. As soon as you get out over the desert, you can toss 'em over the side."

My father propped us. Everyone on the ramp enjoyed the way he could get four or five rotations out of the propeller with each throw while Kern fed in the primer fuel.

"Contact!"

"Contact!"

We took off, did the flyby, and then circled the field while everybody on the ramp below craned their necks and watched us climb.

It was a bitch, being sandwiched into the backseat of a Piper Cub underneath a full commercial crate of avocados. The bottom of the crate dug into my thighs, and as we circled higher over the airport Kern kept frowning back and yelling at me to suck in my "big ass" so the crate could get out of the way of his stick. But it was no good. When we reached

*Old Harold Buck showed up at San Juan Capistrano to wave us off,
and brought us a present of avocados.*

5,000 feet, we needed to raise the nose higher in the thin air,
but it just wasn't working. The stick kept jamming up against
the avocado crate.

"Rink!"

"Yo!"

"I can't climb the plane. Deep-six the avocados. Now!"

I threw open the windows on both sides and perched the
crate up high on my knees, so I had a proper platform for
release.

Avocados away. Visually it was a very interesting experience, watching avocados go over the side and disappear
quickly into the smog. Sticking my head out in the slipstream, I could follow them down for about three seconds.
But I wanted to watch the avocados longer than that so I
started jettisoning them in large pods of four or five, which
allowed me to track them an extra five hundred feet.

Avocados-smog. Avocados-smog. It was fascinating, watching avocados vanish into hazy southern California. Then Kern got into the act too and really enjoyed it, reaching back with his throttle hand for an avocado and tossing it out the left window. We were Piper Aircraft's first bomber, with ordnance going out both sides.

When we could see the bottom of the crate Kern suggested that I hold back a reserve of three or four avocados in the baggage compartment, just in case we ran into another Greyhound in Arizona. That done, I up-ended the crate on my lap and Kern gratefully drew all the way back on the stick. What a relief—we had an airplane that could climb again.

We were worried about safely releasing the crate, because it could easily get hung up on the tail or the wheels. Back home, Kern knew a couple of pilots who flew parachute-jumpers, and he decided to handle it the same way. He pulled the Cub nose-high into slow flight, carried a little power, and made a shallow bank to the left, so all I had below me from the open door was a big space of air and a gentle slipstream blowing by. With both hands I heaved the crate straight down.

It was beautiful, watching that crate fall into the abyss. Spinning crazily and flipping end over end, it disappeared below at about 2,000 feet.

We completely forgot that gravity works all the way to the ground. We were still circling the airport and at a certain point I did notice Harold Buck's limousine depart, but he was probably just tired and needed to get home for his nap. These were just avocados going overboard. Who cared what happened to them after we couldn't see them anymore?

We didn't even think about it until we called my mother from Arizona that night. My father had rushed back to Los Angeles to catch his airline flight for New York and had called her from the airport.

"Gee, Rinky, what happened out there today?" my mother asked. "Daddy kept talking about these avocados."

"Uh oh. Is he angry?"

"No. He thought it was hilarious. I've never heard him laugh so hard."

I hung up and immediately called Uncle Jim. He was laughing too. The scene at that airport, he said, was better than the Battle of the Bulge. The first big pod of avocados, Uncle Jimmy said, had landed on the taxiway, only about fifty feet from the crowd. Splat-splat-splat-splat. Guacamole on the tarmac. It was a continuous volley after that. Pods and individual avocados landed on the runway, on the hangar, and splashed into the irrigation canal. Hildegard Richter dove for cover in the cab of the gas truck. The avocado pod that squashed down on the parking lot coated Harold Buck's limousine with green slime, and the chauffeur wiped it off with one of those little towels attached to a golf bag. But Harold Buck wasn't that upset. In the middle of the bombardment my father rushed over and calmly explained that the Cub was probably experiencing "center of gravity" problems. Harold was okay after that. Considering his background, all the fine engineering work he'd done for Howard Hughes, he said, he should have known that this might be a problem for the boys. Even the airport manager was laughing about it.

Oh! And the crate, Jimmy said. Jesus, the crate. The crate made a real fine touchdown. It came screaming down at a ferocious velocity, vibrating and whining like a flying saucer. Crack! It landed about ten feet from the windsock and splintered into a hundred pieces.

But we didn't know any of that right away. As we cleared the Santa Rosa range, the air pressure changed and the California smog disappeared, and we dropped down low to enjoy the desert vistas of Thermal and Blythe. Over the chalky wastelands of western Arizona, we diverted around a couple of thunderstorms and then cruised down Highway 10 toward Phoenix.

Circling into refuel at Litchfield Park, we chucked the last of the avocados out the window, splashing them onto a hotel parking lot. California had been a real fine time, at least until my father got there, and for two weeks it was fun being the coast to coast kids. But now we just wanted to wander the country for a while and explore some new routes toward home, anonymous again, enjoying the throb of the Continental and the ceaselessly changing terrain.

CHAPTER 21

OUR FLIGHT HOME WAS THE DREAM JOURNEY WE HAD HOPED FOR all along. Through New Mexico and endless Texas the skies were flawless and entranced us into a relaxed state of flying. The prevailing westerlies that generated bracing headwinds on our trip west were now tailwinds briskly kiting us east. The press wasn't bothering us anymore and the only breakdown we had was a snapped carburetor heat cable, which we fixed ourselves. We let the prairie dogs and buses roam free. Everything felt romantic and Kern and I camped out under the wings almost every night. We sat up late in the chilly deserts, talking about ourselves and our plans for life, laughing about my father and the waterbag. In the morning the airport geezers ran us into town for heaping, greasy breakfasts at the cafes, and in the evening they ran us into town for chicken-fried steaks. Our days were aimless, pleasurable, what travel should be. We didn't want to fly the rocky Kentucky swale again and we pointed instead for the Gulf Coast, and so we saw New Orleans and Pensacola.

We even aced the Guadalupe Pass. We deliberately flew hard the second afternoon to make El Paso by nightfall, so we could launch for the pass in calm air at dawn. But when we got in, at six o'clock, there was a pilot tying up his Beechcraft Bonanza. He had just come over the mountains. It was smooth that evening, he told us, without a bubble in the air. He recommended that we not attempt going over the top of Guadalupe Peak, where the air would be rougher, but instead just cruise right on through the pass at 8,000 feet. We fueled and flew like the dickens for the mountains.

From 9,000 feet, a mile from the pass, Kern put the Cub in a shallow dive with the throttle wide open. He timed it perfectly, and there was a good tailwind behind us too. We were still running downhill and clocking over one hundred miles per hour as we whistled through the middle of the pass. There were some nasty turns to make toward the end, down low where the sides are closer together, and some turbulence too once our wings were exposed to the sidedrafts coming off the jagged walls on the far side. But it was definitely a wise decision to cross at low altitude in smooth night air. We were in and out of the pass in about six minutes.

Oh you beautiful old mountain, I thought as we cleared the last wall, you gorgeous whore. You nearly got us that first time but now we have your number and so goodbye Guadalupe. We flew on across the high desert to Wink. That night, the airport manager and his hands took us on a rattler safari, and Kern and I each bagged several snakes.

I was always grateful about one thing Kern did when we reached central Texas. After we got into Junction, in the scrub prairie north of San Antonio, we were finishing up our RC Colas and Moon Pies when Kern flipped me the sectional map.

"Here," he said. "Plan me a cross-country to Austin. You'll fly the whole leg yourself from the front seat, as pilot-in-command. I'm sitting in the back with my arms crossed."

I was jittery at first, taxiing out. I wasn't used to handling 71-Hotel from the front seat. But then I got the throttle open and my tail raised, and I could always hold a centerline and break ground all right.

I was euphoric, flying that Junction-to-Austin leg by myself from the front seat, spending two hours and five minutes as pilot-in-command. There was a large oil field out along the lonely Pedernales River which I had to hit midway, practically our only major landmark, and it was right where it was supposed to be after an hour. Kern kept his arms folded in the back the whole time, not offering a single suggestion, lost in thought and enjoying himself. The route we followed took us right past Lyndon Johnson's ranch, and Kern was excited about the possibility that we might be able to pick out the president's spread.

When we got to Tim's airport in Austin I dropped to pattern altitude and approached the field downwind.

"Here's Austin!" I proudly yelled back to Kern, happy about my navigation and flying. "It's your airplane."

"Rink, I said the *whole* leg," Kern yelled forward. "You can land this Cub."

And I could too. Carb heat, three cranks on the trim, chop the power and hold sixty-five miles per hour. Over the fence I eased back on the stick. As we touched down Kern deliberately stared out the side windows with his arms folded, as unconcerned as a passenger on United Airlines. He knew that I would grease it on.

We flew on to Houston that evening. After dinner in town we rolled our sleeping bags out under the wings and lay there for a while, gazing up at the stars.

"This was good today, Rink," Kern said. "Junction to Austin. You flew it all by yourself. For me, it's the high point of the trip."

My earnest brother. He was always overflowing with enthusiasm about something, making some event from an hour ago the high point of the trip, the sort of thing about him that I was never able to understand. Obviously, there were many more legitimate high points of the flight—Hank, back in Indiana, Pate in El Paso, and crossing the big pass. But if Junction to Austin was the high point for Kern, even though tomorrow he'd have a new one, it was good enough for me. I lay under the wing with my hands clasped behind my head, staring up at the stars, at peace with myself and with Kern. I wasn't uncomfortable around him anymore. Everything between us seemed easier, practically effortless, now that I wasn't wasting all my energy hoping he would change.

The next night, Tuesday, we were already in Florida. A

geezer at the Pensacola airport told us about a cleared right of way for a gas pipeline that we could pick up about ten miles away and follow all the way up to New York. We practically threw away our maps. On Wednesday we reached North Carolina, and after four hours of easy flying up the Shenandoah Valley we crossed into Pennsylvania before noon on Thursday. My father had a reception at the airport and a party at home planned for Saturday afternoon, and we didn't want to disappoint him by storming into our home strip two days early. So we dropped down low over the familiar Pennsylvania Dutch countryside and swung into our old Lancaster County haunt, the immaculately kept grass strip at New Holland. We spent the next two days in Ephrata, at the home of Ivan Martin, an Old Order Mennonite farmer from whom my father had bought horses over the years. We helped Ivan and his boys bring in their wheat and chased around the country roads at night in a horse and buggy.

On Friday evening, after dinner, Kern and I drove a buggy into Blue Ball for haircuts, because my father wanted us to "look nice for Mother" when we stepped out of the plane the next day. Kern was excited about getting back; he couldn't wait to dive right into preparations for his commercial pilot's flight test. I was a lot more reluctant for the trip to end, but there was one outcome of our flight about which I was confident. My father had listened to me back in California, after I told him about the waterbag. We'd grown closer and we understood each other better now. I had proven myself on this flight, and really stood behind Kern. My father would trust me now, and treat me with more deference. Certainly that's what I felt I deserved.

Disappointment, however, was waiting for me when I stepped out of the barbershop in that pretty little town. I called home from the phone booth out in front of Goode's general store.

"Lancaster? What the hell are you still doing there?" my father growled into the phone. "That's south. You're supposed to be approaching the field tomorrow from the west. Christ, do I have to tell you guys everything? Everybody expects a Cub out of the west."

I was crestfallen. A huge gray pit opened in my chest. Nothing had changed. Nothing would ever change. I'd been flying hard all week thinking everything was romantic, that my life would now be transformed for the better, but in fact I was just winging east toward situation normal. But I must have learned something on that trip because I thought about what was happening and deliberately waited several seconds before I replied. Anger and snide remarks just weren't the way to handle him anymore.

"Okay Dad, I'm sorry," I said. "We made a mistake. But I think we can recover. We'll fly north to the Delaware and turn right from there. Don't worry. Everybody will see us coming out of the west."

"All right then. Noon. Noon sharp. Jack Elliott will be there, and a lot of other press. Make sure you both give your mother a big hug. And Rinker, none of this backtalking and awful language you've picked up on this trip."

When I got back to the buggy, Kern was just coming out from his haircut.

"Everything okay Rink?"

"Yup. Fine and dandy. The old man is really happy tonight."

In the morning, our last day of flying, we experienced one of those real high points that Kern was always crowing about. In truth, it was something for us both to crow about.

We were off the grass at New Holland before eight and had plenty of time to make central New Jersey by noon, so we decided to drop in and see some friends at Princeton. The airport operators we had grown up with at Basking Ridge had moved their business south to Princeton the year before, and many of the old Basking Ridge flyers had moved with them and taken their planes down there. Probably, they had all heard about our coast to coast romp by now and would be glad to see us.

Big Eddie Mahler had led the move of the old Basking Ridge flyers down to Princeton, and we hadn't seen him in a long time. When we landed at Princeton that morning and taxied around the corner of the hangar, he was pulling his open-cockpit biplane out of the hangar, getting ready to fly off for his Saturday afternoon show. Eddie Mahler was a regal man. He rarely showed emotion about anything and when he crossed a ramp he ambled, imperturbable and majestic as a big African cat.

But as soon as he saw the Cub with the red sunbursts come around the corner, Eddie broke in a run for us. It was all we could do to stand on the brakes and get the prop stopped before he got to us. He reached in and pulled open the door and pumped my hand. Then he wrapped one of those big tanned arms of his around Kern's shoulder and hugged him like a child.

"Kern Buck, I am so proud of you," Eddie said. "You have done this thing. Everybody followed you all the way across in the papers. Everybody thinks this is just great for aviation. All the old Basking Ridge flyers just can't get over you, Kern."

For Big Eddie, that was a lot of syllables at once, practically all the emotion he had in him for a full year.

What Eddie said that morning built a marker inside Kern that never left. Over the years, whenever we sat out on a porch somewhere and talked about that summer, reaching out with imaginary sticks and kicking at the rudders, Kern would repeat Big Eddie's words like a mantra.

"And Rink, the day we got back, Eddie Mahler said he was proud of me. He *hugged* me that day. I'll never forget it."

A number of other pilots, some of whom we knew and many that we didn't, started piling out of the hangars and the pilots' lounge and surged around the plane. Before we could even get out of the Cub, Eddie stepped back, hoisted the tail up to his waist and started pulling us back toward a tiedown spot on the grass. The other pilots joined in and pushed on the wings and the struts, and it was a wonderful moment for Kern and me, flowing backward in our cockpit seats as all of our old barnstorming buddies—Larry "No Cash" Tokash, John O'Johnny, and "Bird-Dog" Nelson— pushed us along in a crowd and called out questions. It was one thing to have earned the adulation of the news media and the public. But these were pilots, heroes of our childhood, buzz-job artists and famous airshow performers and airline captains, and they marveled at our journey.

"Damn it all, Kern, this is great! Why didn't I think of this?"

"Whoa. Let me just get my head inside that cockpit. No radio! Kern, you're frigging nuts. But I love this."

Eddie wanted to hear all about our trip—the deserts and the mountains, the Stearman men, whether we had any breakdowns, or got lost. We all sat around on the grass in front of the gas pumps drinking Cokes as Kern waggled his hands in the air telling everyone how he flew the Kentucky swale, or smoked 71-Hotel onto those big long runways out west in the density-altitude air.

I felt joyful for Kern. Everybody kept clapping him on the back and telling him what a "hot shit" pilot he was now, and then somebody else we knew would pull into the parking lot and burst out of their car. "Jesus! Is that the Cub? It's Kern Buck!" He was no longer that scrawny teenager running around the airport all day, wondering about what everyone thought of him. Larry Tokash, who ran the airport operation, told Kern that morning that as soon as he got his commercial and instructor ratings, he had a summer job flying for Princeton Aviation.

Then we all enjoyed our old Saturday morning routine—watching the great Eddie Mahler take off for his show. Eddie said goodbye, shook our hands and then wrapped his arm around Kern's shoulder one last time before he stepped over to his plane.

It was the standard Mahler departure. Full show smoke on takeoff, rotate off the ground into a climbing chandel turn, two snap rolls over the windsock and then a hammerhead stall over to the intended route of flight. He was an awesome flyer that Eddie, like a big old stud horse coming out of the barn in the morning. He liked to kick over a few doors as he went by, just to make sure he was awake.

We took off ourselves a few minutes later, and just because it felt right, we gave the crowd of pilots a buzz job low enough to make them duck and then we hammerheaded up and over to our route of flight.

We were accomplished arrival artists by now, and it wasn't hard doing it right for my father and the crowd waiting for us at Basking Ridge. The bit about a "Cub coming out of the west" turned out to be a lot of wasted anxiety on my father's part. It was so hazy over central New Jersey by noon nobody could see an airplane very far anyway. But we did that dumbass thing just to please him, diverting way out toward Somerville and approaching from the west.

When we came over the little mountain in Mendham we could see there was a cloud right over the airport. Kern stayed on top of it until we were almost past the runway and then threw the stick over and down, so we came out over everybody's head in a graceful diving bank. Back with the stick for the chandel turn, kick the rudders over for a short downwind, and we came out of the turn onto final approach with the Cub already sideways in the slip and fell steeply down over the telephone wires. We touched down right in front of the crowd in a puff of dust.

It was mayhem all over again out there, and I had a completely different feeling about it than our reception in L.A. Kern and I had been so free for a month. We had seen everything two boys could see across America, flown the Mississippi, the prairies, the deserts, and then the big pass, and slept under the wings at night. Barnstorming together, there were only two people to worry about—him and me. Now we were swarmed with people, photographers, old family friends, and howling younger brothers and sisters spilling Coke all over the plane. My father directed the press traffic, assigning a pecking order according to the importance of the publication.

Despite my fresh haircut, my mother was annoyed about my hair. It was unruly then and there was nothing I could do about it. I had just flown almost six thousand miles, half the time with my head out the side looking for landmarks or watching avocados disappear. Even Elvis Presley couldn't do that and exit the plane with his hairdo intact. But my mother was upset. She took one look at me and couldn't help herself. The reporters were all right there and they had their notebooks open, and everything she said made the newspapers the next day.

" 'You're home, I see,' sighed Mrs. Buck. 'Rinker, push that hair out of your eyes.' "

Yeah, shit, we were home, freaking home sweet home.

Afterward, there was a big party at the house with all these Roman Catholic priests my father always had around, friends from town, and my older sisters' boyfriends. My father was in his element, and I was happy for him. He needed this, basking in the glory of our coast to coast flight. But after about an hour of the merriment, Kern and I could see that the party wasn't about us any longer. It was just another excuse, like a birthday or a confirmation, to fill up the rooms. We had to get out of there. Our heads were still out in Texas.

We slipped out of the house together and walked out to the barn. The blue Willys was parked in the main shop, in the same spot where we had rebuilt the plane. It had become coated with dust while we were away and we brushed it off with oil rags. Puttering softly out the drive in reverse, we rode over to the Minuteman restaurant on Route 202.

We never planned to do this, to debrief our flight like a pair of NASA astronauts, but that's what we did. It was one of our last long talks together before Kern left for college.

Kern was very selfless about it. He insisted that I appreciate my contributions to the trip, and was surprised that I still underestimated my role. The trip might have originated with him, it might have been his dream, he said, but I had helped "push it over the top." It was an unexpected pleasure for him, he said, getting out to Indiana that first day and seeing what I could do. It was a lot more than just my navigation, or Junction to Austin, or taking over the controls in the middle of the pass.

"Rink, you know what the biggest thing I learned on this trip is?"

"No, what?"

"I'm smart and I don't even know it."

"Yeah?"

"Yeah! I mean, the minute I first thought about flying

coast to coast, there was like this voice inside me. 'You gotta take Rinky. Rinky has to be in that plane.' I was pissed too. I had an argument with myself about it. 'Why should I take Rinky? He'll just be bugging my ass all the time.' But I couldn't overpower that little voice and I knew there had to be a reason. Now I know. I mean, Jeez, both of us had to take the heat on the waterbag together, which made all of the difference."

I didn't say much about that, but I didn't feel that I had to. There was knowledge and satisfaction for me in what Kern said. I'd done what I'd had to for my brother that summer and I was happy about it for the rest of my life.

A few weeks later, when Kern flew off to Red Bank to take his commercial flight test, nobody made a big fuss about it. He always got jittery before an event if people wished him good luck and, besides, this was just like any other morning. Every day that month, as soon as he was out of bed, Kern dashed off to the airport in the Willys to get ready for his test.

I was back working at the horse farm and came home tired that night, and I lay down on the couch in my father's library before dinner. I could tell just from the sound of the Willys entering the drive that Kern had passed the test. The tires squealed coming around the corner and the pickup screeched to a halt in the drive.

"Rink!"

He was calling out to me almost as an abstraction—anywhere I happened to be on the place, even if I wasn't, he wanted me to know. But I was right there, underneath the open library window.

"Yo! I guess you passed."

"Yeah. The examiner didn't like my chandels and lazy-eights, but what does he know, Rink? I got the ticket. I'm a commercial pilot."

"Great. Now you can go off to college and relax."

"Exactly. Now look, here's what I'm going to do. By Christmas, you'll be sixteen and ready to solo. So, I'll get my instructor's rating over the winter for that, and then I'm going to go for my instrument and multiengine. I've got to be all set up by the summer for Princeton Aviation."

Exactly. The thing was, Kern did all this, right on schedule, and he had a pretty good little run of barnstorming blarney going for him by then. Up at Holy Cross, he started a flying club, and he even talked the Jesuits into buying a couple of planes for it. One afternoon, just for the hell of it, he landed one of them on the football field.

CHAPTER 22

THE LAST TIME I FLEW WITH MY FATHER WAS THE DAY AFTER
Christmas in 1966, five months after we returned from our
coast to coast flight. It was last in many respects. My father
never barnstormed again, and he rarely flew in private planes.
But I was approaching my sixteenth birthday, and there was
one more chore for him to perform. That morning, my father
looked up at the breakfast table and examined my face as if
we were strangers.

In fact, we were practically strangers. After Kern left for
college our old threesome had broken up, and my father and
I had quickly grown apart. It wasn't deliberate on his part or
mine, it was just something we knew was wise to do. I was
busy in school all week and led an active social life over the
weekend, having reached the point where an outgoing boy
doesn't want to have much to do with his parents anymore.
My father was preoccupied with work, finishing up a book,
and his increasing fascination with "alternative politics" and
civil rights. We hardly saw each other anymore, but there was
one last respite to enjoy, one more time together in the air.

"Rinker," my father said, "Let's go out and solo you in
the Cub. I always promised myself that I'd live to see the

day both you and Kern were soloed. I just want to get it over with."

I will still three days shy of the legal flying age of sixteen, and no licensed instructor had signed my logbook for solo, but I didn't see any reason to object. Kern would have his instructor's rating soon and could finish me off for my private pilot's test. I wanted to solo and there was no question that I could handle a Piper Cub. And certainly in this old Stearman man I had an able instructor.

Snow had fallen over the past few days, and the runway was covered over in many spots by drifts. A sheet of white ice covered the low area in the middle. But there was six hundred feet of usable space at the north end of the field and a brisk wind was blowing straight down the strip.

There wasn't a heater in 71-Hotel, and my father was shivering in the backseat as we taxied out in the snow. Taking off, we used every inch of clear space and blasted into the air through a drift. Fresh powder swirled around the plane and crept into the cockpit through the cracks by the windows and the door. I remember that like a picture, because it caused a sudden and rapid deterioration of age in my father that I instantly knew to be prescient. He hadn't shaved that morning and the snow blowing in stuck like confetti to his whiskers. I looked back, and the man who had taught me to fly was Rip Van Winkle.

I hadn't flown in a while but I found that being rusty didn't hurt me much in the old Cub. Carb heat, three cranks on the trim, chop the power, and maintain 65. We circuited the wintery patch a couple of times and my landings were okay. Then my father got out and leaned into the front of the cockpit for some last words.

"All right Rinker, go ahead," he said. "There's nothing more I can teach you in an airplane."

I blasted off through the drifts and circuited the airport, euphoric to be flying alone, amazed at the lightness of the plane and the controls without my father in the rear seat. I was shivering from the cold, but I was awed by the beauty of the white, snowy landscape all around me, mounded hills and naked stands of trees rolling off to the horizon in Pennsylvania on one side and over to the Atlantic on the other, with the sun glinting off the black ice on the nearby lakes. The Continental roared, the floorboards throbbed, and the cockpit smelled of burnt oil, and I loved being alone in the Cub.

My father warned me that I might overshoot my first approach—without his weight in the rear, the plane wouldn't want to descend and mush to a stall in all that wind. I overshot just as he predicted, but I didn't let it rattle me. Firewalling the throttle, I flew around again, and on the second try I did a decent job shoehorning the Cub into the short space, deliberately scraping the wheels onto the first drift to help stall the plane. Plowing through the snow and throwing up great white plumes with the prop, I taxied over toward the hangar.

My father stepped out and kangarooed over, shivering and walking sideways in the wind with his pipe billowing out cinders and smoke.

"Good, Rinker. I always said you could handle a plane just as well as Kern, once you settled down. Now go ahead. Take off again and fly around for a while in 71-Hotel."

The wind was really kicking up now and blowing in crossways, surrounding the plane with vortices of snow. But the windsock was pointed directly at me, so I just powered up right there and went off the ramp, Eddie Mahler style. As soon as I broke ground I cross-controlled against the drift, cranked in all of my trim and hung the Cub on its prop. With the plane steeply angled up, I kept my eye on the flagpole down in front of the high school to remain perfectly aligned with the runway. I enjoyed that, climbing almost vertically in the crab and never giving an inch to the drift while my father watched from below. When I looked down to him he waved a couple of times and smoke was blowing all over the place from his pipe. I felt good about it and the strong winds rifling the wings from the side reminded me of Carlisle, Pennsylvania, and Carlsbad, New Mexico, and then I realized something important about myself. In one respect I was just like Kern. The rougher the conditions, the better I flew.

My father told me to fly around for a while and enjoy my-self, so that's how I handled it. As soon as I got up to altitude and had the Cub leveled and trimmed I was joyful all over again to be soloed in a plane, and that just made me very hungry for a hamburger. The Walker family over at Somerset airport ran a very good snack bar so I flew over there. The crosswind was pretty bad there too and cranky old George Walker wasn't happy to see me landing in it, but I got down okay and let him yell at me for a couple of minutes before I went in for my burger. Then I decided to take in Princeton—maybe Larry Tokash, or Big Eddie, would be down there. As soon as I got into the air I remembered that I didn't have a map, but that was another nice moment. I was one of the coast to coast kids. I didn't need a map to find Princeton. Route 206 ran right by the airport down there and the road was practically underneath my wing already, at the Fleming-ton Circle. When I got into Princeton Big Eddie wasn't around, but Larry was, and he bought me a hot chocolate from the vending machine and we talked for a while. Larry was an FAA flight examiner by now, but also a friend.

"Shit Rinker. You shouldn't be flying around in these winds. On your first solo no less. But hell. You got the Cub down here. I imagine you can get her back."

On the way back I remembered that I'd promised the priests up at school to fly over the monastery as soon as I was soloed, so I went over and did that, and then winding my way back over the low hills I became transfixed by the skaters and iceboats on the lakes in Gladstone and Peapack, and I circled for a while to watch them. By the time I got back to the strip it was almost dark and the Cub was low on gas. My father had left hours ago. I tied down the Cub and hitchhiked home in the cold.

When I got in, my father was typing in his library beside the fire.

"How'd you make out?"

"Fine Dad. I did Somerset and then Princeton. Sorry. I should have called and told you where I was."

"Nah Rinker. It's okay. I told you to fly around for a while. I wasn't worried."

I didn't mean for that flight to be symbolic, but it was. Probably my growing estrangement from my father was inevitable—many of my friends and their fathers were going through the same thing—but the turbulent events of the 1960s also had a lot to do with it. My father had always been a public man, changing with the times, and he couldn't resist the siren call of activism sweeping the country. Even before we returned from our coast to coast flight, he was girding himself for his last great crusade.

It began innocently enough, with weekend excursions to civil rights marches down south, then the marches on Washington to protest the war in Vietnam, and before long he had joined groups like Clergy and Laity Concerned and was holding strategy sessions for local demonstrations in our living room at home. He got arrested a lot at peace demonstrations. Other men of his stature and age—writers, ministers, university professors—were doing the same thing by the late 1960s, but they usually had enough sense not to deck the cops. When he was manhandled by officers at demonstrations in New Jersey, and then again at Foley Square in New York, my father fought back. The police and the district attorneys, bringing him up on assault charges, never seemed to understand that there wasn't a judge in the country who was going to throw this one-legged father of eleven into jail, so he always beat the rap. But his trials attracted a lot of attention and were covered in the press, and he soon gained a reputation within the "movement" as a kind of aging firebrand who had made a rather classic transition from establishment politics to radical causes. Invitations for him to speak poured in from all over the country. Defense attorney William Kunstler, pacifist David Dellinger, and the antiwar priests Daniel and Philip Berrigan were now his friends.

Of course, he could never do just one thing at a time. To his delight, he had also emerged as an author. He had finished writing *But Daddy!*, a humorous and anecdotal account of his experiences raising eleven children, the year after we made our coast to coast flight. It was modestly successful as a hardcover book but took off in paperback, and soon he was in demand before women's and church groups on this subject too. To help define and package him, his lecture agent in Washington called him the Catholic Dr. Spock. In 1968 he quit his job at *Look* and lived off his proceeds from lecturing and writing.

I spent my last three years at home in the throes of a most curious role reversal. While my father was radicalized by the sixties, I was the smug conservative, mainly interested in girls, expensive foreign cars, and accumulating enough advanced placement credits to shave a year off college. Occasionally I joined my father at peace demonstrations, and because it was expected of me, I was active in social causes myself, organizing food drives for indigent families down south and tutoring underprivileged children up in town. But I was too numb inside and distracted by something else to know if my heart was really in it.

My father's health had visibly begun to slide, and there was nothing anyone could do about it. There had always been something inadvertently suicidal about his behavior—not just the way he flew, but the sheer variety of his activities, the killer pace he set. His doctors had warned him for years that phantom pains generally grew worse with age, and that his only protection from them was leading a more leisurely life and reducing stress. But my father was never going to do that. The harder he drove himself, the worse the phantoms became, and that only made him feel old and angry at himself for spending too much time in bed. After each successive attack, it took him longer and longer to recuperate. But as soon as he felt better again he accepted another speaking engagement and jumped onto another airliner, almost as if he was deliberately running away so he wouldn't have to face himself. He was a burnout case who didn't know it.

And those phantoms were monsters by now—hard, extended attacks that throttled him into deliriousness at the height of the pain and afterward left him listless for days. Several times during high school, and even after I left for college in 1969, I drove him alone to the hospital for his shots. He needed increasingly large doses of Demerol now—dangerous amounts, as it turned out—and when that didn't work the doctors sent him home with bags full of methadone pills, as "chasers." The medical men had more or less thrown up their hands. There wasn't much to be done for phantoms anyway, and my father was bringing on attacks by overwork.

Those rides with my father were awful. I wouldn't fully understand what was happening until years later, when I finally read some literature on phantom pains. In severe cases, like my father's, phantom-pain attacks trigger deeply buried and even forgotten details of the original accident or trauma, as the patient literally hallucinates the event that caused their loss of limb. Slumped over in the backseat, pallid and sweating, my father mumbled a lot deliriously and then started shouting. Month after month, he was reliving his 1946 crash.

"My God! Get him out of there! He's dying! Get the man in the plane damnit! God, God, God, oh my Lord, he's burning to death."

As I said, it was awful, the most awful part being I didn't know what to do. Many nights, when we got back, my father still couldn't walk very well, and Kern wasn't around to help me lift him up the stairs, so my mother and I made him as comfortable as possible on his library couch, lit a fire, and let him sleep there.

The next morning, my father was curt about what had happened. Either because he really didn't remember too well, or because he was embarrassed, he didn't want to talk about his hallucinations and what he had shouted out the night before. I started facing the truth. My father's big crash, which I'd always believed he handled stoically, was in fact emotionally crippling, haunting him in his premature old age. But we couldn't or wouldn't talk about it. It's a hard thing to admit, but sickness like that in someone you love does drive you away.

In the spring of 1969, during my senior year in high school, my father collapsed from heart failure while delivering a speech at the University of Arizona. Facing the inevitable, he finally retired, though he remained active in politics and various causes as long as he could. My parents sold our place in New Jersey, packing up the possessions and memories of their fruitful, dense-packed marriage, and moved up to Susquehanna County in Pennsylvania, where the five younger children finished school. The old Cub, 71-Hotel, had already been sold, in 1968. The engine needed an overhaul but we had to spend the money to pay my father's hospital bills instead.

During college, and after I graduated and started working as a newspaper reporter in western Massachusetts, I tried to get down to Pennsylvania to see my father every few months. When I arrived, I usually found him up on the second floor of the barn, in the capacious, book-lined study that he had built for himself as soon as he moved up from New Jersey. My father's old flying pictures and mementos from political campaigns lined the walls, and the framed aeronautical chart of the country, with our 1966 coast to coast route marked in red, still hung in its favored place, over his typewriter. Our old Franklin stove from New Jersey was installed on an immense slab of gray slate. In the cold weather we lit a fire, sat on rockers, and talked all afternoon while the shadows from the trees outside grew long on the walls.

My father was quite thin now, his barrel chest concave. One winter he grew a long, snowy-white beard, which actually made him look younger, or at least livelier, the way the older Walt Whitman looked more animated than the younger, shaven man. Conversation with my father was still mostly a business of listening, and I sat as patiently as I could, taking in his long, familiar monologues. Sometimes he talked about his childhood during the Depression, or his barnstorming days, and if there was something in the news—the Watergate hearings were on the radio every day—he launched into politics. He kept forgetting that he had told me during my last visit about the novel he was planning on writing. It would be a *roman noire* with a World War II aviation motif. The Spitfire pilot takes off from England. The Messerschmitt pilot ascends from Germany. They meet over the English Channel and simultaneously open their guns, killing each other instantly and falling together to the water. The mutual sacrifice, my father said, would symbolize the futility of war. I wasn't sure that he was ever going to write this book, or get it published, but I knew what it meant. He was a good old Stearman man, and now he was thinking about dying a lot.

My father was quite thin now, prematurely aged, and sometimes he would doze off in front of the fire in the middle of his own story. All I could do was stare into the flames and remember happier times.

Sometimes, my father dozed off in the middle of his own story. I sat quietly in my rocker as he snored, drinking coffee, and smoking my pipe, staring into the flames. My mind naturally wandered, and that old black Franklin in front of me seemed to anchor our past. Here, by the flames of this stove, I had sat as a boy and heard my father's wonderful barnstorming blarney. Later, the stove was moved into our barn, and Kern and I had sat in front of it every night, racing through my homework before we went to work on 71-Hotel. What I did for my father now seemed passive, even mournful. While he snored in his chair, I stared at the flames in our old stove and remembered.

The ride back to New England, up through the dairy country of New York State, was moody. I was very aware of the need to prepare myself for my father's death. I felt terribly guilty about that, guilty that I wasn't trying to do more for him. But I had my own life to lead and my father, most of all, had always encouraged me to be ambitious. With each passing year it became easier and easier to stretch out the months between visits.

During the first week of April 1975, when my mother called from the hospital in Washington, D.C., and reached me in the newsroom, I could tell the news from the tone of her voice. The reporter who sat in the cubicle next to mine was incredulous over my reaction. While my mother talked I rolled a piece of copy paper into my typewriter and began taking down all the information. I knew that I would be busy organizing a lot of family, and I wanted to get everything down right. My father was dead and I was taking dictation just as if I were writing up another story.

The last two years of my father's life had been a medical odyssey. He and my mother, sometimes with the younger children along, had traveled to hospitals and pain clinics up and down the east coast in a desperate, last-ditch attempt to cure his phantoms. Recently, they had found a program in Washington that provided some temporary relief through acupuncture treatments. They were resting in their hotel room in Washington before my father reported the next morning for treatments, and had just ordered dinner. In the middle of a severe phantom pain, my father collapsed onto the floor. He had suffered a massive heart attack.

The Karen Anne Quinlan case was the big national story that week, and suddenly nobody wanted to let people die naturally in hospitals anymore. Although it had taken an ambulance crew more then fifteen minutes to reach my father's hotel, and their efforts at reviving him were unsuccessful, the hospital in Washington made Herculean efforts to bring him back. All the known procedures, from mechanical respiration to chemical heart stimulants, were administered, and a prominent heart surgeon was even called out of a Kennedy Center concert to implant a pacemaker. It was enough to make anybody a Lazarus. Once more my father's chest heaved with induced breath, but a brain scan the next day turned up no signs of mental life. We all knew that the situation was hopeless, but the hospital was refusing to shut off the machines.

Kern was working in Washington then as a congressional aide, and my first panicked thoughts were for him.

"Mother, where's Kern? What's Kern doing?"

"He's right here, Rinker. And don't worry. He's fine and he knows what to do."

Kern did know what to do. Two days of chasing doctors down on golf courses and threatening legal action finally convinced the hospital to adopt a policy of common sense. They agreed to turn off the vast apparatus of life-support machines attached to my father.

When the doctors and nurses came in to shut everything off, my mother and Kern stood together in the room, holding hands.

"Oh Kerny, don't be sad," my mother said. "Daddy's suffering will finally be over."

And it was. With one last heave of that barrel chest, he exhaled sharply and gave up. He was fifty-nine years old. In the twenty-nine years since his big crash in '46, he had fathered and raised eleven children, joined AA and founded an alcoholics hospital, saved a half-dozen major magazines, helped elect a president, been swept up by the sixties, and he had kicked our butts all the way to California and back too. It was a whale of a record for a man who hadn't even graduated from high school.

We had a nice funeral up in Pennsylvania, with lots of Buck family mayhem and reunions with old friends. Dozens of relatives from both sides of the family, and all of my father's friends from the antiwar movement, descended on the town. One of my uncles got flat-ass drunk and collapsed on the porch, and a bunch of my sisters' former boyfriends carried him upstairs to bed. Philip Berrigan came and entertained us with delightful stories about my father visiting him in prison. Practically everybody was smoking pot by then, even one of my cousins, who was a cop. The night before the funeral, after all of the older aunts and uncles had been escorted back to their motels, we all sat around upstairs in the barn until late talking over old times and Tom Buck. My father had wished to be cremated and his ashes had been sent up from Washington in a ceramic urn. Somebody brought the urn up and put it in the middle of my father's library, and we lounged on the carpet and the chairs with all the old flying photos and mementos of my father's career surrounding us, and passed the bong pipe around. It was a nice time, the way to do it. Everyone had great stories to tell and their own version of events, but we all agreed that this ornery, driven, unforgettable, crazyass man had inspired us a lot and he was impossible not to love.

At the church service, I promised myself that I wouldn't cry. I thought that was what my mother wanted. Besides, I wanted to make myself available in the coming months to the two youngest children, Adrian and Ferriss, who would need me now. Maybe if I cried, they would consider me weak. But then they started crying, and all their friends in the choir started crying, then a lot of people I didn't know, and finally the whole church was wailing away. It was too big a river to turn back and I really was disconsolate for several minutes, devastated that this man was gone.

Later in the spring, over the long Memorial Day weekend, all of the boys in the family met up in Pennsylvania to help my mother clear my father's effects out of the house and the barn. A couple of university libraries wanted his papers, and an antiquarian book dealer had already driven off with his best books. We divided up his antiques and the pictures from his library. Still, there was an incredible amount of stuff left— old wagon wheels and hand-cranked organs, immense cruci- fixes and peace symbols crafted out of barn beams, several broken or twisted airplane propellers and a lot of Texan parts. What we couldn't unload at the dump or the scrap dealer's we decided to burn. Stacking it all on the lower lawn, we threw on some kerosene and lit a match, and then we all sat around drinking Cokes and leaning on our elbows, watching the flames lick up the detritus of my father's life.

My brother Nicky turned for the house, to clear out my father's closet. It was astonishing what he had stashed up there—enough outfits and props for a whole movie set. We each got at least one Irish sweater and tweed jacket and tried them on, and still Nicky came down to the lawn laden with more loot. There were bowler hats and fedoras, more than a dozen canes and walking sticks, a dog muzzle and a driving harness for a pony—there was even an old parachute buried in the corner, which Kern took.

On the dusty bottom of the closet, Nicky finally got to the artificial legs. There was a huge pile of them up there. My father bought a new one every couple of years but he never wanted to throw the old ones away. The older ones, from the 1950s, were made of ash and painted the color of flesh, then tin and aluminum came in, and finally the newer, high-tech jobs made out of fiberglass and carbon-epoxy fibers.

Nicky threw open the window above us and yelled out.

"Kern! Rinky! Brian! Heads up! Here come the legs. Daddy *hated* these things. I promised him I'd burn them as soon as he died. Throw them on!"

Artificial limbs away. Nicky heaved the wooden legs out the window in pods of two or three, so they came down practically on top of us, flailing away at crazy angles, with the waist-harnesses snapping and bouncing in mid-air. Some of the legs still had shoes on them, and when they landed the heels and toes kicked up divots of grass. It was a macabre way to handle the situation, admittedly, but Nicky was still tossing down more legs and maybe we all needed this, I thought.

Laughing, trying not to be too sentimental, we threw the legs onto the fire. The old wooden ones hissed and popped when the varnish caught and newer fiberglass models ignited into angry clouds of black smoke, going up like plastic boats. We stared at the flames some more and talked. That leg there, Kern said, Daddy had on when he built us the rodeo corral. He bought that one there, for practicing aerobatics in the Texan. And so forth. It was a good time for us all, sitting around in hand-me-down Irish sweaters and tweed jackets on a pleasant spring day, saying goodbye to those legs in our own way.

All of a sudden right over our heads a magnificent wailing filled the sky. Somebody was really bending a plane around up there, doing aerobatics, very heavy aerobatics, and we could tell that a lot of negative-G and inverted maneuvers were involved, from the way the cylinders and manifolds screamed from the air being forced backward through the stack. Kern and I had always been quite good at identifying an aircraft just from sound, and this was surely a unique plane, with a big six-cylinder up front and a long aeromatic prop. There was only one plane like that around. Then we looked up.

"Rink!" Kern said. "That's Eddie. That's Eddie Mahler up there."

The familiar red, white, and blue PJ biplane was just piling out of the bottom of an inverted spin. We sent Adrian into the house for the newspaper and, sure enough, Big Eddie Mahler was performing at the Binghamton air show the next day. It was probably his first show of the season, and Eddie must have come up early to blow the cobwebs off his ship and get in some high-altitude practice before he dropped down for the crowd tomorrow.

Eddie wasn't using show smoke and he was pretty high up, but still it was a good show. He did some climbing cobra rolls and check rolls, and then he really hammered the PJ through a series of inverted loops with rolls at the bottom and the top. It was good watching him and listening to his prop scream, and we couldn't get over the coincidence of this. While we were down here, burning my father's legs, Eddie was up there, wailing away in his plane:

We didn't go up to watch Eddie's show the next day, but I did get to see him a few more times. I was living in New York City by then and I would drive out to Farmingdale or Mommouth County a couple of times a summer, whenever he was performing nearby. The airshow circuit had changed a lot by then. Up in front of the crowd, the stunt pilots always seemed to be surrounded by a gaggle of promoters, camera crews, and commercial sponsors. I used my press pass to get through, and Eddie always seemed glad to see me.

He was past forty by now, but he didn't seem to have aged at all. He was still the same strikingly handsome, bronzed Adonis, with perfect teeth and flaxen black hair. But he had mellowed, too. He was married now, with two young daughters, and his face lit up and he pulled pictures out of his wallet when I asked about them.

Eddie's wife, Valerie, had seen a few of my articles in *New York* magazine and the Sunday *Times* and showed them to him. He was excited about that and happy for me, because my father had always told him that I was the "writer in the family."

"What about Kern?" Eddie asked. "Kern. Where's he?"

"Law school, Eddie. He just finished his second year."

"Law school." Eddie meditated on that for a moment. "See? What did I tell everybody? I knew Kern would figure out something smart like that. That's one thing I always liked about Tom Buck. He made you boys toe the line."

Eddie didn't want to talk much about my father. He had heard that he had died and he told me how sorry he felt. But he wasn't the kind of man to linger long on emotion anyway and, like a lot of the old Basking Ridge flyers, he couldn't understand what had come over Tom Buck in his last few years.

"Well, politics was never my bag," Eddie said. "But I'll say one thing. That old man of yours could sure fly a Texan. Nobody was better."

I gorged myself on hot dogs and soda and enjoyed watching Big Eddie perform for the crowd. His finale, the inverted ribbon pickup a few feet off the runway, always made my heart stop even though I'd seen it at least fifty times. I felt refreshed afterward and called Kern and told him all about it as soon as I got back to New York. Eddie connected us to our old barnstorming days as boys back in New Jersey, and I always needed a good dose or two of that when the summer flying weather returned.

Eddie was gone himself in two years. It happened in the fall of 1977 out at the big Easthampton show on the end of Long Island. On Friday evening before the Saturday show, a camera crew from a New York television station drove out to film Eddie's routine, so they would have footage for the weekend broadcasts. As the camera crew set up their gear, the hangars and the small passenger terminal emptied as everyone came out to watch the great Eddie Mahler perform.

In the middle of his routine, one of the PJ's metal tail struts fluttered and blew off. Eddie calmly righted the plane, swung back in and landed to check the tail. The FAA show observer who was present suggested that Eddie remove the strut on the other side, to balance the plane. Eddie had flown the PJ for years without tail struts—they were a recent modification on the plane—so he complied. It should have occurred to somebody that those fluttering struts indicated serious, underlying problems with the airframe, but hindsight is easy when you weren't there. The other strut was taken off and Eddie roared back off the strip.

Over the field, as soon as Eddie rolled the PJ over onto its back, the entire tail section blew off and cartwheeled away, and one of the greatest stunt pilots of all time went straight in.

Kern and I were both living in New York then. I was a staff writer at *New York* magazine and he was finishing up law school. Because Eddie's crash happened on a Friday night, when I was usually out, I hadn't heard the news. Kern woke me at my apartment on 77th Street early the next morning.

"Rink. Have you seen the papers yet?"

"No. What's up?"

"Its Eddie."

"Ah Jesus, Kern. No."

"Yes Rink. Eddie Mahler is gone. Eddie is gone."

I was heartbroken, stunned inside. Few show pilots die in bed, and many we'd known, many of Eddie's friends, were already dead. But I always considered Big Eddie invincible and this would never happen to him.

Kern and I met that night at Minetta's Tavern down in Greenwich Village. Minetta's had a small, quiet room in the back where the waiters didn't mind if we dawdled over a meal and a couple of beers. Dejectedly poking at our food, we talked and reminisced until after ten o'clock, recalling our old days with Eddie. Big Eddie and my father in their twin Texans, roaring off wing to wing for the shows. The day my father and Kern landed in the orchard. The day we landed at Princeton after our coast to coast flight.

"Rink, Eddie Mahler *hugged* me that day," Kern said. "He said, 'Kern, I am proud of you.' I'll never forgot it."

We talked some more out on the street, and then Kern and I shook hands and said good night. He took a cab back to Brooklyn and I walked uptown toward home. I felt very alone and gloomy that night, yet strangely liberated from my past, and I knew there was a lot more to it than Eddie's death. With my father gone, and now Eddie too, an era was over. A generation of flyers, great flyers they were too, had pulled up their wheels. It was a time of passing for open-cockpit flying, for the big, brawny men in their shiny machines, and for us too. Perhaps now I could begin to get past the feeling that something more was always expected of me. One satisfaction, however, did shine through. In 1966, when my brother and I flew our Cub to the coast, we pleased these men greatly and showed a lot of people that they knew how to grow pilots. Maybe we didn't do everything right, or even very well. As a matter of fact, we did it half-assed. But we got there, we made it, we found ourselves, and day after day we really made the country sail by under our struts. That was all we had to do.

I still get out west some and wander around in airplanes. Now and then I like to drop into our old haunts—Cochise County, Albany, and Wink. Of course, it's not the same now. The vast herds of Hereford and whiteface are gone from the plains, penned up instead in commercial feed lots. The crop-dusters have sold off their Stearmans to museums and tycoons. They haul spray now in sleek, turbine-powered monoplanes. New federal airspace rules make it a lot harder to meander the deserts without a radio. These changes, and the new kind of flying I had to do, bothered me for a long time, but I tried not to think about it. I didn't want to spend my middle years like my father, a captive of nostalgia. Then one cloudless spring morning out over the Red Desert of Wyoming, the thought finally occurred to me, and I became comfortable again with memory and flying and wanderlust.

It was the best summer of our lives, and there would never be another one like it. That year, my brother and I flew hard for the Rockies and cleared the big pass, and afterward we no longer had to expend the energy we once did getting to know each other. There is no knowing beyond knowing. I could try and recapture that moment if I liked, but there's no attaining the past and I could never relive that journey. It's the kind of thing that only happens when you're young.

EPILOGUE

On a pleasant, sunny afternoon in August 1994 I taxied out to the end of the runway at Harriman and West airport in North Adams, Massachusetts, with a pretty good tailwheel man in the backseat, Ken Burton. For a living, Ken is an airline pilot, and he has a background similar to mine. In addition to the Piper Cub we were flying, he owns a mint-condition Stearman, which he and his father rebuilt when he was in high school. He likes to use it on summer days to give open-cockpit rides to all the neighborhood kids.

I hadn't flown a tailwheel plane in a long time, but I've found that I don't get jittery about such things now that I'm older. I got the power forward, and once the tail was raised I could feel how the rudders were rigged. That's always a problem in these old planes, spongy control cables, but I held the centerline fine and we lifted off.

We circled left around the field and flew north over the state line. I know the Berkshire Mountains quite well and love the range, and we were passing the spot where the Berkshires merge with the Green Mountains of Vermont. There is a wafer-shaped lake in a small state park, right where the ranges meet. Ken's wife and children, and my wife and children, were frolicking in the water by the shore. Ken pulled from the baggage compartment a boater's air horn that he likes to carry along on such flights and threw open the side window. He sounded the horn for everyone below, in case they didn't recognize the plane.

We flew back south and climbed over the purple brow of Mt. Greylock. The mountain has much significance for me. I spent many happy days climbing it with my friend Roger Linscott, when I was learning my craft as a reporter at *The Berkshire Eagle*. There is a tall, elegant stone monument on the Greylock summit, a memorial to soldiers killed in World War I, which my great-grandfather, John Kernahan, helped build.

The airport at North Adams is built right up against the north wall of Greylock. When you come off the mountain the winds and the steeply sloping sides of the peak naturally force you onto a downwind leg for Runway 29. I eased back on the power a bit and shouted to Ken that I'd shoot some landings.

"No problem," Ken yelled forward. "Just maintain sixty-five."

It had never occurred to me that the old Cub was still flying. Most of these planes get left to rot on a tie-down somewhere, or a student pilot stalls them into the trees, walks away, and you never hear about that plane again. Then one day I flew down to Somerset, New Jersey, to check out some details for this book, and I ran into our mechanic from 1966, Lee Weber.

"Oh yeah Rinker, she's still flying," Lee said. "I've seen her. She's up in the Berkshire Mountains somewhere—Great Barrington, I think, or Pittsfield."

They had an FAA aircraft registry right there in the pilots' shack and we looked it up. Sure enough, the plane was still registered, to Ken Burton and his son. When I called Ken from home that night, my voice was quivering and kept giving out on me and butterflies raged in my abdomen and throat, like I was calling a girl for my first date. I was surprised by how strongly I reacted but I knew what it meant. I was desperate to see that plane again.

When I flew up to North Adams, a couple of days later,

Ken wasn't around, but I spent some time with Pete Esposito, a good old airport geezer type, a stunt pilot, and, as things happen in aviation, an old friend of Eddie Mahler's. He brought me up to date on the Cub. After my father sold it to a pilot from Connecticut in 1968, the Cub sat disassembled in a hangar for ten years. Eventually the plane was restored and flown around Connecticut for a couple of years, and then Pete bought the plane. He used it for sightseeing rides and instruction for a couple of years before Ken picked it up to bang around in with his kids. And it was the funniest damn thing, Pete said. That summer, 1966, when we flew the Cub coast to coast, everybody was talking about it on the show circuit, scratching their heads and wondering why they hadn't dreamed up a stunt like that when they were young. Big Eddie told him that he knew the boys and couldn't wait to see them when they got back from California. But Pete had forgotten about all that fifteen years later and had no way of knowing that he'd bought the same plane.

I returned to North Adams a couple of weeks later. Now Ken and I were just flying around for a bit, two old Cub pilots getting to know each other in the air. It's something I do every few years anyway, bang around in an old tail-dragger just to make sure I haven't lost my touch.

The thing is in my blood and it's not something I can blunder. Maintain sixty-five, Ken said. Carb heat, three cranks on the trim, chop the power. As I turned final, Ken said to land on the grass on the side of the paved runway because he was trying to stretch the rubber on the tires. Good. It's easier that way, because the plane settles better on soil and doesn't want to bounce.

And it's always a satisfaction for me, after a long absence from Cubs, to grease it on and know that I haven't lost my feel for the design. Ken suggested that we go around a few more times, which we did, and then finally I turned back in for the last landing. I didn't want to burn up too much of his gas.

On the ground, when we got opposite the pilots' shack, Ken stood on the brakes in the backseat, opened the door, and got out. Gee, I thought, this is real generous. He's letting me solo it.

"Rinker, I've only got one rule," Ken said. "You break it, you fix it."

There were some men repairing the runway lights on the pavement so I went off the grass.

It was an overwhelming feeling being alone in the plane that I flew with my brother through the pass. Twenty-eight years had passed swiftly. The old Continental roared, the floorboards throbbed and the cockpit smelled of burnt oil. All the old gauges and dials were still in the same place. I wasn't troubled anymore by the waterbag or the El Paso gam, and it had been years since I blamed myself for not being closer to my father, and not doing more for him while he was still alive. I was forty-three that year and over time the truth, or what you declare to be the truth, does arrive. I had done all I could just knowing that man. No, I wasn't worried about a thing at all. Nothing could spoil this reunion. I banked left for the summit of Greylock, leveled the wings, and hung the Cub on its prop. I was up in the sky over mountains I love in a plane that had aged gracefully, and all I wanted to do was fly around for a while in 71-Hotel.

Rinker Buck began his career as a reporter for *The Berkshire Eagle* in Massachusetts. He then worked for *New York, Life,* and *Adweek* magazines, and his writing has also appeared in numerous national magazines and newspapers. *Flight of Passage* is his first book. He and his wife, Amelia de Neergaard, live with their two daughters in Connecticut.